I'm NOT DEAD:
I'm ALIVE...without a body

Volume 2

What's it like after <u>we</u> die?
Find out from these
amazing and genuine
conversations with loved ones
alive in the Spirit World

Channelled by French medium

BRIGITTE RIX

CON-PSY PUBLICATIONS

First published 2013

© Brigitte Rix 2013

Published by

CON-PSY PUBLICATIONS

P.O.BOX 14
GREENFORD
MIDDLESEX, UB6 0UF

ISBN 978 1 898680 61 1

Acknowledgements

I reiterate my loving thanks to my mother, father and my husband for their love, patience, support and understanding while they were on the Earth and since their passing into the Spirit World. I am delighted they were able to learn to communicate with me and have been doing so for many years! I am grateful and excited that they could share more and more of their astounding discoveries and their joy at still being ALIVE in the Afterlife!

My loving thanks also go to my grandma Léonie and grandpa Léon (in the Spirit World too) for their affection and help 'behind the scenes'!

Additionally, my loving and respectful thanks to my 'Spirit Guide and Teachers' who are my trustworthy Friends from Beyond, for their patience and devotion and also for the help and knowledge they constantly offer me. It is an honour for me to be the recipient of their revelations and to be able to offer those to Mankind as evidence that EVERYBODY SURVIVES DEATH.

Warmest and heartfelt thanks to my family on Earth. All my love and gratitude to my daughter Anne-France for her help, patience and artistic talent with the cover and to my son Jim and of course to my very dear friend Stan Pattison for his great patience, understanding, caring and invaluable practical help, thus giving me more time to focus on my work for Spirit.

My grateful thanks to: Angie Jury and BSSK Team at 'BSSK Events', Neil and Ruth Auchterlonie at 'MBS Harrogate & Buxton Festivals' for their generous support and understanding during my UK touring and public speaking at Mind, Body & Spirit Festivals.

Warm thanks to my publisher, Candy Taylor of Con-Psy Publications, for her help and work to ensure the publication of this book.

Finally, all my love to my patient and beautiful black cat, 'Lady', for constantly giving me her unconditional love, trust and devotion.

I'm NOT DEAD: I'm ALIVE...without a body!
VOLUME 2

CONTENTS

I'm NOT DEAD: I'm ALIVE...without a body!
VOLUME 2

INTRODUCTION

Welcome dear Reader! For those of you who don't know me, I am Brigitte Rix, a French language teacher and lecturer by profession, now retired. I have been living in the UK for numerous decades and now live in York, UK. You can find me on Facebook as well as on my website.

I am also a respected clairaudient medium. The way I receive communications from those in the 'Spirit World' is by hearing what they tell me, when I have relaxed and 'tuned in' to their frequencies. But I also have an additional ability: While I listen to my communicators, my hand feels compelled to write down (at high speed, in a kind of 'Automatic Writing') what is said at the very SAME TIME as I hear it. My pen becomes a kind of extension of my ear! And of course, they hear my questions and reply at once! My communicators often provide facts I had never read or heard of before. Sometimes their answers may be the opposite of what I believe or may think! This shows it is not my 'subconscious'! It also means I can argue with those speakers, who always calmly do their best to explain things in various other ways, to put their Knowledge across.

The book you are holding is **Volume 2 of** *'I'm NOT DEAD: I'm ALIVE...without a body'*. The title stems from my mother's comments when realising she was not dead but was in fact truly alive, even though she'd left her flesh body on Earth, so it is the **continuation** of an amazing, enlightening and heartwarming diary.

To appreciate and understand this present book better, you are strongly advised to start with reading Volume 1 of *'I'm NOT DEAD: I'm ALIVE...without a body'*. Volume 1 is the first part of a **lively diary** of the initial five years (out of currently thirteen) of authentic conversations, questions and immediate answers and discussions which I have been receiving directly from my family and various people in the Hereafter, via the extrasensory perceptions of clairaudience and telepathy, as well as automatic and inspired writing. It explains how this series of dialogues came to take place and provides evidence of the exciting progress of surviving personalities from the day of their bodily 'deaths'.

Any new reader unable so far to acquire Volume 1 - or anyone wishing to refresh their memory of the contents of Volume 1 - will be helped by the section 'CATCH UP with VOLUME 1' on the next pages of this Introduction.

MY COMMUNICATIONS

I certainly did not 'imagine' all those years of private conversations with my departed family and did not concoct all the unexpected mind-boggling facts they revealed and shared with me! Definitely not! Hundreds and hundreds of people can vouch for my sanity and honesty.

Moreover, since 1983, I had been training carefully to polish my mediumship ethically and safely in order to ensure I was indeed communicating with personalities who survived bodily 'death'. I also became able to give personal messages to strangers - at no charge - that provide evidence of life after (and before) death.

At first, in those early days decades ago, my main communicator was only my 'Guide', a kind, knowledgeable and evolved personality. He had obviously agreed to watch over me when I chose to come to Earth, leaving behind my life in the 'Spirit' World. (This fact of living as spiritual Beings before being born onto Earth is something all Humans need to get used to, instead of being brainwashed that they are 'only' the product of the merging of a sperm and an egg!).

In my early communications with him, I naïvely asked him to show me his face (if I could be clairvoyant enough to see it!). His instant reply was: "My face in which of my lives?" I realised how pointless my question was. Of course! He had to have lived **many** lives on Earth in the 'past' in order to know what it is like to be a Human Being! Otherwise how could he 'guide' and inspire me, the Earthling, if he had never experienced the human condition and its pitfalls? So I did not bother any longer about his possible appearance, since in the Afterlife you can imagine yourself as anything you like!

He will have obviously progressed away from 'playing' at visualising himself as one personality or the other in various lives. After all, he had also trained thoroughly in the Spirit World, having studied to increase his Knowledge and be able to handle and support his protégé (me!). All the more since he and my other Teachers all link up with many other evolved Minds when they transmit their wisdom. Such Advanced Teachers insist that it is their "message which matters, not the messenger", so they don't see the point of us asking their names! To please me and my human way of thinking, he labelled himself "Silver Arrow". He explained that it is a symbol of his task to help me stay on the straight path to achieving my chosen 'life plan'. Therefore, I was content to listen to my guiding friend's teachings. He and I always converse in English, as I prefer this language, even though I am a French native speaker.

One day, in that early period, French was suddenly spoken from the Spirit World. To my great surprise I discovered that my 'deceased' father had learnt to link up and popped in very unexpectedly, though I certainly had not been 'calling' him! As he said: he did not speak English and he and I obviously used to speak French at home. So, thereafter, the pattern set in: My own French family speak French to me from the Hereafter. All the other communicators I have dealt with so far, speak English to me. But my Guide taught me that eventually, once passed over, we come to realise that languages do not matter, as what functions is transference of thoughts and emotions which are not necessarily expressed in words in one tongue or the other. Both Volumes of *'I'm NOT DEAD: I'm ALIVE...without a body!'* are the printed transcripts of my handwritten diary with dates, just as I received the communications. I allow you, the reader, to eavesdrop on my private conversations, to help you discover how it feels to leave one's body and pass over to a wonderful World of Mind and Light. It gives you an insight into the activities **your** own departed loved ones could be involved in 'over there' - and makes you realise they are **only a thought away!**

CATCH UP with VOLUME 1

A summary of the following events will be helpful to any reader unable so far to acquire Volume 1, to facilitate an understanding of what precedes this present Volume 2.

I have been living for many decades in York, UK. In June 1999, I had to rush to Nice (France) to my mother's hospital bedside, as she had been struck with a stroke and her left side was paralysed. She could not talk but she had all her wits! She could hear me and answered me by using her right hand to write down her comments, yet amazingly she did not seem to realise she was paraplegic! Probably because there was the additional problem of a painful kidney infection, unnoticed and not treated by the staff of Larcher II Clinic, who unfortunately went on strike during her stay there that week.

After a week of my spending days and nights on a chair by her bedside, I had eventually managed to energetically force the nurses to check her better as I could see she was in pain - they'd been ignoring my requests up to that point! That's when they realised she had a terribly painful infection, as her bladder was half paralysed! So, suddenly, that same evening I was told

11

they gave her "a strong pain killer". The next morning doctors declared unexpectedly that the clinic could not do anything else for Mum and we had to go home NOW! At the same time I noticed they had given her some medication and her fingers had gone rather blue, yet they had not been like that before!

When I pointed that out to the nurse, she said: "Yes, that's her blood pressure, which has now gone down. You can talk to her, she'll hear you in spite of (or through?) the morphine!" Morphine?! That was a bit drastic and sudden, wasn't it?! I now wish I had questioned it, but at the time I had to see to Mum.

I dreaded this even worse situation, as there was no way my dear mum, until then active and mentally very alert (at nearly ninety one, she was still giving private lessons to youngsters!), would want to be a 'burden' in a wheelchair! All the more since her house was absolutely unsuitable for a wheelchair. I resided and worked in the UK so I would be unable to be there all the time. She would hate and refuse to be an encumbrance tying down my dutiful brother Jean-Nicolas - aka 'Touky' - who lived in Nice too. Throughout her life Mum always used to say: "Never dump me in an old people's home, I'd rather be dead!". I was sure that the moment she caught sight of the wheelchair she would try to jump out of the window, or would commit suicide sooner or later!

Yet I put a brave face on and told her: "Mum, it's great! Doctors say we can go home. You can go and see again your dear cat! He is missing you. I'll pack your things now. I hope you heard me?"

So she opened her eyes and looked at me, with a faint smile, but then looked past me, seeming quite surprised and inquisitive, after which she closed her eyes again and gave a couple of little sighs. I thought she'd dozed off. No. She'd stopped breathing! Forever.

The following day, on the 27th of June, I was at her/our house. I was a bit numb but not grief stricken because I felt relieved FOR MUM that she was now totally free and healthy! I love her so much and I would not have wanted her miserable and paralysed. Her quality of life would have been awful and she would have lost the will to live anyway! In the end it was better for her and that's all that mattered. To me, Mum's peace of Mind and happiness came first.

So I calmly sat down with my pen and pad to 'tune in' to my Spirit Guide and hopefully converse (in English) with him, as I had been doing (by then) for the past sixteen and a half years - I hear Spirit communicators.

I intended to ask him whether he knew if Mum had realised where she was now. The reason I was concerned was because she had friends in Nice who were Jehovah Witnesses. No problem with that except they kept telling her that when you die you go to a kind of pleasant 'black hole' where you 'sleep' for ages until the Trumpet of Judgement wakes you up! I used to argue strongly with Mum about this, explaining that it would happen only **if** she really believed it, as firm beliefs can create imaginary surroundings when you arrive in the Hereafter! So, when I tuned in that day to get news from my guide, it was to find out whether the Jehovah Witnesses had badly influenced her Mind and she'd locked herself in a 'mental black hole'!

In order to make sure I was well tuned in, I asked him to start answering the first words in automatic writing, as I know how to let the pen write on its own, while I concentrate on something else to make absolutely sure I don't risk influencing it. Once it has got going, it is usually followed by my hearing what is being said. To my great surprise, I noticed the reply was written in French, whereas throughout all those past years only my dad used French to converse with me from the 'Other Side', as I prefer to speak English:

"Console yourself Darling, I arrived safely! I understood everything you told me and you were so right! Dad asked me to warn you straight away as he knew you would be unhappy. I am very comfortable, I am not suffering any longer and I have understood that everything you'd been telling me (about the Afterlife) *during all that time was true indeed... The pleasure to be here is spoilt by the sadness you must feel; I don't know how to make you understand I cannot free you from it, I am not expert enough! You must not doubt, Sweetheart, I am indeed speaking to you myself, as I learnt quickly what to do, because I had promised you I'd communicate, once in the Hereafter!*

"I am certain you know I did hear what you were telling me (in the hospital bedroom, when I spoke to her, in case she could hear me in spite of the morphine) *and I saw some lights in front of me. I went towards them. I grabbed those lights 'with my hand', so to speak and I pulled them towards me! I got the strength to get out of the heaviness around me... I felt as if I was so heavy and I clung onto those lights by staring at them; I felt I was pulled towards them. I managed to get right close to them... then I saw they were no longer lights but people ALIVE... as they were **suddenly transformed into human shapes and I felt my dad and your dad, Nic**! My dad and yours have... er... all in all 'become them', 'become themselves'. I was going to say 'appeared' but they were already there as lights, then **they became solid** in front of me! So I understood that indeed I had 'died...and my life 'Upstairs' had started!*

"Me who thought I was just going towards some lights, I only realised it was the two dads when those lights turned into living Beings! I could not believe my eyes! My dad welcomed me first, as I told you, then Nic kissed me and said: At last! Now I can explain everything to you!

"I did not know what to do; they showed me the

14

'Thought System' to speak to you. All I want is to let you know I feel well and I am sure you'll realise that I have understood what you used to tell me. The problem is: it feels as if there is a black wall between us... I am told the secret is to pierce this 'wall' with my thoughts for you to receive them. That's all. When I know more, I'll tell you..."

This is how, hardly **twenty-six hours after 'dying'** in a French hospital, my own mother made this startling and unexpected 'telepathic phone call' to Earth to me, her astonished, clairaudient, mediumistic daughter. And I had **not** even tried to contact her!

She gave me **astounding step by step descriptions** of:

• Leaving her flesh body painlessly, attracted by and following those two mysterious 'guiding' lights, which swiftly transformed themselves into her 'deceased' husband and father, who cheerfully and lovingly received her in the Afterlife world!

• Meeting up with family, old friends and animals.

• Learning to communicate with me (to reveal she was still 'alive', pain free and looking young again; she was no longer paralysed) by concentrating and sending her thoughts towards me, for me to receive clairaudiently or via Automatic Writing.

Over the following months and years Mother shared her **discoveries** and her progress with humour and exhilaration:

• Powerful thoughts constantly become tangible reality around her, creating her décor.

• Books are movie-like; words become films of actions.

• Colours have sounds; telepathy (reading each other's minds) is the means of communication.

• Extraordinary encounters with a highly evolved Being of Light: her Spirit Guide.

• Discovery and gradual unravelling of a one hundred year old well-kept family secret neither she, nor anyone alive

15

now, had ever heard of! Even in the Afterlife her own mother (my grandmother) is at first reluctant to divulge she had a secret baby from a 'fiancé' who then changed his mind! Her own parents saw this as "a stain on the family honour" in those days, around 1898. She was forced by them to give up her first little girl when they put the baby up for adoption. She later discovered, via hearsay, that her daughter died within less than two years. This tragedy broke my grandma's heart and affected her health all her life. This revelation incited me to start researching French births/deaths/marriages records, a very difficult task so far, as the tombs I looked for had not been kept and paid for and many records were destroyed during World War II in the North of France.

• Time travels into some of her past lives and through history, to view it from another angle. Sooner or later, we all have to analyse the life we have just left, therefore we are NOT judged by some deity but by ourselves. This is in order to understand ourselves better and this leads to understanding that we have lived other/past/lives too! We then can follow the 'thread' of what we, as different personalities, wanted to learn or achieve.

• Her astounding visits to Earth countries as well as touring my own home and go and see my brothers.

• Her practical exercises using Creative Mind Power to conquer Earthly prejudices and fears.

• Her appearing physically via the ectoplasmic transfiguration of another medium's face.

Other 'Spirit people' join in these lively authentic dialogues and intriguing revelations:
- My father's excitement at beginning to study Physics from a new and superior angle.
- My grandma's unexpected participation (she passed over when I, the medium, was only a tot).

16

- Strangers to me joining in the gradual unravelling of the family secret.
- My knowledgeable Spirit Guide offering enlightening explanations and guidance, devoid of any religious dogmas.
- Later on, in October 2004, my husband, Dave, succumbed to cancer. He used not to believe in "all that spooky stuff"! Yet **after** he passed over, he too learnt to communicate with me, to his great amazement! He shared his **own Death experience:** His floating out of the dying body and his pointless wanting to get back into it; his relief at being free from cancer and his appalling time in York hospital; his sadness at leaving our children with me by his death bed; his joy at meeting up again with his 'dead' parents; his delight at being shown**,** in the Afterlife, a **'Spirit Video' of his funeral on Earth!** We also follow him as he has to come to terms with still being alive and even looking younger. He too had to learn to control his thought power and his emotions.

'I'm NOT DEAD: I'm ALIVE...without a body!' Volume **1** also reveals profound knowledge and thought-provoking insights, at times brand-new:
- The brain is not the Mind: The Mind survives the death of the fleshy brain.
- The 'departed' only meet again people they get on with or are on the same wavelength with!
- We on Earth meet 'departed' people and Animals in our sleep, yet we often don't recall the visits.
- Animals feel emotions, survive in the Afterlife and welcome back those who loved them.
- Troubled or frightened souls need help to settle down after their passing over.
- 'Real Light' bathing the Afterlife is vibrations of emotions rather than 'particles'.
- Humans choose every Earthly life as an experiment; each one

is a segment of a kaleidoscope of numerous lives, forming our many-faceted Higher Selves/ Oversouls/Real Selves.
- Thought Energy lives on visibly; it can't be destroyed and is the tool to improve our lives.
- Earth scientists should learn to revive the invisible reserves of life in dying flesh cells.
- Spirit World 'Pattern-Receiver-Thought-Processing-Method' dissects Earthly thoughts' slow vibrations to grasp their meaning.
- 'Death' is just a transition from one state of vibrations to another.

My communicators' spontaneous reactions to questions, events and outpourings of emotions, such as joy and grief, is evidence the 'deceased' still live on; they have only lost their flesh body, but not their feelings, their personalities, their characteristics or their sense of humour!

Those conversations offer reassurance, hope, enlightenment and evidence - these people are still alive in spite of bodily 'death, therefore we shall all survive too! Through those dialogues, I learnt a lot myself about life on the Other Side even though I am used to channelling information on spiritual matters!

This **diary was private** and precious to me, since my loved ones revealed their new lives! It was meant to remain so, but it became evident that the astounding insights and revelations they provided had to be shared and made public. They give so much upliftment and Knowledge - and there are far too many people in the world mourning the loss of loved ones, unaware of what really goes on in the Afterlife! Those must be helped. My diary had to become a book!

So I eventually tackled the hard work of typing neatly all those hundreds and hundreds of manuscript pages, then translating into English all the French dialogues, then ensuring the publication. Thousands of long hours of slog, which I had to fit in somehow, in spite of my busy language teaching to University students and Adult Education classes!

Since its publication, I have been informed by readers appreciating my authentic material, how much my books helped and motivated them, changed their life, gave them hope and Knowledge! This warm and grateful reception has made the effort worth it and demonstrated the great need to help Mankind by opening their eyes to the reality of Life in the Afterlife.

FOR SEEKERS OF EVEN DEEPER KNOWLEDGE

Some readers may be interested to know that I also channel other communications from my Team of Spirit Masters, such as *'Truths, Lies & Distortions'*. This is a book my guided hand wrote down at high speed, at the very same time and exactly as it was **dictated to me at the request of my Spirit Teachers**, who are very knowledgeable and evolved Energy Personalities. As they say, they are no longer focused on the physical world or their physical form (which we call the flesh body) but are now Energy and Mind, though they have previously lived on Earth at some time or other.

Over several years, these individual Spirit 'spokespersons' came close to me to unexpectedly start dictating profound thoughts and facts, most of which were unknown to me! They wanted to create a whole book - I did not ask for it! They planned all the topics. They had done their research and accumulated the Knowledge. They even chose its title *'Truths, Lies & Distortions'*! Only when I wanted clarification did I ask a question and of course enjoyed learning from them. They told me that if I wanted this Knowledge, I had to share it and not keep it for myself! Apparently they had tried to teach the same during their previous lives, aeons ago, but were killed for revealing

19

'hidden truths'. I told them I did not want to be burnt at the stake either - but I accepted to be their 'human scribe'!

Since their answers have provided so much new information that I have never heard before, go beyond my weak grasp of scientific knowledge and have often been the opposite of my own beliefs and expectations, this has proved to me, time and time again, that this information is not coming from my own Mind or subconscious!

Their fascinating and inspirational facts and revelations are explained simply and provided in all sincerity and for the good of Mankind. Their book purposefully avoids obscure or complex scientific angles and jargon, as those Teachers want the information to appeal to and be accessible to the general public. My Evolved Masters do not impose any dogmas. They help you truly grasp Reality and your Life Purpose, **learn why you are on Earth and why this Earth exists**, discover your own inner strength, rid yourself of fears and improve your health. Thus they offer hope, a greater understanding and long-awaited answers to profound questions which have puzzled and frustrated Mankind, who chose to create arguments, wars and religious rifts!

Since my Teachers often came to dictate or discuss those very varied and interesting topics for their book, before or soon after I tuned in and talked to my family, I have included a small handful of them in this volume 2 of *'I'm NOT DEAD: I'm ALIVE...without a body'* as well, so that more readers can benefit from the Knowledge. More details are available at the very end of this present book.

****

Since the publication of my books, I have been touring the UK for the past years as an Inspirational Spiritual Speaker and Medium-Author, giving talks to various groups, societies and Mind, Body & Spirit Festivals where I also hold stands to display my books.

You can keep track of the events I will be attending by looking up my website: ***www. italkwithspirits.com***

I welcome offers of venues and invitations as a guest Speaker. My audiences can be guaranteed a cheerful, lively, friendly, interesting and informative discussion with Questions & Answers on the Afterlife.

To avoid disappointment, it is usually advisable to book in advance to reserve your seat, as (I am humbly pleased to say) my talks sell out very quickly! Talks at BSSK events (British School for Spiritual Knowledge) are free at the time of publishing this book.

Because of my busy schedule and also the need to find time to focus on receiving and sharing Knowledge and Teachings from my Spirit Team of Teachers, I do not have time to do private readings. Sorry to disappoint anybody but this Earthly life is governed by clocks and calendars!

Readers can email me via my website and ask me questions on the Afterlife.

Happy Reading, Friends!

"A candle loses nothing when it is used to light another one."

"Happy are those who have, and still happier are those who are able to share".

FOREWORD
by Brigitte Rix

I am fortunate and delighted to have discovered - around 1980 - that communication with those who have passed away IS possible and real! I became aware that everybody can learn to polish their psychic and mediumistic abilities, since we all have at least a sixth sense. Moreover, we all are Beings of Energy - 'Spirit' Beings, i.e. Beings from a World where the Mind creates and is the only tool; thoughts become visible there! We all come from that world where communication amongst its residents is carried out by telepathy, Mind to Mind transference. (Many examples are given in this diary of conversations with loved ones and other 'departed' people).

When we, as 'Spirit' Beings, decide to be born as Humans, we choose to leave that world of refined Energy vibrations to go on a temporary journey into the physical world of matter, to carry out our individual 'life plans'. This is seen as an exciting and often challenging adventure! Overall, it is to try and appreciate life as a physical Being on Earth. But it is mainly to learn and teach ourselves to experience and cope with various situations and statuses **of our choice** - while hopefully not infringing the Universal Law of not harming any other Being! We also need to grasp that our Mindset and emotions greatly affect our flesh body, which is not the 'real us' at all but only a vehicle and a garment to help us touch, smell, taste and feel physically! We must never forget that **we do not 'have' a Soul and a Spirit, we ARE a Soul and a Spirit,** cloaked with a temporary physical body!

It is important to mention in passing that my Spirit Teachers point out that the creatures Humans call 'animals' - and often use the word derogatorily - are in fact Spirit Beings too; they are sentient and have a Mind and a Soul! To reflect that neglected or ignored aspect and to give more respect to those Beings, I decided to spell it as Animal, since each one is a Spirit Being who chooses to live in a physical body - but disguised as an 'Animal', instead of dressing up as a 'Human' - but with different goals in their life plan.

As I said above, it is natural to be able to use our sixth sense and extra sensorial abilities. Since we are fundamentally Beings of Mind Energy, even when we are temporarily camouflaged as Humans, we still have the same abilities. Not only is each one of us a 'solid' Being with senses that can register through the flesh body, but we also are a Being of Light, a Soul and a Spirit who can do without a physical body and 'be a Mind'. We all have a Dual Personality! So the Soul who drives that particular flesh body - as a Human on Earth - can still link up with its origins, simply by remaining quiet when desired. That allows the personality to 'switch focuses' from one world (the physical life) to the other (the Spirit World) and blend its Mind with others on the same wavelength. That is **'tuning in'**. This is why communication can and does take place between the two worlds!

Why is it useful? Ask anyone who has lost a loved one! Ask any 'departed' person cut off from their Earthly life! Ask anyone fearing their own death! Being able to talk and get news from either world; grasping that we all go over to a wonderful world of Love and Compassion; being able to say once more to your dearest "I love you"; realising that it is only a temporary parting - and not a disappearance forever; understanding that a sick or injured relative or friend (or pet!) is no longer in pain and back to better health than ever... What relief and upliftment! What joy!

When we really love somebody, we should want them to always be happy. So even though we shall often miss their physical presence, shouldn't we stop feeling sorry for ourselves and replace the sadness with joy, knowing our loved ones are

FREE?! They have no more worries, they will never be in pain again, they can do anything they feel like, they have so many exciting discoveries to make in their new world! They'll have peace of Mind - but only if we on Earth don't cry and grieve and send distressed thoughts towards them! Because our 'departed' are only a thought away! So if we wail and sob, we must understand that our poor 'travellers to the other World' will definitely feel and receive all those depressed thoughts we send! Are we being kind and loving to them with our mourning? Will it help them at all? Will it aid them overcome their own grief for being parted from us too? Won't it make them feel guilty to have been obliged to leave their flesh vehicle, since we are letting the temporary parting ruin our Earthly lives? Since they love us, don't you think they would want us happy too?

This is why I feel fortunate to have learnt to develop my mediumistic abilities and to have understood that 'death' of the flesh body is not the eternal disappearance of the person we love. How could I cry and grieve after hearing my own mum's, my dad's and my husband's constant delight at feeling utterly FREE? Free from pain, free from obligations and duties, free from worries!

Talking with my own family, of course, helps me not wallow in self-pity at not having them close to me. Obviously, I would like their physical presence and their hugs and kisses! But whenever a twinge wakes up in me, wishing I had them in my daily Earthly life, I easily squash it by simply remembering Mum or Dave saying to me, from the Spirit World: "It is so wonderful not to be in pain and to be so free! **Please be glad for me**! **Don't cry**! I am thinking of you, I still love you - and we shall meet again for good one day. And don't forget that we meet at night. When your flesh body sleeps, you come and see me!"

24

The fact that I have been communicating with those on the Other Side for numerous decades now is not because I am 'obsessed' with it! It is not because I 'need a crutch'. It's simply because I **can do it** - and **so can you,** the reader, if you practise and train properly! But it also gives a lot of pleasure and upliftment to my loved ones who have so-called 'died'. Especially when they have recently gone over and feel cut off!

Moreover, my receiving great insights into what life is really like in the Afterlife and why, is an eye-opener to the countless people I talk to or who read my books. I receive numerous letters or emails of thanks for the help, upliftment and understanding my publications have brought them, confirming that it is worth doing and continuing to work with and for those in the 'Spirit World'.

As you the Reader, eavesdrop on my private conversations, please understand this book is not a novel and it is not aiming at being a masterpiece in literature! It is simply an authentic modern diary of exchanges just **as they were received**. I want to enable the reader to sense how departed loved ones really feel, the turmoil of emotions they may experience - the joy, but also the longing to have a link with their family left behind, their amazement at discovering their new world and their striving at controlling the power of their thoughts!

This is why I purposefully did not delete some of their statements just because 'they have said something similar recently'. Such sentences may look like 'repetition' to an impatient, cold-hearted academic reader, but I aim at allowing Readers who appreciate emotions the chance to realise what goes on in the Minds of the 'deceased'! The latter find themselves not dead but in fact alive without a 'solid' body - thinking clearly and feeling emotions, in a mind-boggling world on different frequencies, yet parted from their loved ones 'abandoned' on Earth! It's not surprising my loved ones, lucky to be able to communicate with me on Earth, want to share and blurt out how they feel and pour out all the thoughts buzzing in their Minds!

Moreover, sooner or later, all of us will be 'in the same boat' one day - on the Other Side - coping with the same dilemma! So here is your chance to learn what to expect and how to deal with it all!

****

CHAPTER 1

Condensed Light - Lives superimposed, not linear - News from Dave - Colours emit sounds - Objects' impacts on space - Heal Mind and Soul first - Guides blend their Minds with ours

Since my husband Dave's passing 10 weeks ago last October, my life has been rather hectic trying to fit in my job as a language lecturer and the chores involved in sorting things out and preparing to clear the house to put it up for sale in order to 'downsize'. Having to deal with so many tasks is not very conducive to finding time for relaxation and having a quiet Mind!

20th January 2005 - 15.00hrs - *I relax while listening to soft music. The pen starts the first words 'in Automatic' in English, then I hear the communicators' full flow. My Guide 'opens the door' to facilitate the links between the two worlds.*

Dave sends his love to all of you; he does not want to wait for his turn to tell you that! You must tell the children he is well and happy to know they have not been fretting and are steadily living their lives. In my days there was none of this 'music stuff' to relax; we used to simply listen to water in the river or the wind in the trees, to be still within!

BR- Are you aware I am listening to some music?!

We know you have some music on and listen to it with a machine. It's quite interesting to see your Mind quieten and become stiller when you have that playing! It makes quite a difference from the usual 'noise' and bustle of your thoughts! We came to bring your Mum and the others, so here she is. *(Suddenly, French is spoken)* Mum here Sweetheart. At last! The year ahead is going to be extremely busy; you'll have heaps to see to! You also have 'our book' on the go and that will keep you occupied too. So be ready for all those tasks, do not dither, keep things in good order to save you time. Then all will go well. Do not think of sad things as they may never happen, if you do your best to avoid them!

As far as I am concerned, I have been learning even more. I have given myself the job of 'guardian angel' for new arrivals, like both the dads (yours and mine) are doing. There are always people arriving here who don't know where they are, so we need to help the poor souls! When you think how pleasant it is in this world, it would be a great pity if they did not enjoy it simply because they have not understood where they are. We explain and demonstrate things to them and do what is needed to help them.

I had to practise with 'experts' from here to know exactly how to achieve this. What was very interesting and fun for me was to learn how to **transform myself into a light,** like Dad did for me! (*Reminder note- On her last moments in hospital, Mum saw two lights in the room. She was concerned they could be some weird medical treatment she may not be keen on, so she decided to 'follow' them as they moved backwards across the room! Unbeknown to her at the time, doing so meant she could free herself from her painful paralysed body! Her flesh could not last any longer; it was worn out and dying. So she stepped out of the body and left it behind on the bed. Then she realised those 'lights' suddenly transformed themselves into her dad and her husband as she used to know them, welcoming her in the World of Mind and Light - the 'Spirit World.*

They had helped her by disguising themselves as bright 'Energies', because if she had seen them in the bedroom as the people she knew, she could have panicked, suddenly realising her body was dying anyway - that meant her imminently leaving me at her bedside and not seeing her sons again! Her flesh body died but obviously she did not, as she's carried on existing ever since, thinking normally and feeling emotions - as well as communicating with me! See Volume 1 of ND-AWB).

BR- (stunned) Really? You are now able to do that?!
Yes, it's easy when one knows how to.

BR- Go on, try to explain this to me, I beg you!
All one has to do is remember that one is actually just a 'light' who had previously taken on a human shape on Earth, temporarily! Since we all are Spirit Beings, we are fundamentally Beings of Energy. Yet when we first arrive here, we feel as if we've got a body, but we soon know it is not a 'solid' one since the flesh is dead. It's imagined. So all that is needed is to 'go into reverse' and use our Minds to make ourselves become a light again, in order to be a dot of light rather than a supposedly solid body!

I have also done some exploring of my own. There are various 'places' here which one only gets to see when one has acquired a better understanding of certain things. It is really difficult to describe a visit to a particular state of one's Soul, I can assure you! One would need a cine camera or camcorder or some electronic sensor, for you to feel what one feels. It is a Soul state that I need to investigate to be aware of what make things happen around me when I feel in a specific mood...

The only thing required to do is to be calm and to focus on one point of view, one idea, then stay in that way of thinking. After that exploration, we feel much better because we have a better understanding of ourselves. If we understand ourselves better, we can be sympathetic towards others and that's what matters: being able to help other people who don't know what they are doing or why they do it. That way it helps everybody, you see?

Sometimes I go towards places that are different from my own environment, as they were created by other people, for themselves. Of course, it's different, because we don't all have the same ideas. Some folks like to find themselves in an elegant manor, whereas I prefer to be in Nature, as I was saturated with houses, bedrooms and furniture around! I want to see trees, water, rivers and fields - no work, no worries about dust and repairs!

When I go to such places, it's fun to discover others' ideas and what they create for themselves. As I find this out, I understand how and why, here, one can do what one wants with one's thoughts. All that is needed is to 'think about it', as Christopher Columbus used to say! All you have to do is think of it and it 'makes itself', as long as you really desire it. Then it disappears if you no longer care about it. You have to truly want it so that it keeps existing! Everything is like that. What you no longer need vanishes on its own; it's great fun since one does not have to constantly tidy up! If only one could do that on Earth!

So there you are, I am having a good time whilst learning and I learn while having fun. That's my life here. So much to do, to see and to uncover! What an amazing place! Nothing better, in my opinion.

BR- I am so glad for you. May I have some news about Dave? (Silence for a short while, then the pen starts again but in English this time. My guide has stepped in).

We have Dave here. I'll tell you his message to you: He says he wants to say hello and give you a big hug and kiss for being who you are now. You will have problems in life, no doubt, when others pay no attention to what you say and you'll suffer from it and because of it... He says he'll be there to send you good thoughts because he's learning to do just that. He still has to learn to communicate directly. You probably wonder why he can't do it 'properly', i.e. without help from guiding intermediaries. Because it is a question of stilling his Mind and focusing in the right direction.

BR- I would have thought he could do that by now?

You think he could do it? Well, he is not quite up to it somehow. He is doing well but needs more practice. As he works at it, he discovers he has not got as much patience as he thought he had and he gets impatient if no results occur at once!

I am now passing on what Dave is saying to you:

"Life here is very pleasant. We have all met and enjoy each other's company. I have found a few friends who passed over before me and wish to say hello to the Earth. We have so many people around us; we could never be lonely! All these conversations are very pleasant indeed. I learn a lot from them, as there are always explanations given on how to cope here with what is on offer.

"As I like to be alone too, I can go wandering like a cloud over vales and dales and see the daffodils and other flowers we have here. I could have done some gardening all my Earthly life if it had lasted longer, and still not seen such wonderful flowers as those here! There are hundreds and thousands of beauties who would have won all the trophies at the Flower Shows indeed! *(Dave used to win at all Flower Shows. I found 115 cards for 1st/2nd prizes and he often won the Cup)*.

"My mum is here and says hello to those on Earth who believe and understand she has not gone. She wishes to be remembered for her love to all of them. My father has always been a quiet one but he finally says hello to you too. He wants you to know he did like you! He hopes you can cope with the upset and distress my departure has caused. We are all here and have lots to say and to do.

"It is interesting to look around and see what can be made with one's Mind if you set your wits to it. I have made a whole garden of wonderful flowers by just thinking of the ones I fancy here and they appear and grow on their own if they want to - though I can still play at looking after them, to make sure they keep flowering for me and my friends around me. We have quite a few gardeners around here, and ramblers too, as the landscapes are wonderful: hills, rivers or lakes, it all depends where you look or go. My favourite occupation is walking around all those, simply by thinking: "I want to go there"…and I find myself there!

As I do not require a home as such, I have not built one. I was told there is no need to do it, for no one has to sleep or eat or live in a house... but some do because they think they should! My needs are more for freedom and fun with no problems. Just fun doing what I want. No ties, no restrictions or 'necessities'! So I go around my new world and enjoy it a lot!"

BR- I am so delighted for you! Please send your loving positive thoughts to Jim and Anne-France (Then I give Dave some news).

All your thoughts reached me. I am pleased to say I heard every word.

25th January 2005 - *During mediumship home practice circle. My guide pops in to talk to the group.*

Let us begin with a lesson on quiet Minds. The Soul is like a mirror we look at when we look at you. We see your Soul, not your body. In your Soul, we see your lives before this one, or after, or **all mixed up, all superimposed!** If you wish us to be able to contact you and stay in tune with you, we need that life which is 'now' for you, to remain present in the mirror. But on top of that, it needs to be a clear 'Present', as a jumble of thoughts is to us like a muddy soup, or fog, or an entangled ball of string! You cannot imagine how difficult it is for us to reach you, when the barrage of your thoughts interferes with the ones we want to send you! So, do not ask that we accept this. We cannot do anything until you have a clear and quiet Mind, absolutely still, devoid of bits coming in and out all the time! You will have to control that. Then we'll have a plain piece of paper to write on, or a pure mirror to reflect our light into and reach you.

14th February 2005 - 23.30 hrs- *The pen starts the first words in French. Then I hear the fast flow.*

Your dad here, if you want to speak to me! You have your work cut out! I'd like to point out you will all have to be careful with the monies you will receive. *(Note: From the recent inheritance after Dave's passing).* There will be a large sum, more than you've ever had, so you will need to be very careful where you put all this and how you will use it and invest it. In my opinion the best way is to use a small amount to make life more pleasant but a larger amount should be invested to bring interest as time passes, otherwise you will never have enough! Each one of you should find some high yield investments; it would be best to seek advice from a financial expert to guide you. I am only telling you this in case you and your children didn't know what to do for sure.

BR- Thanks, it's very kind of you to be concerned about us. I shall also have to help Touky.

I see Touky's problems will soon be over, I have been told. There will be a little bit of worry then it will be fine, it won't be discussed any more. Touky will be free from it. He will have got rid of that burden and will be able to live more freely, as life was not fun for him ever since he had that boat, and it did not help poor Mum either. I am told it will be a positive result and all will be well soon. He won't have any more problems on that score. *(Looking back, this turned out to be correct. A few weeks later the sale of the land at St Y- provided the enormous sums needed to free him from the stupidity of French 'red tape' and the deceitfulness of the crook Mr Trouillard).*

BR- I hope he won't escape from it by dying?!

The truth is this, that problem will no longer exist because he will have solved it. That's all. Nothing else. So you will all be able to live more comfortably and I hope you'll have more time to do what you need for Mum's book *(Volume 1)* and for the other spiritual things you deal with. It is very important to make people understand that no one dies! It must be done, because when they arrive here some are so disorientated that we wish they'd known it earlier!

(A long silence follows, during which the pen seems to have fun doodling...then it suddenly writes again, still in French). The main thing one must remember is that the written word lasts longer than a word sung or spoken. It is there, sitting on a piece of paper and one can read it again at leisure. It will be available for centuries if it is not destroyed.

BR (Surprised, as I thought I was talking to Dad) - Who is speaking to me?

Your mum of course, didn't you realise?! Therefore, one must respect written words and have them published as soon as possible. There is so much to do to get something published, that's why one must not dither. One must find an outlet as soon as possible and the moment one gets known, one must be ready to give them what they want! So be prepared for when it happens, but for that you must have everything as organised as possible so that it looks professional. There is so much to do, it's essential to get down to it early and do it well. So you'll have to start soon to manage to survive and not miss a good opportunity. We can only warn you in advance so that everything is all set for when you need it. The best is yet to come - the day you'll be invited to present your book to the public so that people see you sign your work!

BR- I wonder whether this is my ego or my 'subconscious' telling me all this!

No! You can believe me Sweetheart, this is what they tell me to pass on, to give you courage: It will happen!

BR- But it is not translated into English yet, on top of having to type it!

The joy of seeing it published will be what matters in the end; the most beautiful day of your life in a way!

BR- Which book? Your book, Mum? Or the dogs' story? (It's another book. A story dictated to me long ago by a Spirit Teacher).

The 'dogs' life' is not in sight. It is my book I am talking about, my book of conversations with you, what I do here and I tell you about. Can you see the effect it will have to say: "Madame Suzanne Bondaletoff, the 'dead woman', wrote this book, from the Hereafter, by dictating it to her daughter?"

I would love to watch the faces of people hearing this, especially the poor Jehovah Witnesses. But for now, you should go to bed, as you'll be even more tired tomorrow if you don't get some rest...

22nd February 2005 - 10.35 a.m. *The pen starts in English. My guide speaks at length about my material life. Then he mentions Dave.*

Dave is doing fine; he is learning fast and loving it. His anger and frustration have gone at last. He was so angry to have been bed bound, in pain and restricted, all for nothing *(in a York hospital bed),* but he has recovered from that now, as his new life is so much better than before. The last months *(on Earth)* were horrid, he recalls, but now we encourage him not to think about it and not to look back, but rather look ahead, as he needs an anchor in front of him to pull him forward.

He has his family with him; they help him a lot. He loves his folks and he loves the fact that he found them again, not having realised it was true indeed that you could go back to them after your bodily death! He thought it would be at best "some airy-fairy love in the sky type of thing", not realising they were actually living here, like one can live on Earth, but better! He had a real shock at that discovery. This is something he did not expect.

BR- Well, I did tell him or try to!

You told him, yes, but did he take it in? No. He thought you were making it up. He assumed they were 'just thoughts'! Possibly at times from another Being but, to him, it was still like an airy-fairy world of Thought, rather than understanding the world here is solid to us, as much as we want it to be solid.

So he is learning and enjoying it, amused by it all, as one usually is after coming from Earth knowing little or nothing. He has made real progress. He wants to send his love to all of you; he says that now, as he has picked up my thoughts to you about him. He knows I am talking about him, so I've received his thoughts to me: "Send them my love. I am happy now, not suffering, but I am sad they are not here to enjoy it too".

He'll be in contact himself one of these days, don't worry. He'll pick up your thoughts if you send him love and healing and he'll feel better for it! But you need to give him a bit of time to concentrate on his new learning, then he'll be able to cast his Mind in your direction, as well as tuning back here, without feeling unsettled. All is well, he is fine, is not suffering, is not miserable and is not pining. He is looking ahead, creating a new life for himself, therefore learning to use the 'tools' here. He'll be all right. He has his family, they look after him!

36

11th March 2005 - 21h.35 - *After the pen drew quite a few 'doodles' in 'Automatic writing' I dozed off... then woke up and within minutes the pen wrote in English.*

You went to sleep and that's helped things tremendously! We have some 'new news' for you! As we told you last time, your Dave is busy organising his life with alacrity. He has a new 'job' that keeps him busy and able to concentrate on the aspects he is working on, meaning: he can't grieve as much, which is good. We cannot have him crying for having left you all; he would reduce himself to a torn rag. He must have a happy project planned which feels useful and creative and productive, then he'll feel better.

BR- A project? What is it?

He has many little jobs to make his plan work. He needs to create an environment he is happy with - doing so teaches him to use his Mind and his thoughts the correct way. He had to learn things he'd never heard before, and that's where your mum had an advantage - she'd been told about it before by you and that's helped her so much. Dave is all right, he has his parents and family with him - he is not alone, he is doing well.

BR- Please pass on to him our grateful thanks for all he did for us and all our love. Could you tell me about his environment?

All around him he has a beautiful countryside, full of birds, trees and landscapes he'd love to paint if he had time to do so now! But he is very busy looking at his landscapes, his surroundings and wondering how his Mind could possibly have created that! He is learning from those near him, who explain to him what the Mind can do and what his has done.

He had a rather tough time initially, coming to terms with the fact there was a great divide between us and you all.

37

That's why he wanted to talk to you all first, to feel he had not really lost you, or at least not completely. So he did with our help. Now he has understood that making his project work is vital to him and for him, so that once he feels he's settled mentally and he has understood how things can be done, he'll accept more 'amazing' things (that's what he'd call them!). Therefore, he is doing the landscaping of his environment.

BR- Do you see it?

We all see it. He is in it and we are in it with him, those of us who look after his welfare. He has beautiful mountains on one side and lakes as well as the sea. He makes them change at will, like the weather can change on your Earth. He decides whether the mountains will stay there or move elsewhere... and that way it shows him that the Mind you and we all have, has tremendous powers and can do things he'd never dreamt of! Once he has finished accepting all this (it takes him some time to accept, to absorb it all and to conjure up new things), he'll be willing to do something else. We want him well settled in his environment - he is in need of something beautiful and steady. He has to make it steady for his concentration to turn upon something else. He is not ready for something else yet.

BR- Doesn't he go walking anymore?

He goes walking at times, when his landscape has changed into somewhere he has gone to before, so he goes to inspect it and feel and 'live' it, absorb it. Then he'll come back to where we usually meet and he'll discuss it with us, so that we can explain to him anything he is not sure about.

BR- It seems different from my mum's experience. Can his parents do all that and more?

Many years ago, when his parents came, they were just as lost as him - or even more! They had to come to terms with

38

the same things. But we all taught them and now they have understood of course, so they are the ones who help him at the moment - as well as our teams of helpers here who are dedicated and experienced in the matter. All help all. We all help each other doing what is new or difficult at first. That way all is 'Love', as you would call it.

BR- Actually, I don't like that constant use of the word 'love' by people!

You may not like it but we call it 'Caring and Helping', as we are 'all in the same boat' when we come from the Earth, or from elsewhere for that matter - and have to adjust.

BR- You said 'elsewhere'. Can you explain? Are there worlds other than Spirit World etc?

Everyone is Spirit, whoever one is or whatever one does. All and everything are made of the 'stuff' you could call **'Spirit'**. **The basis of any kind of dimension**, level, state, place, domain, world or whatever word you use is the 'substance' so-called 'Spirit' is made of. That is to say the element is basically the same - we are all made of this same stuff/cloth, wherever we are.

That 'stuff' is the electronically charged Matter of invisibility for Earth people, but visibility in our world and in others on the same vibrations. If you took one of us elsewhere, without any warning, the others would know what we are, where we came from - because the 'stuff' is recognisable, in as much as its electronic pulses and power would be understood, accepted, grasped, recognised and 'read', so to speak. The bulk of the Universe is made of that. The difference with the Earth and worlds similar to it is that the physical appearance has been made 'hard' to the eyes or senses, but is in fact hollow! That was the clever trick of those who engineered it! The use of **hollow Matter**, built on wavelengths which are different from those we use here, made it possible to organise a different type of 'Matter' from what one can do elsewhere and certainly here. *(Note: A concept hard to grasp for some people. More is explained by my evolved Spirit Teachers and Masters in their book 'Truths, Lies and Distortions', which they dictated to me)*

BR- Another question. For example, Dave, how come that once back in Spirit World he does not remember he was a Spirit who lived in that world (before being born) and knew then how to use his Mind Power etc?
All those who have been to Earth come back here and remember eventually! It all depends on how much they have forgotten when on Earth.

BR- Why did they forget?!
Many people choose to blank all memories of previous lives on Earth, elsewhere, or in Spirit World simply because they prefer to think of one thing at a time! But once the shock of transition in either direction has dissipated, or the lesson/experiment is over, they will begin to remember where they were when they first started that original step, why they did it, how they did it, who or what they were. All that is not very important in the long run, as it is only a small matter of adaptation again, that's all - like someone falling asleep and waking up feeling a bit 'out of place', or so it seems to him. That's quite normal, most people do.

BR- Just people? What about Animals? Are they confused? Do they reincarnate too?
Let your Mind rest before we tackle all this. It will be a long subject with many pages and many questions! You could ask again if you like.

BR- (Disappointed at the unexpected answer). Couldn't you give me a little bit of an answer to start with?

Any 'Spirit' Being wishing to become what you call an 'Animal' on Earth needs a good reason of its own to want to do so, usually not to help himself but to help others most of the time.

BR- I wonder why my cat Timmy, or say a snail, has chosen to come?!

It is all a question of what is needed to learn and experiment and why. If they chose to be a large Animal, it won't be for the same reasons or experience as being a much smaller one. So the law of incarnation and/or reincarnation follows the same 'rules' as for 'Humans', but the Soul who chooses to go into an Animal body has usually a different agenda from some Humans' aims. Agendas have to be worked out and planned in advance before anyone makes the big journey to your Earth.

So be good; have a rest as your Mind is beginning to lose its concentration, then we can re-start this conversation when you are fresher mentally and physically. You will understand and hold your attention better then.

30th April 2005 - 20.40hrs - *I had a snooze earlier so I feel fine for now. Mum comes to have a chat.*

I really have great pleasure in speaking to you my Darling. It seems it's been such a long time since I last did. You've have a lot to do and I hope you are not worn out; you looked tired lately. All I can tell you for the time being is that your Dave is well; he is getting used to his new environment and copes well with his practices, which are pleasurable but useful to help him become familiar with what happens here. You'll have to speak to him one of these days. I think it would be good for you to know he is fine but is upset to have lost sight of you all, otherwise he is ok. He is not in pain anymore and this is what matters when one was suffering on Earth, you know!

Most of the time he works at having fun, if you see what I mean? He has his own family, so we don't bother him and don't nose into what he is doing...but we see him from time to time. He appears quite happy, I reckon. He is still shocked to have been separated from you all and to have left the Earth, as it is not something one does every day, so it is a great surprise when one arrives here! He will learn quickly as he is very intelligent and copes well, but we are very aware that it hurts to find ourselves without those we love, who are still on Earth. So that's it for now, he has his exercises and we have ours.

As far as I am concerned, all I have been doing here since my arrival is to enjoy myself, so I should be ashamed, shouldn't I?! There is so much to do! The pleasure I get chatting with you is still the same as ever since we first spoke, long ago, when I left the Earth *(Note: Nearly six years ago)*. You have always been on my Mind and I have always enjoyed talking to you.

So I'll now tell you what I've been doing recently. Most people I see are here to help me. They are here for themselves too, as by lending me a hand they help themselves, I reckon they learn to be of assistance to others. Most of the conversations we have consist of so many intermingled topics that it is difficult to separate them!

I have learnt a lot by seeing things from a point of view that is different from mine. I used to think I was right about so many subjects! I now realise that in a way I was wrong to reject what was not beautiful or 'sensible'. I mean, I thought if you could not judge something by reasoning, it was not correct. However, here we see things differently. If it is evaluated by the 'brain', or to be more correct by the Mind (since the brain

42

is only a tool of the Mind), it is probably false. One must judge and size up with one's heart, one's affection and feelings. If one cannot do or say anything good, one should wait to be able to do so before expressing an opinion, thus it is quite different from what I used to do!

But I reckon the most interesting thing is to discover oneself. It can be painful or embarrassing but it's worth it, as in the end that's what we need to achieve when we are here! We must know ourselves to be able to comprehend why we do or did such or such a thing. This is how to progress, by understanding ourselves better, as it makes us want to do better and no longer make the same mistakes.

BR- What do you have to do to get to know yourself?

The hardest part is to recognise what we should do, rather than what we've done wrong. To know how we should have behaved is much harder because we need a comparison point. If there isn't any, we do not always grasp why it is 'wrong' and how to rectify it.

It is when we see the effect it has on others that we comprehend the harm it has done. We do not always have a comparison point, of course, yet we can then try to imagine the effect of our actions if we keep acting that way and what would happen if we did. The spirit in which one does something is what matters most; the reason why one does it, what one is thinking at that time and why. All that is like a big puzzle, the pieces of which hook onto each other and shape the reason and the results.

All this is very interesting when you tackle it, especially if you have not done anything really bad. You can then examine and analyse it without being too ashamed or filled with remorse. Studying your own temperament is a little like analysing the characters of a play or a novel and giving yourself marks for each action or reaction!

(As it is getting late, I struggle to concentrate in order to listen properly. I briefly lose the link but Mum is still there when I tune in again). It is most wonderful to know that you and I can still talk to each other, think about each other and not lose contact, otherwise eternity would be unbearable in my opinion! Fortunately we can still do it and...'thank you' for doing it! I hope you'll be able to link up more often and the 'line' will be better, I am sure. You have perhaps worked too hard lately. That's why you lost your concentration?

Anyway, I am so pleased to know you are still all fine and things are fairly good for you. My little Darling, we can only do our best to send you our loving thoughts. We hope all will be well and you will all have enough money so as not to have any worries.

Worries are constant Earthly problems - whether to do with money or else health and it spoils one's life. Mine here is so much better than before, as far as worries are concerned! None now, except to know you are all safe and trouble free yourselves. I give you big kisses, Dad does too. I look forward to chatting again soon more easily.

(Before I stop, my guide slips in a few words, once more reminding me of the need to have a calm and rested Mind in order to provide a good reception to the thoughts they send. As I am going to bed, he adds: If you are not too tired, you can easily meet your loved ones in this world while your body sleeps. It you are too tired, even your Mind wants to 'sleep' and rest! Let yourself be relaxed and you'll all meet happily.

15th May 2005 - *Have been trying to free myself since 22.00hrs! Finally by 23.00hrs I settle down again, but the pen only writes three words in English: "Off to bed!" I have a Guide as strict as Mum...*

44

28th May 2005 - 23.55 hrs. *I don't feel too tired so I try tuning in. The pen draws two spirals, the centres of which are linked up to one another. When French is spoken, I realise Mum is on-line.*

This centre point is you and that other point is me. The two points are linked up because the vibrations between them are superimposed at the right place, therefore we can hear each other easily.

BR- How does it work?

Quiet and peace of Mind allow the sound of one's Soul to resonate at the correct frequency, so that the other Souls can absorb and receive them on the same frequency.

The main thing is to understand that when two points are linked up on the same frequency, one no longer has any difficulty in communicating. The majority of people would not know or understand this, but we thought it might help you calm your Mind to know how it works.

Most people would like to be able to do what you can achieve, so do learn to do it better and better. That way the results will be so impressive because you receive perfectly such clear and precise communications that they'll leave no doubt as to their origins - that way everybody will believe what you tell them.

The pleasure in communicating is comparable to the pleasure of loving: there is nothing as good! When you love truly and deeply you don't feel like doing anything else or being with anyone else! That's why the pleasure we take in communicating with each other is similar, because once we've learnt to do it, we no longer fancy doing anything else, the rest feels and seems to be so poor, doesn't it?!

BR-Oh yes, indeed!

The very fact of being able to speak to each other between two worlds which are so different and practically invisible to each other is a miracle in itself! We need to pinch ourselves (nearly!) to check we are not dreaming. Therefore, you see, it isn't unlike loving someone who is worth it.

Moreover, this has even more value as it is eternal, since it has to do with eternity; we can no longer be parted when we've linked up again between the Hereafter and the Earth and vice-versa. For us to meet up again, my darling daughter, all that is left to do is for you to go to sleep (for your night rest) and for me to wait for you, so it's easy! Yet what is even more exciting is to have also the possibility to speak to each other when you are awake and you being able to write it down to create a book out of our conversations - because you are aware that you are actually talking to me! People should realise that if you can do it, then they could too, if they tried and had a go!

Life here is the same as the last time we had a chat - happy, useful, amusing, interesting, rather fascinating. Life here is the one we should live all the time instead of going to have problems on Earth!

15th June 2005 - *Mum comes to chat.*

You'll have your work cut out with the books you will be writing for us from here! There is 'mine' (yours and mine of course), that will take some time. There'll also be the other one from the gentlemen wishing you to take down in writing their ideas about the future, about the 'invention' (!), conception and creation of the Earth and lots of interesting things they were unable to make people of their own era understand! If they succeed this time, apparently they will be really very pleased. *(Note- She is referring to my Teachers book: 'Truths, Lies & Distortions').*

BR- Who are they?

I only know what I am told about this. They seem to have waited a very long time before they could find someone who would accept to receive their dictation! Let them talk and you will be thrilled to receive that Knowledge, because what you'll want to know will be in what they say. So, let them talk and do not interrupt them, so that they do not lose the thread of their thoughts. Apparently the work is complex and difficult when three people have to dictate the same book! *(Note- There are three main Spirit 'authors' heading the Teaching Team).*

It will be interesting for everybody, you included. You'll have to get on with both those books, so that everything is published at the same time - that way it will have more effect. Of course, there will be some people who will think you are mad etc! But there will also be so many who will appreciate what you did that they'll be grateful to you for helping them, once they've trusted the information you'll have given. When you are well known for that, there will be other books to come which will be as or more interesting!

BR- Are you talking of other books dictated to me?

Yes, of course. Other books that will show people the path towards a life which is more spiritual and less materialistic, so that their Souls develop better. You can guess it's my friends telling me all this, I cannot see that in advance! They simply want to encourage you not to be afraid to give up your job or part of your job, to have the time to do all this! You and I will indeed have our work cut out. Me dictating the rest, you writing, typing and publishing it...and of course translating it, as there will be that to do too! But first of all you must sleep now, because you've had long hard days and we don't want you to risk being ill out of fatigue. So have a good sleep soon. We'll meet up again during your night. All our loving kisses. *(Typical of Mum! She spent her Earthly life telling me to go to sleep. She still does!)*

BR- Before leaving you, do you know whether Dave is ok?

(Brief silence then I hear his message!) Lots of love from me, darling. I hope you will all have enough money to keep you going and get the kids started on their way. They should have plenty to get them going. *(I give Dave the latest news about our children and ask about his activities).* Mainly on my allotments and gardens. I look around and plant more, I change things, I grow wonderful plants and veggies I'd never seen before. I only have to wish for them and they appear!

BR- How can you wish if you have never seen them before?

The list of what can be done here is enormous, so when I wish I could grow something different for the pleasure of it, it appears in front of me! I look after it and water it, or pick a special feed for it and it helps it be even more beautiful! All that is just for the sheer pleasure of it. It is great and not back breaking nor thirst giving!

BR- Anne-France, Jim and I are ok, knowing you are still alive and hopefully happier. We hope you are not grieving. Have we met at night?

Lots of times, otherwise I would not have been able to go on here without you all! I had to see you all again and I have, so now I feel better knowing you are not gone and I have not really gone. You have my love and I have yours and we are all 'a thought away', as they say. So you have nothing to worry about me: I am ok, am flourishing, blooming like a flower or a good cucumber! *(Typical of Dave! Managing to joke to reassure his family, even in the worst times).* I have lots to do here and plenty of people to help me. I love doing what I do and it is very exciting, so all is well in both worlds, mine being better than yours though!

You still have some time to go before we all meet here for good, they say, but you will all have done some good on Earth and me here. So we'll all be happy in the end. We cannot fail to meet, that's good to know! All my love to all of you, the three of you. You cannot know how much I missed you when I left! But now I have understood we are not really completed parted, so we'll put up with the interim situation until we have our rightful time, which is not now, not yet, but we shall be together one day! Not yet, not yet, I know, but that's ok. I understand, I accept, that's fine now. I can cope with that now.

BR- Anne-France has bravely got stuck into understanding and comparing mortgages etc!
Anne-France is brilliant...like her Dad, I know! *(I could sense the wink and his guffawed laughter as when he used to joke. Still does it!)*

BR- Jim could do with some healing sent, to protect him from sick people around him at the moment!
No worry, we'll look after him and them and you too. We cannot leave you out alone to struggle. All is well. You have our love and support. You can go to sleep now, you need it.

15th July 2005 - 8.15am - *It took me a while to relax enough to get a link. My guide steps in*:
There at last! Lots of thoughts going through your Mind are blocking the way to our conversation. Make the journey slowly but surely. Try again and again until your Mind is able to remain quiet for a while. Lots of people have this problem, you are just unlucky since you want so much to talk to us. Many try and fail. You've succeeded now, so be of cheer!
Lots of folks here would like to communicate with you. We'll try one at a time. Your Dave is all right, he has plenty to do and is enjoying it. We've got to let him get on with it, as

49

communicating for the time being would bring him back to thinking of the Earth time and we would rather have him think ahead! He is still fragile on that score, better for him to focus on the path in front.

It is a difficult situation to be here in a new world, so to speak and yet have the possibility to link back to one's previous life on Earth and have people still over there! Everybody suffers from it, in a way. It is good because they know you are still there and they can have a word with you; you are not lost forever! But it is painful too, because it makes them long for the old ways and old life instead of concentrating on the new one and building upon it, as there is a lot to build here!

They have to learn to think in a very special way, unlike on Earth. It is a question of concentration and focus and need for upliftment and calmness of Mind at the same time. So, at the moment, he is better left in peace for a little while, at one with the new world he creates for himself. Yet do not think he is forgetting you, he is NOT! You are all in his heart and thoughts, but **we** want him to concentrate on the good sides of his stay here, which is real life. We wish to let him build more to consolidate what he has already achieved.

BR- Ok. I understand. Any news about my mum?

Your mum is fine. She's always busy and active, learning more each time we meet! Make her happy by trying to link up more often. She is fine and enjoys doing what she likes best - learning. We have plenty to learn here, so she'll never be idle! She can come if you like but you'll need to be concentrating well, as it is 'painful' for her to be left hanging if you cut the conversation off! Lots of people want to talk to you, including all those helpers you don't really know of, but who care about you and try to inspire you.... *(Suddenly French is spoken. It's Mum).*

50

Let's hope you'll have more time to speak to me, my Sweetheart. You have so much to do, I 'forgive' and understand you, don't worry! I am enjoying myself as usual here so don't fret, I have lots of activities but they are always pleasurable.

BR- I am pleased for you! You deserve it.
There is only enjoyment in Paradise, you see!

BR- Do tell me more about it please.
As usual, it is more 'mental exercises' rather than physical activities, if we can say that here! All we have to do is think in a certain way and thus get some astonishing results!

BR- Can you give me some examples?
My 'entourage' consists of a group of very pleasant people, who are kind, intelligent, interesting and know much more than me. I can ask any question at any time and they'll give me an answer. If I wonder why the 'shape' of a thought is different from another, I am shown either in my Mind or through being given explanations or examples which make me understand. Thoughts always have a shape when we look at them, because here they materialise! As soon as we think, we see the result. It's very amusing and used to intrigue me, but one gets used to it very quickly, so it is not new any longer if one does it often.

I learnt to really make great use of my thoughts because I wanted to be able to utilise them for you all, to do you some good and also to explain the power of thoughts to you. We create just by thinking. By creating, one has fun or one does something useful! It is so easy to do here, one wonders why it is not used more on Earth! I think Earthlings lack practice; they are not used to it, whereas here we are.

51

I have seen lots of people, new and 'old' ones, ever since my arrival. My main occupation and also recreation is to have a chat with them, exchange ideas, have fun trying what they suggest or tell me and see the results I obtain. All this does not really take much time. As we talk we give each other examples - and the best way to explain and understand is to see things we have just discussed create themselves! Only a few people around me practise it, others don't try, they simply watch or listen! But, personally, I need to try it in order to understand better, so I do it with those who want to have a go.

We do have other activities too, it's not all chats! Activities depend on what people like to do. Those who like gardening do it, those who want to practise playing or learning music go and deal with that elsewhere. I stay in my beautiful garden/ park, with its animals, my cats and my friends from here. My parents come from time to time but they do have their own activities too. Dad has always a lot to do.

BR- Your dad or mine?

Yours, Dad Nic. He is always so busy with his research in physics. I lose my way when he tries to explain something too complex!

Your mum is no longer a little old woman sitting on the edge of her bed reading or watching TV, you know*!* *(Unexpected comment! It shows how Mum hated her old age).* She is now a rather good looking young woman, I think (I hope!), who deals with various subjects which are not only interesting and useful but fun, most of the time anyway. There is so much to learn one cannot get bored. The only thing needed is to want to do it, get on with it and at once, one gets results and more discoveries.

My life in Nice was so boring compared to this one now! When you come and join me here, you will see for yourself that everything is really so exciting and fascinating.

Don't worry, you are not ready to come over yet, though, of course, one day it will happen, but it will really be worth it! So don't have any concerns about it. You will get the best teaching one could receive!

BR- Do you know whether Pierre is still on Earth or in the Spirit World? (My eldest brother in South America). I have not heard from him for a good while!

I haven't been told anything about this, I don't think he is here as I would have been warned, I am sure! Well, that's all for now. I'll let you know if I have anything new to tell you.

(I give Mum some news of us all. Then my guide pops in). All is well, she's got your news. You told her lots, but she says she could follow them as she received them as pictures in her Mind. So it is best to send them by thinking of each piece as a picture; they reach better the person you communicate with. Let's call a halt for now, but you may want to say goodbye to your mum? *(Suddenly, French is spoken again).*

My darling daughter, go and deal with your activities and no doubt your chores. I'll carry on educating myself and enjoying myself! Thanks for talking to me. Don't worry about the future. I am told things will be all right. Life is shorter than one thinks so make the most of it, before coming to enjoy yourself here! Lots of love to you all. We are keeping an eye on you!

30th July 2005 - *The conversation starts in French. It's my mother.*

We send you all our loving thoughts. Remember there is no need to cry for Dave. You know he is fine here now. So do not grieve, what happened is over, his illness and suffering are over. All you have to look forward to is meeting up with him again one day when you come here and he will certainly be there for you when you arrive with us all. But it's not for now so don't worry about it!

Life for you should be much easier now with more money? The children will certainly settle better with their own 'wealth'. I hope they will be sensible with expenses and will not go overboard. As for you, I know you will be anyway. I'd really like you to manage to finish typing our book and publish it! You will then feel so much lighter and freer on that score. Moreover, I am told by my knowledgeable friends here that you will have others to type and prepare (which will have been dictated) so you need to make time and place for them! All you have is to reserve certain hours or days just for that in your diary as if it was a class you had to teach somewhere. That way you won't miss the opportunity.

BR- Yes, I have started doing this.

Thanks. You'll see it will be really exciting to see it in print and selling! My own mother was very excited when I published the short stories I had written during the war. She still remembers them! It tickled her that I was a member of the Writers Guild. My mum is never far from me. She is quite busy like my dad. They always have interesting activities, so do I. We deal with what interests us, so you see there is no risk getting fed up here!

BR- What have you been doing lately?

My life is chock full because I look into what one can do with one's thoughts, whether travelling in Time as I have often done, or creating things, or analysing oneself more and more to discover what kind of person one really is! The most difficult thing to grasp is to forget I am not just (for example) your mum, that Suzanne Leclercq, who was born a long time ago and 'died' not so long ago... but I am another 'person' in a way, as there are heaps of various facets to my personality if I study them!

54

I do wonder how one can get around to accepting oneself as one personality made of several facets. All this is beginning to get rather confusing! One has to constantly remember one is not only from the last life one has just had, but from another one... and many others too! It can become complicated! I reckon one must do it in little pieces, small mouthfuls.

I think of the four of you as 'my children', but there must have been other 'times' when I was not that and you were not 'mine'! I have been told this and it was explained to me simply, just to try to make me understand that we do not have only one life on Earth! Otherwise it would be very boring, hardly useful and quite limited!

On the other hand, by having lots of lives, over centuries, one learns loads of very useful things and one discovers other points of view. One does not feel one is just one person of only one gender, one learns to understand others' ways of thinking. But all that takes a lot of time, probably centuries and it doesn't stay in your 'head', you forget it from one life to the other. Yet the Soul, the Spirit, remembers a little or a lot. So you begin to accumulate this Knowledge gradually and to improve yourself... and that's what matters, I am told here.

Personally, I would prefer not to bother with all that stuff and only think of what I have discovered up to now, then tell you about it so that you too learn and write about it for the public! Yet there is much more, my friends keep telling me, so I do what I am told, I listen, I learn as well as I can, though I don't always absorb everything at once! There are things one must ponder about and also analyse with someone near you, who helps you, encourages you and explains what you are seeing.

BR- Have you discovered some more of your own facets?

The life I examined first was the recent one with you, because it was important I understood why I had come to Earth and had you all. Now I know why - you were my 'raison d'être', my reason to be and my life. The rest was simply revolving around that. I wanted to be your mum; my life was the four of you! My choice had been to be a mother as I had not been one like this before. But there were other lives and this is what I am beginning to examine a little, from time to time. I don't have to do it all the time, it's only when I think about it or get interested in it. So, that's what I have been doing up to now!

Little details are not precise. Overall, I have been a man several times before! But I no longer wanted to be a man because I did not know what it was like to be a woman as a mother! As the life when I had been a woman before was childless, that's why (after it) I wanted to be a mum, to understand and learn what one feels when one has children whom one loves.

My 'visions' and glimpses of those lives are only short visions, impressions and brief memories, rather than long detailed films. We are not interested in little details but in the main feelings which have shaped that personality, that life. After living it, we always find ourselves back here, to analyse it sooner or later and ponder on how we could improve what we have or have not learnt! Yet there is always the possibility of returning to Earth **if** we wish to do so, though we are not 'obliged' at all. We decide that when we want, if we wish to!

There is no reason why I personally would go back, considering you are still there and you won't have the time to wait for me. I would have to be a baby once more and grow up, meanwhile you'll be getting older! It would be very silly to do that! Moreover, I don't see why I would want to go back when I feel so good here, having fun to learn all kinds of things without any problems or disease or worries. Personally, I do not want to go anywhere! I only want to wait for you (when you are ready!) while occupying myself usefully.

After seeing all those little pieces of 'old or previous' lives, I understood there is only one thing to do in each life: **Do our best all the time**! That way there will never be any regrets, as we risk feeling obliged to return in order to repair stupid mistakes or learn better. All that is needed is to listen to our conscience and tell ourselves that if we cannot do some good, at least we must avoid doing any harm to whoever. After that, the main thing is to improve ourselves in every possible way and I am not talking of money in this case! Money is very useful and allows you to be comfortable, but you must not live **for** that as, after all, where is it once you've passed over to where I am, hey?!

So this is my 'new' opinion, as I used to want to be able to earn money or at least have some, but I must admit I have always thought and acted as I should, concerning not to harm others and do one's best. So it helped me and I was right after all!

BR- You have always been kind! Did you discover more details about one particular person you were?

Not really. It was more impressions and getting some comprehension rather than lists of facts, dates, genders, jobs etc, do you understand? So I'll have to delve into it gradually, several times, to understand it all better. After all, WHO I was is of no importance! It's mainly how I lived before and how I reacted or felt which matters, you see? So there is still lots to discover about all this!

BR- Very interesting. Do you see Dave? I assume not often, of course.

Everybody's life is 'enveloped' and wrapped up in their own thoughts. It's only when we think of others that we find ourselves 'transported' towards that person.

So, as I know Dave is busy with his own discoveries and his settling down, as well as having his own parents and others who look after him, I don't go and bother him, being only his 'Earthly mother-in-law'! Yet he was very kind to me when we met again. Straight away he gave me a hug and a kiss, gave me a lovely smile and said: "It's so good to see you again!". That really touched me to see he had not forgotten me completely! He also saw your dad and introduced himself by saying: "I am Brigitte's husband", a fact which amused us because he introduced himself 'via you'! We hugged him and kissed him, welcomed him warmly and congratulated him for what he did for you all on Earth. We loved him as best as we could to thank him wholeheartedly to have endured all that to help you. But he was modest as usual and said: "I've left them behind, it breaks my heart not to see them again." It brought sadness to his Soul to think about it, so we changed subject. Then we let him talk to his family, as he had lots to say and do to catch up!

Now I'll leave you in peace to go and do what you have to see to. I give you and your children big kisses. Sleep well tonight!

17th August 2005 - *My Guide wants to give some advice and explanations.*

When the sun goes down, the air is usually stiller. When the air is stiller, our vibrations reach the Earth more easily, because the Earth vibrations are not 'shaken' and disturbed as much and we can 'flow' more easily from one world to the other.

So if you want to be a good medium and channel, you'll need to be able to stand still inside yourself and listen to us, as if there was no wind or storm within you. A pure blue sky would do as a picture in your Mind. The vibrations and the thoughts we are sending you are often disturbed; it is frustrating - but if you listen carefully, it is wonderful both for you and for us, do you understand? Life has to be quieter at times for you and us. There **must** be a time devoted to us. We'll keep you to it if you promise us to do so.

BR- Do you want me to give up going to M.? (A practice circle away from York I started attending in the hope of improving my link to get messages for others).
How you do it is your choice, my friend, it is your life! You'll have so much to do with the book writing and typing and sitting with us, you'll be obliged to give up some things less important to you, if your books and sitting matter to you! Make the time - we'll provide the goods! Once or twice a week would do. You need not give up all your life for us and our meetings! So be as good as you can, let's start having some discipline and regularity... then you'll find it will be easier and fall into place. You have a job *(for Spirit)* to do on Earth; we want to help you do it. We can do as much as possible our end, but if you do not provide the time, the will and the dedication, you will find it a big struggle. We are here by your side - you just need to ask and work. *(The tragic past eighteen months have made life very hectic for me, hence his reminder).*

25th August 2005
Mum here! We are once more together, at last. It's been a while since we last spoke, hasn't it! I'd like to tell you what I have been up to recently. I saw ancient countries and people with different civilisations! This is to make me understand that, whatever the race or the era, people are basically the same!

Of course there are some small differences but, deep down, people are alike, with all the same emotions in those days as the ones we feel nowadays! So in the end, it means we are all similar and we must not make any distinctions and create differences, therefore we must not fight and have wars, because when we fight and kill, we kill part of ourselves, since we are all alike with the same human desires and wishes.

Yet ego, stupidity and selfishness come in and destroy everything; people argue, come to blows, kill one another and do a lot of harm to their own Souls in the end! So the moral is not to kill or fight because we do not really have any differences!

Seen from here, feelings look different from what we think or feel when on Earth. What matters is the moral behind all this, you see. Facts are not that significant, it's always the feelings, the impressions which matter and which one remembers when one comes here. One does not care any longer about facts, details, 'techniques', who was what! It is no longer important at all! What really matters here are the feelings others and yourself have!

28th August 2005 - 22.45 hrs. *I hear English spoken. At first I am not sure who is speaking!*

Greetings from this new world of mine to your old one. You have all wanted me to give you news of my new 'holiday'...which I'll have to take without you or anyone else, this time, until you all join me!

BR- (The jokey tone is familiar) Is it you Dave?

You've guessed right love, I am here and really happy to be able to talk to you. You've been waiting a long time for this, I know, I was told. It's been very painful for all of us, this sudden parting and all the illness before *(he passed over 10 months ago)*. I can assure you I am fine now, no more illness,

60

as you know! But you must make sure the kids are ok and safe. We've worked hard for them, both of us and now you are alone to make sure they are all right. We can do it. You have the material needs covered now I hope, with all the dosh I left, hopefully and carefully saved in the right place. Make sure the kids don't waste it on silly things like Jim could do if he did not think enough. Though I am sure he'll be careful, because he's got his dad's head on his shoulders (ha ha!). He is not daft, he thinks well when he wants to.

I am all right now, not perfect as it could not be perfect away from you lot, but "I am all right", as my brother used to say! *(Family joke: That sentence used to be as much as his brother Ray would say on the phone!)* I have learnt a lot since we last spoke. You know all about my arriving here, don't you! I told you how I got here - quite a surprise for me but now I've found ways to occupy myself and ways to cope with the separation.

You've done well, all of you, I hear. I am so pleased you are coping fine and have done a good job of all the chores etc *(hectic moving out and selling the house)*. You did and do deserve a medal, all of you! But I hope you've been rewarded with all the dosh, so that should make you feel better!

BR- Thank you for all you did but we do miss you a lot!
You miss me?! I miss you all, silly billy! You know I do, I am not a stone, you know. It hurts to be such a long way away somehow, but we'd better not talk about parting and all that, as it makes us both feel sad. Let's keep it happy and enjoy the reunion! I am glad you've chosen to come tonight. I was not sure how we were going to talk again. I was told to rest and 'gather myself', to hold on to my new surroundings because I was walking all over the place, looking for you I suppose, in my Mind and heart...but that's settled down now, I think.

I still miss you but we've met many times at night, when you are asleep. Yes, you know it helps me bear the new situation and the distance between us. So we need to have that contact; I've always loved it and I hope you'll keep coming now and then. My life here is a bit different from the hard slog of allotment digging and pruning of roses or hedges! We've got gorgeous gardens here, full of amazing flowers I've never seen before, which means I can grow them easily because I love the look of them and that helps them to grow. Their beauty is beyond description. I'd need a film, a camera, to show you how beautiful they all are! That's one part of what I do here. Then there is the listening to beautiful music. I could not play myself but others do and that's what I enjoy most too - listening to lovely sounds of colours!!

BR- You do... what?!
I can **listen to the sounds of colours**. I am told you know it is possible, so why are you surprised?

BR- Can you give me more details about it?
When they play those lovely tunes, I see colours around them and that's like painting with music or listening to colours of enormous quality and numbers! I've stopped trying to list the colours - there are some with no name I know - because I cannot ever recall seeing them on Earth. What I see here is incredible! My Earthly palette was practically bare compared to the amount of variations there are here. It's never ending, so that's why I say I listen to music and colours, as well as gardening with wonderful flowers who play at growing for me!

BR- They play at growing?!
It feels like playing, because when you try to grow something normally on Earth, you have to prepare the ground and sow and feed all the plants, whereas now I only have to

wish them to grow and they do it, as if with a smile for me! You have never met plants and flowers willing to grow even before you start dealing with them! They are there, ready to flower, bloom, grow, attach their branches or leaves to the right stick... without me having to do much work!!

BR- It must be boring for you then!

No, it's not really, because it is so amazing, amusing and funny, for now anyway! I am beginning to get used to it but it is great to create a great parterre, or wood, or field without all the slog and the backache! As to watering them, don't even think about doing it yourself!! All you think is: "I wish it rained"... and it does for the sake of the plants! All that is to show me that you can think of something and want it strongly enough for it to happen, as they often say!

BR- Who says that?

My parents are with me. My dad is still gardening and also a few others here who are interested in that too. They've shown me a few tips - how to cope with this new life here, without having to struggle with a flesh body. I am getting much better at it. I had so much to learn and am still learning. That's what it's all about: Having to discover new things without worrying about it, because there is no point doing so!

My little Darling, you know I always loved you and you've helped me to the end more than you'll ever know, because I could not have coped on my own without you by my side, encouraging me and Anne-France and Jim lovingly caring for me. I'll never forget what you all did for me, especially when the times were awful. You all pulled together to try to help. We were all one loving family; that's what I'd always wanted and I had it right to the end. That helped me go without regrets in a way, without feeling we had not made peace. We had made peace and still loved each other, all of us. That's all that mattered and matters.

So I could go without regrets, I suppose, but it is not quite true, because I do have regrets to have had to leave you. Yet it is how it had to be, I reckon. If you think about it, all of you could not have had enough money unless I 'died'! And in order to 'die' I had to have a disease, or accident, or something, so it happened! Let's make the most of our times together from now on. You tell me about you all and I'll tell you about 'me all'! You've got some of my news, so tell me yours now. Keep talking *(I explain to Dave how Anne-France was able to purchase her first new house in Kent, then mentally I describe it by visualising slowly every room... as if I toured it with a video camera).*

BR- Could you follow me Dave?

Fantastic! Thank you! I could see it as I was shown the pictures in your Mind. It was great, like being there! We'll have to do that again, it's amazing, you could have had a video camera and it could not have been better! Make sure we do it again another time - that will be wonderful. I find myself in her house that way; it's really great to have been able to see it. So she has settled well by the sound of it.

BR- I went to help her move in and her friend S. helped also. (I then visualise Anne-France's garden and the outside of the house as well as the nearby view, explaining what I was showing. My guide steps in).

That was fine! We could follow you. He had to be helped to pick the pictures but it was feasible because you explained as you went along, so it was ok. You could slow it down: to have one small picture at a time, with a short gap in between, so that it had time to register here - but otherwise he's got it and is delighted to have an insight into his daughter's house.

BR- Didn't Anne-France do it before, herself, some time ago?

Dave here now! Yes, I'd had some glimpses and bits shown before, so I had an idea. But it helps to go over it again and again, to build up the picture of the place in my Mind. So that's fine. I got the overall picture before and get more details every time we speak. Can you do it another time? That would be good, so that I can reinforce the image in my Mind and keep it safe, like a photo or a film, you understand?

You can always talk to me, you know. No fear of upsetting me now. I know you have a busy life and dare not distress me by reminding me we were all parted. But I have understood and accepted what has happened. So, we can all meet often, now and then, that way the parting will not be so painful. It will be eased and made more interesting by sharing each other's lives. You tell me about yours, all of you and I tell you mine!

I bet you can't beat what I'll have to tell you! You'd never get to do things like I do here...unless you turn up on the doorstep here yourself, one day! But that's not for now, don't worry. Think of me and my musical flowers and colours; think of me as not suffering ever again, that's what matters. You be what you need to be and want to be; you know what it is.

Forget the past, now is the time for your new future. I still love you all and always will, so why fret? Do what you all need to do and have a more comfortable life now, I hope. Go ahead with your present life and close the door to any sad times. Only the good times stay in my Mind, so keep them in yours too, but don't cry over them! One does not cry about good things, surely! Be happy!

7th September 2005 - *The pen starts in English. It's my Guide:*

All that is needed is a quiet Mind, that's all we ask! We'll do the rest. Then see the difference it makes when the two worlds are joined.

BR- Am wondering whether I'll be getting the part-time teaching work I applied for?

Life on Earth has its own pattern; we cannot always see the details. If it has its benefits for you, it will happen because you want the best solution. If it has not, it won't! So do not fret if you don't get it! We'll see to you, all along.

The last time you spoke to your mother, you seemed to doubt or hesitate about the facts she was giving you - you must not do that! If she comes to talk to you, she'll tell you what she has done and did, not what she is inventing or what you think your Mind invents! So, please do not disappoint her by doubting or being concerned it may not be her.

BR- I am sorry. Am concerned if something could make Touky think it is my Mind influencing things!

Make the leap of faith once and for all, as they say. Please stop doubting or being concerned your Mind might interfere. We would not let it happen, we would tell you! I am always there and I supervise the conversations, to make sure your mum gets it across correctly. So please feel reassured and safe and worry-free, all right?! *(A brief silence then French is spoken).*

Now it's me, Sweetheart! Don't worry, all is fine. Do you recall my telling you before of my impromptu visit to your brother, my son, with his big boat, because I wanted to 'quench that thirst' too! I had not really seen his boat in detail when I was on Earth *(she'd only seen the schooner once briefly, from the quay, she could not climb on board).* So I had to go and

66

visit it to see it more clearly, to know where it is and how Touk is feeling. He looked very busy, but he always is, isn't he? I suppose it must be a nightmare to have so many things to do so that it works, or does not sink, or does not cause accidents, or stays in good condition! It's worse than having to do some housework at home every day, in my opinion!

Poor Touky seems to feel very lonely within himself. He puts on a brave front, he looks efficient and he is that too indeed, but it seems to me he feels alone, having to solve everything on his own and struggle against the outside world. He appears so self-assured but I reckon he can only count on himself, can't he? Other people have so often let him down or disappointed him!

I would have liked to be able to tell him that I was there, near him and kiss him... but I could do no more to let him know than come close to him and look at him with great love! That's all. I hope he felt me... I wonder? It's so sad to be so near each other and yet so far through lack of communication! I do hope I'll manage to make myself heard in his head, though I expect he will doubt! Yet perhaps he'll believe it...one day!

The only reason why I tell you this is that I hope he will read this sometime and will understand I had been near him when I visited him unexpectedly, as I was wondering what he was doing and where. That's it. If he does not believe it, well, too bad. Personally I do know that I went there! He will eventually know it is true when he too comes and joins me and Dad here! We shall then say to him: "You were wrong to doubt!" But for now, that's all.

BR- Did you see the accident Touky had? (I give her more details).

No, I didn't. But I know about it. I am really sorry not to have been able to prevent it, but it's not always possible from here and I wouldn't know what to do for that at the moment. But I am - and we all are - sending him all our loving healing thoughts, as you can guess! It's awful for him.

I am pretty sure you must have some things to do, so I should not delay you any longer. I have my eternal life here to do what I want! Poor you, no doubt you have chores to see to. What a life that Earthly life! Why can't we just have pleasures like I have here? I assume it may be as a 'reward' for having done one's best to be a 'good pupil'!

BR - Sorry if I disturbed you by talking to you!
The main thing for me is to talk with you and teach you what I do and what there is to do here, even if I don't always understand it all! So it's ok for you to call me and 'disturb' me, as you say. I have nothing fixed here. If I stop doing something, I can always start again later on, you know. So don't worry Darling. Life on Earth can be a bit of a nightmare, can't it, if we have to tackle too many things we don't fancy?! That does not exist here; that is one of the great differences between the two lives! I'll let you get on now and hope we'll soon have another short or long conversation, when you are free and your Mind is calm. Mine always is, except if I am excited by all the marvels I am shown here or I discover. Long live Earthly death! Long live eternal life! Your mum loves you Darling.

7th November 2005 - 23.45hrs. *Tonight will be the twenty-third anniversary of my dad's passing. After doodling joined up spirals, the pen starts the first words in French, then I hear the full flow. From what is said I guess it may be Dad.*

The light we see here is not the light of the sun. We are surrounded with superb light which does not dazzle us! I know where it comes from. It is not created by one or several persons or any other 'Being', but by their own individual kindness. It radiates from the core of each Being's heart, even though they obviously have not got a heart of flesh. It is always a pleasure to watch those lights of different colours emanating from each individual here, as it looks like some rainbows, or even better!

Each personality seems to have his or her own colours, thus creating a marvellous range of incredible hues, which I could not name as there are no words to describe some of those beauties! In order to grasp the effect given, one needs to know how to look at them without analysing them but by absorbing them yourself with all your Being, to be able to sense the subtle vibrations which shine forth each time you look at them! One may get used to it but personally I still and always marvel at this wonderful and spectacular show!

This is what life here offers us: A display of beauty and kindness, intelligence and superior science. True paradise for intelligent Spirit Beings, thirsty for Knowledge! My passion is researching all this, researching and understanding all I can in order to be able to grasp even more and therefore research even more what there is to know, learn and discover! As there is no time limit, it may take me quite a long time!

Last time we spoke to each other, we discussed new theories about the formation of atoms and their expansion towards other worlds.

BR- Did we? Sorry, I have forgotten. You have a better memory than me then!

Yes, I told you I had seen that atoms in cells could divide themselves, or wake up if one activated them, in order to keep life going in their complicated structure. But there is no need to do that if the Spirit Being who created them decided to no longer use that physical body (if we are talking of a human or animal body of course).

So, supposing someone was ill, we must remember that somebody (physically) ill is somebody whose own Spirit and Soul is ill, one way or the other. Therefore, one has to try to deal with healing the Soul before wanting to tackle the cells of the physical body! To do this, the Energy one sends to the sick person is and must be directed towards his Soul and Spirit, so that he can 'recharge his batteries', buck himself up, reconsolidate the internal structure of his very core. When the help given to him to invigorate him manages to have an effect on his Soul, then and only then shall we see an effect on the flesh body!

This is why we also say: "Heal the inside so that the outside can be radiant with health". Even children have psychological problems - mental, spiritual, and emotional. One must not ignore them or reject them, but understand what comes out to the surface **started within** them. This is why one must always look inside a lighthouse to see whether the light still shines as well as it should, otherwise the lighthouse will be dark or perhaps gradually or suddenly switched off! The Internal Light is the one which counts, at its source. It is the source which must be in good health so that what shoots out externally is clearly projected, 'well understood', do you get my meaning?

BR- Yes I do. Is that you Dad? (Suddenly the pen sketches a rectangular box and my question is ignored!)

The apparition of a box in your text won't be very clear, but if you think about it, a box has six well-defined sides. If they were removed, there would no longer be six visible sides, there would be a vacuum, a hole, in fact 'nothing' in front of you!

Yet the imprint of those sides will have had an effect on the canvas, the 'texture' of what one calls 'air', empty space. Yes indeed! Though one cannot see it with eyes of flesh, there is still that effect of imprinting its shape and Energy in the invisible 'form' of space and its Energies! Its Energies indeed, because the Energies of an object are at different frequencies according to the dimensions, the thickness, the length of its 'texture' etc.! Therefore, an object seen as 'solid' in terms of Earthly physics has a texture which will radiate in different ways according to what it contains, what it is made of, how it is made etc. All that has an influence on its environment, invisible to human eyes. Do you grasp what I mean?

BR- Possibly... I am not too sure.

Just a minute. Wait. An object is a mass of atoms (electrons and infinitesimal particles) which are constantly present and create their own environment by the very fact they exist. Because they are there, that creates other micro-environments around them, which have an influence on what surrounds them, whether they are physical or non-physical objects - and certainly on what is called 'space' , 'vacuum'!

So how can one understand physics as taught on Earth if one does not grasp physics known here? One cannot make head nor tail of it as something invisible cannot in theory (if looked at with eyes of flesh) have an influence on empty space. Yet it does - this is what I want to tell you. What has 'disappeared' to your eyes, you Earthly people, has **not** really disappeared! In fact, all it did was change form, from visible to invisible, which does not mean non-existing! It still exists, but at such a fine level and vibrating at such a speed that eyes cannot see it, instruments may not pinpoint it and people will not know about it!

Therefore, if an object can do that, so can a body, a Being, whether human or not! This is why once the human body is dead and destroyed **an imprint remains in its entourage** - an imprint left by its existence, its identity - yet the true identity is the one of the Spirit and the Soul which 'inhabited' it, because they are the ones which gave it life.

This is why one sometimes thinks one is seeing someone who has 'died', say, in an ancient castle, but they are not always really there: They may simply have left a very strong impression during their Earthly passage, during a particular era. That impression still lingers on; the imprint was not erased on the fine and sensitive web of 'Space-Time'... time which does not really exists but which is an idea created by men to enable them find their way on Earth, during day and night.

The totality of my 'discoveries' is only infinitesimal compared to what one must be able to know when one has been studying that here for quite a while! I enjoy finding out about all this; it enriches my knowledge, but it also allows me to understand better what one must be able to do in life and for life.

BR- Can you explain this more?

If one grasps how everything comes to be in existence, why it exists, where everything which seems to disappear goes, well, one gets a point of view and comprehension that are very different from what one used to have! So, any Knowledge is always welcome, as one simply adds to what one had learnt earlier - never subtracts! One step forward propels you onwards, often by ten steps in fact, because it opens even more doors for you towards other discoveries as or more fascinating! *(Then Mum pops in suddenly)*. Darling, please go to sleep now. You'll get too tired if you stay up any longer. Good night from both of us. Personally I don't always understand what he is talking about... but he seems to know what he is on about, so let's believe him!

26th November 2005 - *I asked my Guide for explanations, regarding a comment made by someone I met who fancied himself knowledgeable and said our "guide/door keeper comes on our left".*

This is an excellent example of how Mankind sees things in black and white, right and left, blue and black etc! **We** see Love, Caring, Teaching and utter Truth! That's all.

So, whoever comes close is the Teacher of Love of that time; whoever decides to be there to help is the Teacher of the 'day'. Whoever is near is automatically the protector of his protégé.

An idea of how it works or takes place is this: Imagine myself (your 'Silver Arrow') beside you. If someone from my world wishes to come and talk to you, I make sure he has something 'safe' to talk about - nothing disturbing, frightening or untrue (which would not happen in my vicinity!). He then approaches you and if he knows how to reach your Mind directly, I'll let him do it. But if he is new and doesn't know how to, then I'll be the person who talks to you. I'll say: "He says he was in the war" or: "Your mother is here and says she loves you etc.".

On the other hand, if the communicator is a far Superior Being, filled with Knowledge, he has no need for my intervention and he can go straight to your Mind and come to you with his communication. Another communicator or inspirer will always be welcome to draw close any time he wishes. That means you can be well surrounded with Love and Knowledge!

Whether it is 'on the right or left side', or 'front or back' is of no consequence whatsoever! **We come close to your Soul and your Mind and let the Knowledge and information seep into it.** If you are very receptive, the flow is good, easy flowing and delightful. But if you are not, as your Mind is too full of other thoughts, then we all have to chip in, to help pave the way for the higher thoughts to come through.

BR- How do you do it?

The main thing is to send you lots of healing and peaceful Energy, so that the good communication resulting from the exchange can be fruitful. If you were constantly being disturbed or too upset or unsettled to maintain the link then there isn't much point keeping it going or even trying at times!

It is not our job to force you to receive! We are here to **help** you receive, if you wish to have the information or are ready to have it.

A good example is your mother. She has so much desire to do well and succeed, indeed, that she tries very hard, no matter what you offer her! If you are not very receptive, she'll still try really very hard! But we cannot let her exhaust herself mentally as she could lose her self-confidence. So we stay near her and send thoughts in the right direction or intensity, to help her own thoughts travel where they need to be or go... so that you receive them, in spite of everything! We do know you don't refuse to have information from your mother, so we are not 'imposing' it on you! We are facilitating it for both your sakes and for the sake of Truth and Love of the Spirit World.

BR- Many thanks (I then send loving thoughts to my family in the Great Beyond and send a thought to Dave, assuring him he is not 'a faint memory', hoping this is passed on to him).

They are all around, safe and happy and prepared to talk but you may need to rest more now. *(Suddenly a conversation starts without any introduction! I soon guess it might be Dave. Incidentally, he left us 13months ago).*

An incident to be told: My mother went to see your mother, out of sheer politeness, as they didn't really know each other well! They've become quite friendly now; they have forgotten the Earth details and concentrate on the Spirit World aspect of things. My mum says your mum is very nice indeed and quite helpful, as well as excited about her discoveries here! So we are all in the same boat, sooner or later, at various levels. We all try to discover and understand more! If you could give me a bit of your news I'd be delighted.

BR- Now or after yours?

My news is not very complicated. I have a lot to do in order to grasp how things work here. So, I spend quite a lot of time not only with my new, magical garden here, but also with new people I have encountered, who help me comprehend what I did not know.

BR- Do you do any 'practice exercises'?

Making my Mind control its thoughts may be the main thing, but also enjoying the fact I do not suffer anymore! We all have our life ahead of us, without risking death anymore; it is a wonderful feeling to be treasured all the time! My feelings for you are still strong and I will not forget you, don't worry. You will always be my little 'W—' in my heart, you know that. So will our kids - they'll always be in my heart and Mind! I hope they have recovered from the shock and sadness they may have felt from my departure - they were very strong and brave, so I hope they don't suffer anymore from it. My love for you all is still as was, if not stronger, as I miss being able to phone you or see you all, but my news is not sad. I am settling down and constantly finding new things to do and learn, so it is an interesting place indeed!

BR- I told you so, long ago!

My regret is not to have listened to you more! But that's past now. I have to concentrate on the present and future, they tell me, so I do. Now it is your turn. What about your news and the kids?

BR- Anne-France is studying, goes to dancing classes, has made new friends etc. I am due to go and see her soon. I have less work to do thanks to what you generously left us. I do more work for Spirit and receive psychic drawings. Did you get this clearly?

(My guide pops in briefly!) We helped but he got it. It is always harder to receive than to give out, so we help him and he is doing well.

(Then Dave came back). Better say goodnight now, love, you know you are tired and I may not be able to maintain the link, as they say. We have quite a lot of helpers here, always ready to give us a hand for doing things of this kind. You have plenty of people around you too, I gather.

My Mind is full of those facts you gave me and I'll think about them for a while now, to 'digest them', let them sink in. My Mind has to think 'Earth-wise' now, to remember those details. That makes a refreshing change from constant mental concentration here! I hope Anne-France finds her 'true love' at last, so that she does not get any more disappointment and heartache, as she's had plenty. What is our Jim up to then? You did not say. *(Unprompted question showing how well he followed what I said and how 'with it' he is!)*

BR- He's busy doing recording for clients. Thanks to you he's started building his own recording studio, buying various pieces of equipment.

Yes, I got the main points you said, no problem. Have got to go now as I can't concentrate for long. Love to you all, tell them! My love to you, little wife still mine, hey! And love to 'Jim-Bop' and 'Franssou'. Love to all of you, my family! Let them know one day that I can communicate, will you? They may be shocked but it may be worthwhile. Love you...bye.

12th December 2005 - *Tried to sit earlier but had some chores to do first. I now put some relaxing music on. The pen starts in French.*

Lower the music, the noise is hard to dominate. Mum here, Darling. My friends advise me to speak 'in one block' so that I don't lose the thread of my thoughts. So I'll do so.

One of the most beautiful moments here was when I succeeded in showing myself to Touky (I think!). It seems to me he saw or sensed me. He looked very busy when I approached him and looked at him with lots of love, so that he tried to feel it. He turned round and stared at thin air, as if he had the impression that something or someone was there. I do not know whether he was able to see me, or whether he has only an impression of a presence or a shadow or a light... but I could see him very well!

It happened towards what could be the end of 'last week', I think, but it is difficult to give a day so I am wary! There was a bag near him, he was bustling about, looking for something I reckon... (*Unexpected news! He had not told me anything. Probably doubting himself! Suddenly English is spoken - it's my guide*). He had lots of things in his hands, she says. It made him jump to think someone was watching him. He looked around to see who was there but did not quite catch your mother's appearance. He knew within himself there was someone but he had misgivings about it! Mother came to see 'Touky' because she wanted to try again and do what she did with you or for you. But it is difficult for her, she needs a lot of practice.

BR- Can you explain how she did it?

She went to her quiet place and saw him in her Mind, then wished herself there. He appeared in her vision and she saw an amount of objects near him and his hands. He was looking for something he wanted and was annoyed he could not find it. He was leaning forward over a bag or a box or some other object and was searching, but suddenly turned round as if he felt someone was watching him. That gave him a start and a shudder, she says. She smiled at the thought he had realised she was there...but then she knew he had not actually seen her as such and she was rather disappointed!

The experience did not last very long but it was a good exercise for your mother and it gave her hope she could do it again, better another time and with her other boys too. The incident was worth it in her eyes, even if her son did not quite see her as well as she would have liked him to. Yet you could try to tell him she was there indeed! But do not despair if he denies it. He may not have realised that he had reacted like that. All experiments and experiences are worth the effort, you know that. Let us try again with your mum now. All you need is to listen quietly and be still within. *(As it was 23.00hrs, I was getting tired and was unable to link up as well, so I stopped, then sent a long email to Touky to inform him).*

17th December 2005 - *The pen starts in English, then I hear the rest.*

Oh, the joy of being here and not suffering anymore! Can you understand it? It's such a wonderful, indescribable feeling. You cannot imagine it until you live it and this is how I still feel after whatever time I've been here! You cannot doubt it, it's me Dave talking, you know I am here Darling! You may wonder why I speak directly to you, without an intermediary? I have learnt to concentrate my thoughts on you and now I see you can receive me.

The purpose of my visit is to tell you what you wanted to know. You asked whether I heard Anne-France talking to me. I did, of course, I always receive thoughts sent to me. She seemed very relaxed, not upset. She had something to show me, she said and she started going round her home, as she had organised and decorated it. She wanted me to share her Xmas tree and decorations and paintings. I felt her thoughts in my Mind and heart - it was warming and uplifting!

As Anne-France showed me her house, I took great delight listening to her talk, as she felt very close to me as if we were in Fulford *(where we lived in York)*. That brought a pang

78

in my heart because I miss her here! I wish I had you all here, we could talk so much more easily, without worrying about concentrating our thoughts. My 'little girl' was really careful to space out her thoughts. I would have assumed she would have blurted it all out, but she took care to do one bit at a time and she made me see her tree in the corner with her paintings nearby and mine too, she said. I felt the pain she must have suffered but she still seemed calm and composed, as she spoke to me in her head. My Mind had joined hers so I could understand more easily that way.

You have tried to link up with me before, but I was not able to come because I was doing some exercises, would you believe? I was shown some things one can do here, which explain why we have to practise thinking in a certain way. That's what makes it so interesting and strange but I am getting used to it, gradually. It all seems so weird to have to think in such a manner for my thoughts to turn into reality! Easy? No. Simple? Yes. Like I said earlier, I was doing some practice exercises to show me one can only improve by honing the details of one's thoughts. Then your thoughts came to me but I could not respond at once, because I had people around me demonstrating to me how one can progress from one stage to the other.

7th January 2006 - 08.20 a.m! *The pen doodles, then words start in French. Mum is online.*

Once you are relaxed it's much better for us to meet up, you know. If we have trouble getting through it's because your Mind is so busy. No 'new' news here but we can still chat, can't we? I want to remind you I love you and give you and the boys a big kiss for your New Year and wish you the very best. Actually, I constantly wish that for you! I would really like you all to be here, so that I don't have to worry for you and I know you would be much more comfortable and happier than on Earth!

My mum has been coming to see me now and then, to have a natter with me and tell me what she's been up to recently. She looks after little children who arrive here rather lost. She ensures they understand there is nothing to fear now; they can be happy if one looks after them as she does. There are a lot of them around her; she is a very good 'mother' for them. At the beginning they often cry if they have lost their real mother but after some time they get used to things and she wins the battle against their grief! Of course, she's always got cats around her; that does help the children to calm down and have some fun!

An interesting incident: Recently I met some people who had just arrived, who did not know what I've been learning since my own arrival here. Therefore, I saw myself become a 'teacher of new arrivals'! It's weird and fun and encouraging too, as it shows me I did not stagnate at the 'baby level'; not only had I learnt heaps of things, indeed, but I could also explain them!

Not that I know as much as my friends, of course, but you see it's pleasurable to be able to do it and it also helps other people. After all, we are all here for that: Help each other but also enjoy our happiness here, free from pain and problems! Yes, we regret not to have our family here - we all do, of course! We can only think of you all with love and try to surround you with good protective and positive thoughts. That way we are at least doing something for you! All those who have got families on Earth do the same.

A man here told me there have been lots of accidents and horrible events on Earth, even more than before. He lived there and has just arrived recently. He talks of bombs, attacks and murders. All this is incredibly awful... and poor you have to live through it, be aware of it, possibly fear it! How sorry I feel for you all!

80

Pierre must be fuming in his 'hole' *(Note- He lives in the rain forest),* knowing that the rest of the world fights and yet he still manages to get some information and be concerned about it. Personally I think I would pay no attention to it if I was in his place, in my little forest!

Just a moment...a young man (in my world) who practises drawings with and via you would like me to pose for him, so that you have a portrait of me from here!! Are you happy with this?

(Note- What unexpected information coming from Mum! Indeed, a Spirit artist had started practising doing Psychic Art through me - all I have to do is be very relaxed, let the pencil draw and sense where it wants to go. So both he and I need to practise at polishing our link. I am useless at doing 'normal' portraits on my own. In fact, I am not interested in them at all! To me photos are more useful nowadays - so it won't be me drawing! But if Spirit Artists can eventually reproduce 'deceased' people whom I have never seen, it should be excellent evidence of survival! No doubt it will take time and a lot of patience for the adjustment of vibrations to achieve such a feat).

I would be, too, but no doubt I'll have to recall what I looked like when I was old, as you will not remember me as a young woman?

BR- Think of a photo.

My photos are so old in my head... I don't know whether I would remember them!

BR- You could show yourself as you imagine yourself nowadays! (My Guide pops in)

She has difficulties staying on line.

(Later on that day, I sat with a pad and pencil to allow my Spirit Artist to practise with me. I did not know what he was

*going to draw. He produced a simple sketched portrait of a lady... which turned out to be quite a good resemblance of Mum as a younger person! Something I certainly could **not** draw myself on my own at all! I left it lying around the house, forgetting about it, then each time I caught sight of it unexpectedly, I thought: "Oh, this looks quite like Mum!" So now, later on in the evening I tune in. The pen soon starts in French).*

Mum here. I announced this 'morning' (for you) that your young friend from here wanted to do my portrait, to make you understand and believe he does work with you. Well, it was done! What do you think of it? I posed for him, looking at him face on and trying to think of 'me, long ago', when I was younger than the old hag you knew during the last years, yet not as young as I feel now!

BR- Yes! I recognise you Darling Mum! Bravo to both of you!

So we've succeeded, hey? That's incredible to be able to show oneself from one world to the other, without making an error as to what one used to look like years ago! And for this man in this world to be so skilful and send it by thought, in fact, so that your pencil draws it, without you knowing what was going to come out...and without yourself seeing it, according to what he told me...that's amazing. I am not too sure how he does it!

BR- That's correct! I just relax and allow the pencil to go where it 'feels right' for it to go. It's only when it's all finished that I can see properly what he drew. But both my Spirit Artist and I are learning to tune in to each other. It's still early beginnings!

Well, well, I can't get over it! Don't you think it's a miracle?

BR- Very extraordinary indeed!

My main friend here - meaning he is the one who is there a little more often than others - tells me that if you had been able to relax even more, he would have possibly done even better!

BR- Sorry! I thought it was just about 'sensing' where the pen wants to go. I am still new at this!

As for me, I don't know what has to be done, but you can be certain they will always be saying one must be relaxed, calm, concentrating! Same old tune with them here... so probably for you too!

BR- Will you pose another time just to show me how you see yourself nowadays? I'd like to know.

The amazing thing is that we succeeded at the first go! I was expecting to have to do it again. I am really pleased for you, you can 'have me' more that way!

BR- Well done to you for remembering what you used to look like!

It's just a question of thinking about oneself, of remembering good times in one's life or photos, or to try to visualise it mentally, strongly, so that it projects itself on your face as you think. Do you understand? This is what happens each time we think of something very strongly as we want it - it makes it happen. So I wanted so much to be able to show myself to you and to have the 'miracle' of having my portrait nearly painted from an absolutely incredible distance, since it is between two worlds, invisible to each other. I simply cannot get over it!

BR- Me too! It's probably 97%? But it's still jolly good since I was able to recognise you!

What is unbelievable is that one can do such things! I had never heard of that before! You had of course, but it's really nearly inexplicable, because I do wonder - how can someone send you a drawing without using a photo or even a fax? It's absolutely mind-boggling for me - I keep marvelling at this amazing feat! Yet, I must remember that after all, we are in Paradise, at least my friends and me, therefore how can one wonder, since everything is astonishing here anyway? Yes, it is actually absolutely marvellous and I congratulate you for being able to receive the picture though I don't know how you do it.

*BR- I just let the pen draw by 'sensing' where it wants to go. It is certainly **not me** who does the drawing!*

Yes, I know, it is 'our' young man, as he belongs to both of us, doesn't he? My artist and yours too! It is truly unbelievable, I must say it again! Sweetheart you must be tired after all that concentration?!

BR- Have you got something else to tell me? (Silence... then my Guide pops in).

All is well, don't worry. Better rest before you become too tired to come and join your mum here during your sleep and share her joy to have shown herself to you in this way.

****

CHAPTER 2
Using ectoplasm - Mind power creates - My past life link with my guide - Fend off others' nastiness - Communicating helps departed - Tennis game using Mind!

28th January 2006 - 18.50 hrs. *In case somebody wanted to communicate, I tuned in. I never know for sure who will come close to talk with me. Suddenly I hear French spoken.*

Mum is here, Sweetheart. You've managed to link up with us. We are here and we love you, of course! We have a few interesting things to tell you. First of all, I must say I met up with some 'new' people whom you did not know. It gave me great pleasure to see them when they visited me.

They arrived here relatively recently in a way - or they perhaps took some time to become acclimatized, so I've only seen them now. It was pleasant for me, no doubt it's not for you since you did not know them. They were very kind when on Earth. I knew them in Paris in my days as Giberton *(her first married name)*, yet we recognised each other and it was really enjoyable to meet again and catch up after all that time! We had so much to talk about!

The other matter I wanted to mention is that the anniversary of my 'death' must probably slip by unnoticed in a way, because, after all, for you it is terrible. Yet as far as I concerned, one should celebrate it as the return to Paradise, to happiness, to lack of pain, to the joy of being free from all worries! Of course, there is a price to pay - being separated from you all for some time, but, one day, things will be rectified. The rest feels so good here! Therefore, I think you should have a big party on the anniversary of my 'death' to say: "How lucky she was to be able to get out of her old wrinkled, battered and useless body!

She is free now and with Dad!" Yes, it's a pity one does not celebrate with joy. The other 'other thing' to tell you is that I have just been learning what one needs to do to show oneself and be felt and heard. I had studied that a little, with the carry-on with that sticky, dusty ectoplasm thingummy, but I would like to be able to do better than that!

*(Note- Spirit Scientists call **ectoplasm** 'Living Energy'. It is a cobweb-like substance which a 'physical medium' can release as scientists from Beyond use its unknown components and Energies - but human scientists are unable to reproduce it! It can look a bit like thin 'cheese cloth' and can be very strong, e.g. lifting heavy objects etc. It is extremely sensitive to light, [in the same way as one used to be unable to develop a photographic film in full light but needed red light]. But sometimes red light can be used in a genuine séance room if the medium's health is not affected. People in the Spirit World can learn to cover themselves with ectoplasm to 'materialize', i.e. be more tangible and appear 'solid' to Earth people. More in further chapters of this book and also in Volume 1 ND: AWB).*

So I've started learning more. It will no doubt take quite some time, as far as you are concerned, but I shall manage, you'll see! So, I do hope to succeed in showing myself to you again and making myself 'felt' when you are where I'll be. It won't be for tomorrow! I am still learning heaps of stuff, but I am certain I'll get there.

BR- What do you have to do to cover yourself with it and become more visible or tangible?

The most interesting is that in order to do this, I must first learn to project myself mentally, like a kind of photo of myself. Then I must remember this very strongly and keep the image in my 'head' or rather in my Mind. Afterwards, I'll have to use that as a 'mould' or 'pattern' in order to shape a recognisable physical body, if I want to show myself 'out of thin air' like a ghost! There are lots of things to do, of course. It has to be learnt step by step. It's a matter of knowing how to use the Energy of one's thoughts, so that they travel only towards that operation, that creation of oneself into a visible shape! Yet it will only be visible without being tangible.

On the other hand, if I wanted to be 'smelt' and touched (and also me touching you!), there will be heaps of other extra things to achieve, like learning to envelop my whole body, or at least a good part of it, in that sticky stuff you call ectoplasm, but here they call it 'the veil', or something like that! Don't forget, we do not really have words for things here! It is not necessary; we understand each other without using any.

So there we are. There are several possibilities and I'll try to see what I can do best to start with, then warn you if and when I think I manage to make myself be recognised. It would be smashing and sensational if we succeeded in kissing or at least touching each other, if only once, won't it? I am sure neither you nor I will forget such a happening! Unfortunately, I assume it is not for straight away. I'll have to learn quite a lot.

BR- Well, you did manage successfully to do the transfiguration? (Note - Transfiguration is when Spirit Scientists create a kind of thin mask out of ectoplasmic film, over a medium's face. They can then shape it to make it to look like someone else. Departed loved ones who have learnt to do this can then be recognised 'physically' by their family on Earth - See Volume 1 of this series).

That time was indeed such a special opportunity! I'll have to practise more to do it again. But I reckon my friends want to make me do something more 'complicated' (in my opinion) so that you can really, truly be certain it **IS** me indeed in front of you!! We'll see, won't we? Personally I am always ready to be a good pupil, so I am sure I shall do my best and the result will be really worth it.

That's the main thing I wanted to tell you. It is very exciting to think I have all that to learn in order to succeed and there is a possibility I may manage to do it one day. I am practising and learning. I am doing it with friends and acquaintances here, but, of course, it's essential to be able to do it within and for the 'Earth atmosphere', as apparently it makes a big difference to come close to the level of the Earth with its 'slowed down vibrations', as they say here! As for me, I used not to realise I had 'vibrations', fast or not! So, to start with, I must become aware of the rapidity of my vibrations!! Then I have to know how to control it!

BR- How will you do that?

I have to concentrate, as always!! It's a matter of concentrating on myself, as I told you before. I must 'sense how I feel' then increase or decrease those impressions in order to learn to control them. I use my Mind for this, of course, as that's all there is here to do it - no tools, machine or brain! Therefore, there is a lot to practise, to understand, grasp and remember to become aware of the difference of sensations! Do you see what I mean? I must say I do my homework very attentively! Truly like a good pupil... and I give myself good marks - that way I know when I've done well, better than usual! One day we'll see the result and it is you who will be able to give me at least one good mark, I hope!

BR- I'll give you thousands, even kilos of them!

I admit that kind of work is fine. It looks complicated and difficult and one could think: "Why bother doing all this? After all, we have the whole of eternity in front of us to rest!" But there is a very important point: If I was not doing it for you, I would at least have to do it for myself. Because now, I too want to be able to show Earth people that I am happy here and truly alive! Even if I was not showing myself to you, if I

88

am successful, I could do it to other people or perhaps even strangers. It is absolutely essential that we manage to convince people that we do exist and live on here, in a real world which is full of life! But doing it in a different way - different from mediumistic messages and from this book.

I would never have thought some time ago that I would have 'bothered', we could say, to try to convince total strangers on Earth. No indeed. What for? Yet, now I can see what happens to those who arrive here sobbing, because they've left their loved ones on Earth and cannot communicate with them the way I do with you! I also see those who did not know at all that one 'survives' the passage of 'death'. When they arrive here, they feel totally lost at the beginning, so disorientated and unhappy because they used to not believe at all and refused to accept it - a fact which delays them at the beginning.

So, I reckon one must make a little effort so that as many people as possible are briefed! That way there will be less unhappy folk, either because they have lost their loved ones, or because they are scared to die and imagine all kinds of dreadful happenings, or because they believe they'll find themselves in a big black void! That's why I tell myself: "Why not teach yourself something new and thus help others?"

Of course, it's to you I want to appear first and do it as much as possible, **if** it is possible. Then perhaps my sons will begin to believe, when you tell them that you speak to and hear me?

BR- You'll find that to be able to speak aloud, when materialised, you need not to use too much Energy in building up the body, so reduce how much body you show! (Unfortunately I am suddenly interrupted. I am so annoyed by this, it takes me quite some time to be able to link up again. Then the pen starts in English. My Guide has stepped in saying: "Plain sailing from now on".

BR- What do you mean?

We've got through now. We had to try hard but we are here now. Your mother is still close by but we wanted to come and help break through the wall of thoughts, even though you tried to dismiss them and assumed you were quiet within. We still had to fight the 'fog' of their shadow that was left behind. *(Note- That's something I did not realise!)* There is a 'rule' we can tell you: If you can catch one word, hang on to it! If you hear one word, please keep it on a hook for us to add more words to it, so that it forms a sentence. Then we'll probably be 'online', as you say and the rest should flow. So try that, whenever it may happen.

BR- I am so sorry to be such hard work!

You can only do your best, as we do ours. It may not be easy but we've survived so far! As we are 'tuned in', you could be told a couple more things. The programme your mum is referring to is a great plan to help her manifest herself in a more tangible form; for you to have the joy to link up with her, at least once, if not more often. We'd be pleased to do that for you, as you so much wish to see or hear her 'really', solidly. It is not impossible to do, as you well know. It is only a question of her learning to cope with the necessary steps to take and get the hang of, as she progresses towards full materialisation, or 'solidification', as we sometimes call it.

It is not just a matter of throwing some **ectoplasmic substance** onto oneself as you may imagine it to be. Wouldn't that be simple? Everyone would do it then! It is an elaborate operation consisting of careful itemisation of every part of a body and one's body...so that one can **recall exactly one's persona, one's physical representation, one's way of thinking and doing things!**

To be able to cover our so-called 'body' with a **veil** of a strange substance ('strange' in the sense that we do not have any physical substance here),we need to create such material every time we need to use some, to be represented physically in the World of Matter. So what is required, is for us to use what our physicists and chemists make here, as well as what we can obtain from your World of Matter. This means we need to play with and handle lots of different vibrational rates, which, as they are manipulated, will change from high to low and **will create various chemical substances**, so that we can use them in an appropriate manner. The use of such substances has always puzzled Mankind and its Earthly scientists, as they have never been able to reproduce what we make here for one good reason - they are not here with us! So they won't ever be able to get hold of, or understand, how we can make it!

We need a great concentration of vibrations, of various frequencies, so that the scope is wider to create something which suits the personality of the Being wanting to show himself/herself. We know it is hard to comprehend and it is hard for us to explain too, as you would neither have the knowledge of our physics nor the understanding of something you cannot see. All in all, it is a mixture of very fast vibrations reduced and concentrated into a thicker, slower rate mixture, which you humans can see or sense - basically that's what it comes to! You know roughly what it looks like, but this is only to give you a vague idea of its manufacture.

BR- Does it depend on the medium?

That final result will depend on the structure and essence provided by the personality of the medium and its physical representation. It has to blend with his or her characteristics. We need to extract certain particularities, which are hard to explain to you, for the formation of ectoplasm to take place. So you could not provide any if you did not have those particular specifications, or 'ingredients' if you like. It's all a question of fine balance and timing in various vibrations for success to happen!

An extremely complicated operation which has to be recognised as such. Rules have to be respected scrupulously, so that one does not jeopardise the health of those involved in the making of and using the substance. The Energy provided and released as it is used has to be very carefully weighed and balanced! Having said that, it is exhilarating for all those involved when the personality can show themselves to the World of Matter and be recognised as that person was when on Earth! All the hard work has been worth it and it gives encouragement to others to do the same or, to those who make it happen, to tackle the delicate task once more.

We are all happy when someone is happier for having experienced it on both sides. We are also joyful when we can show ourselves to our family or friends on Earth, in the same way as you'll be happy, we hope, to receive not only communication but evidence in solid form of the existence of your mother/father/husband etc. in our World of Light and Happiness! You can start thinking about it and wishing hard for it, because the Energy of your wishes and thoughts - your hope - will help build an even stronger representation and likeness of your mum or whoever wishes to show themselves. That will help speed up the process of creating this materialisation.

BR- What about first appearing as a 'phantom' only?

An exception to the rule of materialisation is the appearance of the personality in a non-materialised form, but visible to the person on Earth. That requires the Earth person to have reached a certain degree of sensitivity to our vibrations in order to be able to sense what is shown to him/her. That is obtained with sheer practice of opening all the inner senses to our vibrations.

You can hear us, that is one of our vibrations, except that is the one within you, as a recipient of our thoughts poured into your 'Thoughts-Receiving-Process'. Not your thought mechanism, as that is used to make your own personal thoughts. We act outside that process, we do **not** use your 'thought creating mechanism', **we use your 'thought receiving mechanism'.** That has been perfected over the years preceding the time when you started picking our thoughts! You had examples now and then, but until the latter years you had not really used it, or you assumed it was your own thoughts! Now you know better!

As to seeing us, it is only a question of practising that same sensitivity development, so that the vibrations sent are received by your inner sight, that is the one you do not see with outwardly, you see inwardly. *(Note- That is clairvoyance).* All that you need to do is simple: Make time for it and sit quietly, sensing whatever you can sense around you. Feel the air, feel the peace, feel the silence or the noise, if any. Absorb them within you and open your inner senses to them. You will thus develop a better affinity with the higher frequencies of vibrations we emit and you will become more receptive to them.

An example: A flower looked at is beautiful to the eyes of flesh. But if you sense that flower in a different way, like feeling the healing Energy coming from it, you will begin to open the inner senses more fully, so that they all open up. You will feel you can contribute more by knowing, in different ways, the same thing others may describe. You **will** see as well as hear, if you try to practise more and more. You will succeed if you tell yourself you will, instead of doubting your capabilities. You will know what you can do as soon as it starts happening to you and then there won't be any stopping!

Once you've opened to them all fully, you will be able to keep them open, as long as you have those moments of peace and quiet to recharge the inner batteries, so to speak. You cannot go backwards in your development. Once achieved, you can easily stay on the path leading to more discoveries, of course!

BR- Can you tell me more about Mum possibly communicating through a trance or physical séance? (Note-Trance is when the Medium looks 'asleep' - is in a deep altered state of consciousness - as she/he is unaware of goings-on and of communicators impressing their thoughts on and using the medium's vocal chords. A Physical séance is when materialisation or phenomena involving lights, objects, people and/or independent voices are witnessed by all in the room. More explanations in further pages).

You can rest assured she is trying to learn and practise what to do. It will take more sessions with us and on Earth to get all the details perfect but she is managing well. Of course you will need to find places where such events are going on! When it happens the results will be good if you allow your Mind to open up to what is going on. Let them speak first.

BR- Who are 'them'?

Those who will talk to you to introduce your mum. Let them talk to you and prepare the path for her. She'll need a 'path' of Energy paved by someone speaking in front of her. So if you speak to them as they speak to you, you will help prepare the path for your mum to build up the ectoplasm over herself. She then will be able to come to you with great excitement and no doubt she'll also be nervous about it!

You can help by listening carefully and talking loudly and clearly so that she knows where she is going and that will be all that is required of you. We provide the direction and the intensity of Energy needed for her to build on it her way, i.e. the way she's been taught to do it. All you'll have to do then is enjoy the conversation and the closeness while it lasts. You

94

may not be able to stay together very long as it will be her first time with you. It will be good if you can maintain the voice contact all the time and build up the Energy constantly, since it will deplete itself as she talks or moves - so you build it again firmly and lovingly. As she withdraws, you will be upset to lose her again, I warn you! It will feel like a 'death' to you since she'll be gone... but you will not need to cry about that because she will come back another time.

Look forward to the momentous event for you to speak aloud to your mother and to know she is there, in a room full of people.

BR- Thanks. I know it is very difficult for her to learn to do that! Even her just coming through in a trance séance would be great.

(1st February 2006 – At the Spiritualist Centre's Practice Circle, as I was going to give a young man a message from his 'deceased' grandfather, I distinctly heard clairaudiently - but like a voice outside - a deep male voice saying: "Ok then!" Then I received a helpful detailed message to transmit to the lad, who was a total stranger to me).

4th February 2006 - *I wonder whether I can find out whose 'voice' it was. The pen starts in English. It's my Guide.*

The link is always brought on by you and me together. We create the link for others whom I tune into or link with, you see? You and I need to create a bridge for them to find their own wavelengths towards you. If your Mind is all over the place, they have difficulties. I am more used to it, you see?

BR- You mean you are used to suffering from it?

Yes, 'suffering', as you say! Not really, but used to coping with the problem. So I said: "Ok then", when we started talking about this young man's problem. His grandfather was present, making himself heard by telling him what he wanted to say. I was the link, the communication between you and the 'old gentleman', as you'd say, but he is not old here, of course, as we all feel younger, healthy and happy! So, I said those words and the fact you heard them augurs well for later on, as we may be able to be heard more loudly in your head. It would help you keep your concentration, I imagine.

BR- I heard a deep male voice, yet you don't have any vocal chords, no real voice?
The sounds you hear normally are sounds of us talking to you but made as 'noise' in your head by your brain. If you heard my 'voice' as deeper and exterior to your own thought-like sounds, it is because my Mind imprinted on yours the attitude, the personality I project when I want to make a point or give serious information. Your Mind manipulates your brain as its tool, so it may have sounded like a 'serious man's voice'. I was projecting serious male thoughts as we spoke about the other gentleman, who is a serious man, especially when it comes to discussing his grandson's future! That is how it came across and that's very good. I am pleased you heard it. It's a step in the right direction.

BR- Could you do it now?
Lots of thoughts are still floating in your Mind.

BR- I wish I could do something about it! Could you explain more what 'Mind' is? How does it differ from 'Spirit'? Is each one of us 'A Mind'?
Allow my Mind to tell your Mind what it is! *(Note- I think it is so wonderful to be able to ask such questions suddenly and get answers from a knowledgeable Teacher!).* My Mind will think the answer and your Mind will receive it. The Mind of everyone is a part of each personality. The Mind

96

is 'the-thinking-that-processes-things' part of the personality who is a 'Spirit' (as you call it) here on Earth or elsewhere. **A Mind is a thinking process,** an active part of the Energy which one is made of.

Each one of us is a 'Spirit Being', as you well know. So, since each one of us is a Spirit, we need to express our thoughts by sending our Mind in the direction we want the information to go, whether to create something or to tell someone something. If you and we did not have a Mind as part of our personalities, we would not be able to converse, contact others and create what is wanted or needed. It is a tool within ALL of us, all of Creation. The Mind of an Animal is as powerful as the Mind of a Human, but at times it has different goals or aims. If you wished to think like a horse, you'd be a different personality from one thinking like a cow, or a Human, or a bee. You need to have the right kind of Mind suited to your personality.

Therefore, a Mind is a part of your personality well-matched to your needs and a potent tool, which has such power within that it can constantly create around itself what it thinks of, or half-thinks! It is therefore important to think carefully and be aware of what you have within you! Otherwise you are relentlessly at the mercy of an inner tool rampaging and creating left, right and centre, without any control! It would possibly create situations you don't really want and probably fear or at times dread. Yet you are thinking about them, so **you** make them happen, because the **lifepower of a situation is given by the Mind thinking of it!** The moment you withdraw that lifepower, the situation loses the strength it needs for it to be created! It cannot achieve its created state when you lose interest and do not have it on your Mind.

You must NOT concentrate on something you fear to happen, as you will make it happen! You must not concentrate on the disease, you must think of the health state! You must not think of someone as being nasty to you, think of that person

97

with a totally different attitude towards you, so that you only see them as either kind, or at least not unkind to you.

BR- I understand. So, the Mind is part of the Spirit. Please define 'Spirit' a little more.

A Being of any kind has a Life Force within itself, to make its existence possible, for it to exist whether in Spirit World or on Earth or elsewhere. That Life Force is what you people call 'Spirit'. It is that which means there is a personality who is different from another personality. All those Beings have a power which allows them to think and therefore to create - as you think, you create life events around you! As life around you changes, experiences vary and provide opportunities for various possibilities of action. That's what Creativity is all about!

So, that power, that Mind creating things with Thought Power, is what is within the Spirit personality, as part and parcel of its being and existence! The personality cannot exist without a Mind if it wants to be able to produce action around itself. The Mind is indeed part of the Spirit personality and Being and would not be of any use on its own! It needs to be linked up to a 'Spirit' Being.

A Mind is the 'engine inside a Spirit Being', to make it create. But it needs that Life Force with it, linked to it, the Mind. Otherwise the Mind alone would not really be able to function. All rather subtle and yet complicated, especially for an Earthly Mind, or rather Earthly brain used by a Mind, which has often problems grasping subtle, invisible concepts and happenings!

An example: A Mind is like an engine in a vehicle for transport. Unless the person (i.e. 'Spirit' in this case) decides to drive the transport vehicle, the vehicle will go nowhere. If the Spirit (person) decides to use the Mind (engine) to its full potential, it can do great journeys or great speeds or clever manoeuvres! But the Spirit (person) could not do all this without the Mind (engine)! Nor could the engine/Mind do anything without being empowered and kicked into action by the person/Spirit. Well, that's as much as I can think (with my Mind!) to say in order to explain and answer your question.

BR- It's very clear. Thanks. Can you calm my Mind?

Someone's Mind is his own engine. No one else can step on the brake pedal to stop it! But it can be helped a little by pouring love and affection and 'healing' into it, to soothe it. Soothing it will slow it down a little and that may help you link up more easily.

BR- Please do so!

The times we've done it, my dear! You'd never be able to count them; too many figures to it! One last thing to add: That example about an engine is not completely correct because to have an engine in a working order you also add some fuel, don't you?

BR- That's true.

Well, that's an extra help for the engine, so it may not be completely 'correct' as an example. But I meant the person starts the engine, which he (and the engine attached or linked to the wheels) drives around. You see what I mean? It was only a figure of speech, a symbol, a general idea more than technical accuracy - just in case someone tried to 'nit-pick', as you say!

BR- May I ask you several questions? 1) Which was your last life with me? 2) Was it your last one on Earth? 3) What was our relationship?

We heard them all ok. So, when was I 'last' with you? When the Dukes of Normandy were reigning or imposing their laws on this country, you and I suffered from it and ran away, so to speak. We could not cope with the injustices and the terrors at times, so we left the main towns and kept ourselves out of their way whenever we could. Why? Because there was no need to suffer under authoritarian men when you could live on your own by your own means.

Secondly, was that my last life on Earth? No. I went back afterwards and did various things, but the life when you and I had a strong bond was the one with the Dukes behind us! So, we linked so closely and suffered together and died together that I swore I would never leave you in this current life of yours, to guide you to your own goal, until you come back to me and others here.

What was our relationship then? I had a very strong bond with you, my son. You were my son, I was your father. We had to leave not to be conscripted into waging wars against others whom we did not want to kill, since they were not really doing us any harm in the first place! That was the main reason for us to run all over the country, away from searching troops. So we became humble peasants, but on our own. Not a bad life but a poor one - we had no comfort at all, as we could not settle in one place for long before risking being noticed and grabbed to be made soldiers... or rather murderers! That was the Earth life with you.

19th February 2006 - *(16 months since Dave's passing). My Guide pops in.*

Let's start with the news for here. Mum is doing fine, father is busy, as usual, with his research - and little cats are all ok awaiting your return here! But Dave is the one who could do with some boost. He has some highs and lows and we are concerned he does not speak enough to you all. He will have to be made to link to you more often, to sense and feel he is not 'cut off'. He needs to have news from home, because he can be homesick at times and we know it is only a lack of communication. Look out for him trying to talk.

BR- How will he do that?

Anyway he can reach you. He may be thinking of you or he may try to talk to you, but he still has to learn more about that kind of communication.

BR- I am very sad for him to still be in that state!

Allow your Mind to rest more often, it's hard to reach you from here.

BR- Am sorry! But I need to work to earn a living and teaching is stressful.

An excuse for work is money needs! You may not need as much as you think you do! Check your accounts and finances. You'd then be freer for us, wouldn't you? My task is to help you understand the great necessity for communication between our worlds! This is both for your own sake and also for those here, who need to feel they have not lost you and their family altogether. That's what I am trying to make you understand.

20th February 2006 - *My Guide starts the conversation.*

We would like to help you link up with your loved one who is waiting here.

(Sudden change of communicator) My little wife, I am here at last, at long last! If you knew how much I need to talk to you and feel I haven't lost you all! We do see each other at times in your nights, but it's not regular and you say you don't always remember it happening, or rarely! We meet but we can't talk in quite the same way. It is lovely but it is different! We do not see each other as solidly as we did on Earth. I only know you are there but it needs to be more solid somehow. You can talk to me now, I need to know you are all right.

BR- We miss you of course but Jim is ok, so is Anne-France and I am too.

They are, are they? I hoped they would not grieve for me too long, because there is no need to mourn for me! I am fine here, no more suffering! I only miss you all a lot, so much! I wish I could see you more or at least talk to you more. I think of our kids and try to come close to them, though I am not very good at it yet. I send thoughts as I am shown to do, to help them be happier than before and I send you some too, don't think I forget you my little Darling! But it is difficult to concentrate hard like this! I know you struggle too to get into communication at times when you are tired or stressed. We both need to work at it more, don't we? I have made some progress, they say!

BR- Who are 'they'?

'They' are my tutors, my mentors, as well as Mum and Dad, who have always been near me since I came over here. They are there to steer me to learn to cope with the newness of it all.

It is indeed a beautiful place, with magnificent sceneries and many amazing things happening when you don't realise what you are doing! I think my main task here is to find my feet at my own pace and to learn what can be learnt when I feel like it! All along, it's a kind of special process for me to grasp what one can do in many different situations. I only want peace and quiet at the moment, though I enjoy my easy gardening here.

It is such a shock, you know, to find oneself 'all done with' in a way - and yet still alive in spite of everything that happened to one's body! I can't get over it yet. I am finding it difficult at times not to think I am still in that body which has 'died' after all! But that is silly talk really, because I am fine, you know. It is just a question of adjusting to everything. It is all so new and still is! Often more new things appear, so I investigate, learn, wonder, don't always understand why, get help from someone or other, then move on to the next thing which comes across.

It's also weird **not** to 'have to' do things! One can ignore everything here and not bother about anything if one is so inclined! Just the job for a lazy person! But I like to find out what this is all about! I cannot arrive here and not go on 'recces' to map out what we have on offer! *(Note- He used to organise rambles with his Ramblers Club)* But to come back to my first point, I miss you all, all three of you. I want you to know I am very close to you in many ways, because I think of you strongly and wish I could hear you better and more often.

The year it all started, I had no hope left in me. It killed me to think I was going to go away to... where? And never see any of you again! I could not bear the thought of it all and that is what killed me probably, even though the bloody cancer did its job too. I could not bear the thought of not having my kids near me anymore. That ate me up from inside out. As I laid in that hospital bed, I saw it happen in a symbolic way, I suppose. I was eaten up by despair and that was a kind of vicious circle.

(Note- How perceptive of him! He guessed that the unstoppable weeping of his enormous wound - from a double stomach by-pass imposed on him by surgeon Mr W- totally useless at that late stage - was symbolic of his Soul's and his inner tears!)

The thought of seeing you again eventually (when you all pass over) and also to meet at night and when you talk to me makes it more bearable, though it takes so much time to get going. I'd like to have you all here, every day of my time here, that way there would be no more regrets or longing! The longing is painful, you see! The longing and the sadness of what could have been and what has gone... but I suppose we all suffer from that, even on Earth!

My life here is not bad, you know! Only doing what I want when I want, talking to people a lot, learning new things (or new tricks, you could call them) and finding out why I could not do something before and now I can.

BR- Can you give me an example?

An example? My 'head' tended and still tends to be filled with facts from life on Earth. When I think of them I see them appear here! So it is more like a nightmare at times, because you know you cannot have those things happening again, yet they are there! Therefore, I have to learn not to think of Earth events in the past, as this is not productive at all - in fact it can be Soul-destroying, with regrets gnawing at your innards! Not that I have any innards here, fortunately!

Last time I thought of you all, I recalled we were on holiday in France, in Carnac, or around there with a tent, in a large campsite. It was very sunny and very good! But if I think of that, it appears like a strong dream and does not last very long, so just enough to make me regret not to have it all again for real! Not much good, is it? *(Note- Dave must have misunderstood my question. I was not asking for an example of 'longings' but of new things he could do! But I don't want to interrupt him).*

Now I really need to have contact with you all, if we can organise that better? Could you make sure you talk to me often, because I don't think Jim and Anne-France know how to, not the way you do anyway. Maybe they could learn too? It is not so hard to concentrate... if one does not have anything on one's Mind! But if you are all busy, it might make it much harder for all of you. So, I hope you can manage to come to me and we could have a bit of a conversation... keeping each other up to date with what's going on both sides of the dark fence which seems to separate us in a way. We may have more luck and ease if we do it more often I think, or so they say here.

There are lots of people I knew when I was young who have come over too. It's amazing, as I thought neither them, nor me, were old enough to 'die'! But it was good to see them again! We could at least have a few jokes about the old times. Lately my thirst for painting has gone down a bit, I am more a gardener in the gardening section of activities, though I don't know how long it will last!

BR- Do you eat what you grow?

My vegetables here are more prize-winning than eating stuff. I would eat them, of course, as they certainly are organic now! (Ha ha!) But I find I don't feel the need to eat anything, or not much anyway! It is not a body one needs to feed; there isn't the hunger or the thirst. It is more for the pleasure of growing them and watching them grow, all of a sudden at times, in fact! There is no real need to want them to grow, if you think about it, because everything is **not measured in time but in feelings and sensations**. You forget about time here, it's bizarre. You go about your business and get so engrossed in what you do, you just do it and enjoy it! But you don't think of actual time and its limits, because there isn't any 'time' as such! Just feelings of 'longer' than another period, if one could call it that... *(As it was very late, I unfortunately dozed off, but it felt as if the conversation carried on during my sleep, though I could not recall it when I woke up!)*

24th February 2006 - *It is useful to note here that an older man J.M, whom I had kindly invited months ago to join my Friday physical mediumship experimental group right from the beginning, suddenly revealed his true self and surprising hidden bitter jealousy (which he must have 'bottled up' for months) by unexpectedly pouring abuse at me at the end of a séance, for no reason whatsoever! Sheer ego! The members present, including his family, were shocked and disgusted and* *told him so. Yet he imagines himself to be 'spiritual' and a healer! I was taken aback, shocked, shaken and very hurt as I had always been kind and respectful to him, thinking he was a friend! Of course, that now automatically excludes him at once from the group, as we need sincere harmony to reign! How upsetting! Then only a few days later, on 4th March, I slipped on a very icy pavement and broke my left wrist.*

6th March 2006 - 17.00hrs. *The pen starts in French. I realise it's Mum.*

Once more, the enormous pleasure to have you on line, Sweetheart! If only you knew how happy it makes me! My darling little girl who has been so grown-up for a long time now! I am longing to be able to kiss you for real and hold you in my arms and tell you I love you and think of you!

I think one of your last birthdays was a 'milestone'? I recall being that age, very long ago and I used to think I was so old! In a few years time, you'll see this present age as young, when you look back! Then when I reached eighty and even ninety, I realised how young I was several few decades earlier! So don't worry about ageing! You still have plenty of time in front of you.

My friends here often comment on the 'age' people imagine they have, yet what matters to have is the maturity of Mind and accumulated Knowledge rather than years. Knowing more at twenty years old than a seventy year-old man, **that** is being mature and adult! Unfortunately, I don't think there are many people like that!

I would like to tell you that if **you** have had problems lately it is apparently because there were several people who concentrated negatively towards you! They've had negative thoughts towards you and you've received them and 'absorbed' them. By doing so, it injected and enveloped your Energy field with 'negativity'! Yet if one rejects other people's nasty thoughts, one straightens up as a stable 'positive heap' instead of reducing oneself to a 'negative heap'! You must have positive thoughts to be well balanced in life. If you let others perturb you with their either stupid or negative thoughts, you are doing yourself some harm. This is what I was told to tell you!

There has been a lot of unpleasantness and negativity from other people around you and you reacted the wrong way. You did not push them back mentally and emotionally as soon as you encountered them, you have sort of 'accepted' them and let them reach you. You MUST protect yourself from what others send you. If not, you'll find yourself bombarded with 'a deluge of dirty waters' instead of a pleasant warm shower! The pleasure to know **one can protect oneself** is immense because, thanks to that, one feels safe and in control of events. Otherwise you get the feeling everything falls on your back unexpectedly and you are helpless and unable to do anything about it! This is a major error. You can do a lot - constantly protect yourself, even in advance, against any future or possible bombardment!

An accident happening out of the blue is caused by a succession of others' nasty thoughts which knocked you off balance and made you act in a way different from usual. If one falls, it's because the mental, emotional and physical bodies are out of control and not interlocked. So it unbalances the whole system! It is essential that those bodies are engaged and interlocked, fitted together correctly so that equilibrium is possible and normal functions can carry on. If one or the other of those bodies is out of its niche, its recess, its line of characteristics, there will be conflict and then it will definitively cause a problem, whether mental or physical depending on the seriousness of the effect on one or the other of these bodies.

This is what I am taught here, as you can guess - it is not me inventing all this! I would not know where to start if I had to talk about that! The main points have been given - one needs a good mental, emotional and physical balance for everything to go well. This is what 'good health' is. The moment one or the other of those levels is disjointed and disturbed, there will be conflict, problems and unhappiness, one way or the other.

I was told you wanted to know why you had fallen. I am told your broke you hand or your arm*? (Note- Amazing diagnosis, yet it makes so much sense, all the more after the unprovoked attack on me).*

BR- My left wrist.

My poor Darling! I suffer for you. It's so painful and such a problem! It must cause you some hassle now! Do your best to rest, so that your body regains its strength after the shock you must have had. I am told to tell you we are sending you some healing Energies and you will surely be in less pain. It is essential to really grasp that business of 'thoughts and healing Energies' and the physics behind all the positives and negative thoughts! It is so important! I do realise it now!

Had I known that when I was on Earth, I may not have had so many accidents and mishaps! Who knows? We don't really realise what we do with our thoughts, do we? We cause ourselves heaps of problems, whereas we could constantly protect ourselves so well and so easily! All that is needed is to do it at any time, as if one was in danger of being 'under attack'. That way one does not risk anything - no more problems, no more accidents! My friends tell me that's the solution. You had perfectly understood because we told you about it when your body was asleep.

I think when we had a chat some time ago you wanted to know what Dave was doing. I went to see him to please you and to help him if I could, of course. He was in good health emotionally. He still had regrets to have gone and to have left you all, but he wanted to talk about you and what you did during the last years and what you told him fairly recently. So his morale seemed to be quite 'healthy' mentally, though perhaps still feeling a bit sad, but it is normal here, you know, we feel cut off from our loved ones and it takes time to 'pull oneself together' emotionally.

There is so much to do when one is a newcomer; one has to constantly watch what and how one thinks! We also have to be careful and not be too sad, so as not to spoil all the good work we achieved when we managed to grasp many other things! So we definitely have our work cut out!

Yet Dave is not alone. He is looked after too and he has his parents close-by ready to help him if he wishes. He can only progress towards an increasingly calmer and more satisfactory state of Mind. My visit did not disturb him, he appreciated it. We always like having kind people supporting us here, you know, as it is such a huge leap to make! It is rather awful to have to adapt oneself to something so drastic when one did not expect it. So much to accept, put up with, change, observe and understand!

Personally I am beginning to really cope well here now, but I do know how much poor Dave must be suffering emotionally from not having you close to him any longer! Especially not being able to speak easily to his children. That is the biggest sorrow - being parted from one's family.

The saddest thing is not to have any news regularly, or at all, like in some cases where the families do not know how to communicate like you can! So one has to survive here, with the hopeful certainty that we shall all meet up again 'one day'. That feels so good, yet one knows it may be very far ahead for some people! I can't see any solution to this problem except ask people to learn to **better communicate with us all here!**

But I am diverting from the topic of Dave. You wanted to know how he was faring and what he was doing. He does what he feels like at the moment. He seemed to like painting like before, but does less now I think. He also really enjoys gardening; he has fun watching plants grow so fast, without any problems! He will probably get weary of it, because, after all, it's the possible complications which make things more interesting apparently! Personally I would say: "No complications, it's Paradise! Why want some?". However, if one has nothing to do to ensure everything goes well, I suppose it must become a bit boring and humdrum! Even if one likes what one is doing! The way we think here is weird, isn't it? On Earth you'd say: "I do not want any problem in order to be happy." Here it's sometimes: "Blast! No problem, that's boring! I have nothing to solve!" I wonder how many things one decides to give up because of that!

BR- What did Dave look like to you?

Dave looks exactly as I knew him - young, kind, smiling and attentive. He does not look tired or ill of course, because the flesh body is no more, so he feels 'normal'. He still marvels about it, as that is the secret of eternal youth - never age again, never be ill again! True Paradise, isn't it?

As for me, I am fine. I have not made any great discoveries recently. It's more a question of practising what I have been learning for some time, understanding it and doing it without thinking about it. But I have also enjoyed myself simply doing 'nothing which is a chore'! Just chatting. I also read, I listen to my friends and other people I meet.

I have not really had any 'Soul Rescues' to do. It was just conversations with new arrivals, to help them find their way round, yet perhaps it counts as 'rescues', I don't know! There often are newcomers so I do what the others do: I talk to them and reassure them and help them understand the weird things which happen, because it is really disconcerting at first, you know? You'll see when you come over yourself!

110

But fortunately Dad and I will be there to help you, so don't worry! In fact you'll already know quite a lot, won't you, with all the stuff I will have told you ever since we started communicating, you and I? So there you are, I am having fun, I keep busy, I learn and I talk to you when you have time for it.

BR- I am so sorry I can't do it more often!

Don't worry Sweetheart, it's not serious. I realise you have so much to do! You understand I absolutely love talking to you, yet it is not the end of the world if you cannot manage it often. You are there, I know you love me and you know I love you, that's all that matters! *(I am suddenly disturbed by someone coming in. When I can link up again the pen starts in English. My guide has stepped in).*

Let bygones be bygones, whether recent events or older ones. You cannot be constantly churned by other people's actions! Otherwise you'll be the one suffering from it in the end! It is most important you learn to let it go out of your Mind. The best way is to think of what else worse could happen and then compare. There is nothing so important which could not be worse or compared to something worse! Then you get a feeling of perspective and importance and futility...and you'll forget or forgive what has been done or said! You can do it, if you only started to try.

BR- It's so maddening it happened!

It is most frustrating at times, indeed, but the side of your personality which cares and heals can overcome the other side which rages at every stupid or careless thought or event or annoyance! You can do it if you really want to try! Because you will never get peace of Mind if you let others rule you by churning you, upsetting you with everything they do wrong! If they do real wrong and harm, then they'll suffer themselves in the end... so why have two of you suffering from something which should not have been done in the first place? All is in the learning of control of emotions.

You control = you win! You let them control you = you lose. As any **imbalance 'within' will lead to imbalance 'without',** 'without' being and meaning the physical body of course and also the world outside... as the vibrations of anger and resentment will carry on moving around you, in a circle of devastating forces which will sap at your very core!

You need to strengthen your inner core, so that the other layers of your own Self are not attacked or even touched upon. That way you will resist all diseases and accidents. You will not be unhappy and you will be more successful at everything you do. So please start trying to do this, you will see you can do it and we talk sense. It is only a question of patience and perseverance. An accident like the one you've just had has happened everywhere, in many cases, simply **because** those people were not at ease within themselves! Their bodies could not withstand the imbalance caused within by the raw emotions and the mental turmoil. It is all a question of balance!

BR- I might end up 'not giving a damn' about most things and people!
Let it be. Let things be. Let them (whoever) say this or that. Let yourself relax and bathe in the knowledge you know they may be wrong or hurtful and you may not be as nasty or ignorant. It may be hard at first, but eventually you'll find it easier!

BR- Don't I risk becoming haughty and 'feeling superior'?
A little story: One day a man went fishing for big fish. He left early in the morning to get there in time to catch his fish, as he needed them to feed himself and for others. But on his way people disturbed him, delayed him, stopped him,

112

possibly hit and hurt him. Yet eventually he got to his river to catch his fish. As he threw the line in the water, the biggest fish ever seen jumped into his net, without even being hooked! He had a miracle catch! Why? Perhaps because he overcame all the obstacles, perhaps because if he had got there earlier he would not have caught the 'big one'?

Whatever comes in your way is to be ignored, or put up with if possible and discarded if not important. **Keep your Mind on the goal and give it priority**. Ignore the rest. That way you'll have a sense of perspective and importance. So, even if your goal is damaged or delayed or interfered with, you still have your goal in your Mind and heart - that's all that matters! Your goal in your heart, your heart full of caring and loving for those in need and the end result **will** be 'the big fish'!

BR- (teasing) I am one hundred per cent vegetarian. I don't catch or eat fish!

You know what I mean!

"Place your hand in the hand of the one who guides you,
Place your heart near the heart of who loves you.
You will never ever feel alone my dear friend,
If you place your heart and your hand in your friend's heart and hand. I am your friend, you'll never lack any thing, I'll be there to guide you."
(I had the feeling he was singing this made up 'song'!)

A final point before you leave me: Last night's dreams should have taught you something.

BR- I can't remember at all. Please remind me.

You were with us but we showed you some gentlemen in need of help. You were willing to help but could not find the solution, as they kept changing their Minds and goals. It was symbolic of what people will do to you! You'll want to help them but they will say yes at first, then possibly reject the help, simply because they are not ready for the change that the new Knowledge will make in their life! If it happens you must not be distraught or disgusted. People are what they are and can change their Minds according to their free will, which they use a lot (unfortunately, sometimes!).

So be sure you know that you do your best to help, you don't push Knowledge, you offer it and that's all. It's up to them to take it, leave it, absorb it or reject it or make use of it. It's all in the learning for both of you. Then you'll be free to help someone else, if that first one has gone away from your presence. Simply move away instead of staying or asking for more.

Let's leave the profound talking and see whether you can let your poor mum come back once more, hoping she won't be 'kicked out' by sudden interruptions. *(Just then someone from the RSPCA phoned me, to ask me to help as usual at some fundraising for the local shelter!)*

11th March 2006 - 20.00hrs. *My Guide comes first.*

Make yourself available more often. Your husband would like to talk to you now. Can you receive him? Help him by keeping your Mind still. *(Swift change of communicator).*

I am here, Love. I have wanted to talk to you for quite some time, it's not easy indeed! I thought I could do it more easily! You can rest assured I don't forget you or the kids. I have faith now that we shall meet again one day, as I met both my parents, so that's what matters - we have not lost each other! Yet you must make the effort to talk to me if you can, as I need a link to keep my strength, mental strength.

We have to have faith in the future here, otherwise we'd go to pieces if we thought we'd never see our loved ones again! My mum keeps saying not to worry about the future, it will not matter because we'll understand where we are. But

114

you and I know there is a big void between us and it's a miracle to start with to have been able to link over it, like over the Grand Canyon, in spite of everything that happened!

BR- I think of you every day, we are certainly not forgetting you!

Last time we spoke, I said I was not too bothered about painting, not as much as before I suppose. I have to achieve something to feel I am getting somewhere. My friends here (new and old ones) try to show me what can be done by simply thinking of one thing and seeing it materialise, so to speak, in front of my very eyes! It is indeed very strange, interesting and amusing at times! A magic trick of some kind! I still have to do quite a lot of practising to make it happen smoothly, but I am getting better.

There is always something new to discover or to want to learn to do, if one can be bothered to do it. They say here: "It's all in the learning and the practising!" One always needs to practise everything one learns; it's like learning a language isn't it? So if you don't, you don't move as fast as if you did practise! *(Note- Apt comment from this University language lecturer who spoke four languages!)*

BR- Can you give me an example of an exercise?

I can tell you of one we did, my new 'mate' and I. It was a question of sending a 'ball' to each other. A tennis ball type of ball. He **thought of it, threw it to me mentally** and I had to receive it and hit it back mentally, that is without a racket, but as if we had a racket! That's a new kind of tennis I had never played before! *(Note- Very unusual! I had **never** heard of that one! Fitting indeed, since he used to play tennis when on Earth).* Well, it's hard at first, I can tell you! It's like thinking you are a diver who needs to hit the bottom of the sea to surface again! A real shot in the dark, but gradually you feel it coming and you can sense where it's going and how to hit it back! Not a bad game actually, as you cannot get tennis elbow with that one! But it's fun too... eventually! To become good at it, it's all a question of practice and focusing your concentration on that ball you 'know' is coming!

BR- Do you see the ball?

At first you are not too sure where it is, because it's like sensing something in the dark! Weird stuff! You know it's coming, it's 'there', but you are not sure where it is!

BR- Are you sure the other man manages to send a ball?

The other guy is ok, he sends the ball all right! But it is the realisation there is one 'over there' which is hard to grasp at first, because you have to make your senses more receptive to its vibration - the vibrations of that ball of Energy, which is not at all like the ones I used to play with on Earth! My tennis days were over, I thought - until I came here where they make me start again in a different way!

BR- Well, it's good and useful!

Yeah, it's good. Must be done for a reason. I suppose it's to do with opening one's senses and sense of direction and appreciation of distances and use of thoughts as a tool rather than using your hands. It's all in the new learning, as they keep saying! Learning to make sense of it all is the first one!

Another example of making use of your thoughts: If you are meant to meet someone, you only need to think of him or her and say to yourself: "Where is X? I want to see him now." That's how you find yourself directed towards that person. Somehow he appears in front of you as you start going towards where **it feels** right to go. I am making good progress with this one. Now all I need to do is think of someone and they'll appear in front of me before I have time to think any-more! That seems to work!

BR- *Well done! (I give detailed news of Jim, Anne-France and myself. Silence, then my guide steps in).*

He heard it all. We have to transpose our thoughts over yours, so that he picks them better.

BR- *Can you explain this please?*

He needs us to pick your thoughts first, make them clearer to him, so that he can read in **our** Minds more easily than having to read them in yours. It's all a question of practice and degree of intensity, clarity, vibration etc. He's got your news and now is quite happy to be up to date with the children's lives and yours, he says. You can carry on speaking to each other if you like. *(Sudden change of communicator again!)* Help me with your thoughts coming towards me all the time!

BR- *I think of you as on a nice photo I have of you young.*

That's right, I keep you in mind that way too. So, I was saying, we had some fun throwing balls at each other and talking to each other. I said I got your news, didn't I? I said it to the man here who does help with the communication. He is a nice kind of chap, he means well and helps with the link. He has some practice at it apparently and makes it easier for both of us.

BR- *You are happy with the news?*

Many pieces of news if I recall. It had to be like a newspaper rather than a news bulletin, but it was good to get all those details! I gather Anne-France is doing well; that's a good thing she has not stayed with her S. *(Note- Ex-boyfriend).*

117

There wasn't much hope in that direction, so it had to happen one day, for good this time! If it helps, I send her my love for a new, steady, lasting relationship. It's what she needs to buck her up and back up her work and efforts in everyday life.

As for Jim-Bo, he's doing what he wants and likes by the sound of it. So he should be all right. It's never been very straightforward with him but if he is happy there then that's all that matters, isn't it? Make sure you look after that hand of yours, you must be more careful if falls occur like this.

BR- It was icy on the path and I was walking very carefully, with flat shoes!
There isn't a lot of that here, we are lucky!

BR- Have you met Uncle Alfred or any other acquaintance?
Have I met Uncle Alfred? Yes, of course, he was there when I arrived, soon after anyway. There was Aunt Ethel too. They were happy to see me and me to see them. It was really good to meet up again after all those years. There wasn't much difference from when they were on Earth. We talked gardening as usual and orchids of course, though I reckon he may be getting fed up with them now! I think he has other interests. He is as friendly as he was before and has not changed much, though his hair is probably not as white in reality, as he hasn't got a flesh body anymore! He is just like me - **we feel we have one but we know it's not quite true or real**, is it?

Another example of practice here is the tuning in to the sounds coming from the Earth people we have on line! If we can communicate, we have to recognise the sounds the communicator makes, not just by talking, but by the sounds of the vibrations of their thoughts! The thoughts we all have make sounds which are beyond the noise of the words heard on Earth. The sounds of thoughts have a special vibration I am told. That's what we have to learn to recognise. In the same

118

way as you recognise a phone ringing compared to a door bell ringing!

25 March 2006 - 19.45 hrs. *My guide discusses things with me.*

We are here whenever you want us to talk to you and if you are 'on line' properly. Do not try when you are too tired if you want good quality communication. There has never been a communication from your loved ones which was not genuinely from the person you wanted to hear from or chose to come to talk to you. It has always been them talking to you. They may have been helped to do it, or their message was passed, but you had their love, their thoughts and their message.

BR- How is Dave? Is he busy? Would it help him to have a chat with me?

He has been told you are here online, so to speak, therefore you can have a word with him if you wish.

BR- Of course, but also if he wishes!

Has Dave told you he is trying new ways to talk to you? He is practising learning to use his own Mind to reach you, rather than giving the message to one of us to pass on to you.

BR- I think he has had a go.

He is still trying. He is not quite an expert as he would like to be but is doing well in his efforts and attempts. *(Sudden change of communicator. Dave is online!)* It is very difficult to keep one's Mind still, I can tell you! It is so hard not to see the person you are talking to and yet talk to them in your head!

BR- It's a bit like on the telephone.

Yes, like on the phone. I am making slow progress, though. If I disappear it's because I've lost my concentration!

BR- Don't worry about it. I am sending you a big hug and kisses.

It is a question of staying on one spot mentally; it's not as easy as it seems! Let me say that every time you come and talk to me, it makes me very happy, because I know you have not forgotten our good times and love. We did have a lot of love for each other, didn't we, and it did not die out!

I am pleased you are here. You can tell me about Jim and Anne-France afterwards as I think you said they are ok, but let me talk first. *(Brief silence)* My goodness it's hard work! You see, I am progressing more by being able to tackle this on my own - it's not easy! I think last time we spoke I still used someone to convey my words. You have to understand all this may be easy for you, but for me it's all so new and such a challenge! I have so much to think about to do it!

All I can say is time does not seem to exist here. I can do loads of things yet I don't seem to feel time passing; it's strange but it's interesting. I have lots of chats with Mum and Dad, Uncle Alfred and Aunt Ethel and my grandparents too at times, though I don't see them as much. We reminisce but we talk about here as well, because it is important to be able to cope with the new situation and surroundings, especially for me as I have not been here long really.

As I am talking to you, it brings back memories of Earth life and it may be painful as well as good! It's good to hear you and think of you, but it makes it painful because it reminds me we are all parted. I hope my family is well, my sister and hers, my brother etc. I know they won't actually believe you can talk to me so I don't expect to hear from them, sadly. If you can do something for them, please do. Don't let them think I don't care as they did care for you, you know.

My mum has a lot of her friends here as they were all older and they often meet and have a chat. My dad has his family - his brother and father and is happy pottering round with them. He isn't bothered about trying to fathom out complicated things, he is happy just enjoying the rest and the peace after his hard life on Earth! My mum is content to chat with all; she is her usual self.

I am aware you and me have not seen things eye to eye about this topic of Afterlife, but now I understand why you wanted to make me find out, to help me once I'd arrived here! You were so keen to talk about it and I was reluctant or was not interested, because I think I was a bit scared of what it meant and did not want it to happen... I was not old *(69yrs)* and was younger than my dad! I can't understand why I had to leave so young! You'd think a son should go at least at the same age as his father. Mine was older than that!

BR- (Trying to change topic to uplift him) How do you occupy yourself now?

Let's remember the good days, hey? That's what will keep us together forever. We need to keep that going for both our sakes. We had good 'good times' and that's all I want to always remember! Now, you were saying: What do I do? Well, I learn what my parents and my friends here show me. I made some new acquaintances and they are very helpful. Others are like me, so we learn with and from each other, we practise little things to make life more understandable here.

BR- Could you give me some examples?

Every time you think of something strongly, it appears! So, you need to be careful how you present your thoughts. If you think of something you really want, it will become visible. If you don't care much it won't stay or even come, but if you are serious about it, that makes it visible!

I have pondered a lot about this, because it is interesting if you reflect on it. It is so easy to create things to make life easy and that applies to gardening too! I've tried various things, as you don't really need to do any gardening here, but it's fun to see plants appear and grow at a rate you'd never see on Earth! You could imagine the seed you've just planted turning into a giant sequoia in minutes, if you wanted to! Rain is only needed if you decide it is required. It only rains on demand here, not like in England!

Making sure the plants are not eaten by insects is a thing of the past! They don't really exist as such here, anyway not as pests. **You** would not have to worry about killing them as you used to fret and probably still do*! (Note- He remembers my gardening dilemmas! Indeed, I am a one hundred per cent vegetarian Animal lover and do my best to respect all living creatures, even 'pests').*

I am free from all those chores. I just enjoy seeing beautiful plants grow fast or slowly according to my wishes! My pears never rot, my dahlias always win prizes like before and I am getting rather blasé about this now (Ha ha!). I must say it is comforting not to suffer anymore and not to worry about one's health and tablets etc. A thing of the past!

BR- Do you listen to music?

Bearing in mind I don't play an instrument, not yet anyway, I'll have some scope and choice here, because I could learn to do anything I like. I thought of trying but it won't be difficult, I guess, because all you'll have to do, I expect, is to pretend you can play it, imagine it, and you'll be a virtuoso! My sister would be jealous if she could see me play the piano a thousand times better than her! I am not too much into playing music for the time being. I have heaps of other things to do to occupy my 'moments', which are not things I have to do but I choose to do, to suit my mood at the time.

It has been very hard, you know, to go away from you all who have been my life. It is so hard not to see the children and my thoughts are often with them, wondering and hoping they are all right. That's good to hear they are - you said they are busy. That's fine, it occupies them and gives them a goal. No moping about, but it must have been hard for them to lose me and see me 'dead', or rather see my body dead, as **I know I am not!** Very hard, I am sure. Poor kiddos.

But you must not worry about me. I have some sadness at times because it is painful to be parted but I also know it's not forever and we'll see each other again, all of us one day! So it's not as if it will be never ending. I'll miss seeing them grow older, all the things they'll do, no doubt... Anne-France will possibly get married one day?

BR- She is still looking for the 'right' man!

She is sensible, she won't choose a wrong one, but it's sad not to take her to the altar and hear her say "I do" when I could have given her away... but I'll be there in thought and love if and when it happens one day! Same with my lad. Can't imagine him a married man, though... sounds strange! He must have so much to do with his job, he may not have time for girls, I guess?

BR- He is very busy as he runs that studio on his own! Anne-France is very grown-up but no doubt she grieves and analyses; she is afraid of losing someone again!

Has she got someone good for her now? Is S. still around?

BR- She's split up for good but they are still 'friends', though I advised they do not see each other often. She dates other lads but no one is 'perfect', yet! Also she knows she has to work for her Nutrition Therapy degree, so she keeps them at bay, as she got hurt by falling for the wrong guy.

Better be free and single than with the wrong fellow, so she's doing all right so far, I see. Well, my little wife, that's all

I can say about me and perhaps you don't have any other news. *(I gave more news, including my broken wrist and that I miss our Scrabble games together!)*

Lots of love to all of you. Yes, I know what you've just said, all understood. Sorry to hear about your wrist, I hope that will heal quickly and painlessly. I'll take my leave now as I am rather worn out trying to concentrate for so long..

BR- You've done very well! It's great.

Give a kiss for me to the kids and let them know I am not forgetting them, far from it! I can't wait to see them again but it must not be yet, of course. They still have plenty to do with their lives. Love you all! Dave xxx

1st April 2006 - 18.45pm. *The pen starts in English as my Guide steps in.*

We'll let your mum come through. She's been waiting for a long time for a chance to talk to you. *(Silence. So I hum to myself those childhood songs Mum used to sing to us. Finally French is spoken).*

At last, Mum is here! Phew! I thought I wasn't going to make it! It's been hard this time! I wanted so much to get down to it, as it's been a long time I have not spoken to you. I wanted to know how your hand and wrist were and whether you are in pain?

BR- I am ok overall.

You'll have to be careful after the plaster is removed, as your hand and wrist will be weaker, they won't have the same strength as before to carry heavy weights. You'll risk dropping things more often. Beware of hot dishes and breakable objects! *(Note- Wonderful! Mum talks and tries to help, just as she would have when on Earth).* I'll keep talking so as not to lose the thread of my thoughts. I have seen lots of people recently

124

and it's been very interesting because they are folk I did not know, who taught me fascinating things. They made me do unusual exercises to teach me to think about myself, by exteriorizing my thoughts aloud. It is not that easy because **we do not really have a voice!**

BR- Please explain this more?

I did such things as visiting someone as if it was night time, in 'darkness' and telling them I was there and describing myself in great detail so that they recognise me! As those people here knew me, it was good because they could check whether I was making a mistake or I forgot a detail.

BR- Is that as a preparation for séances?

It's good practice. Yes, of course, it's to be able to do it properly when I come to Earth in séances, as you said, where you receive communications from Beyond. But I want to be able to show myself to be recognised by you, of course, as I don't care about the others in the room! So, I am working hard so that all the details are correct. You'll see, one would have to be an idiot not to know it is me! I mean, I shall give lots of details about me and you and our life together, so that you won't be able to doubt it's me indeed! *(I suggested a few private details).* You are right, that's good to mention it. So, we'll work hard at this and you'll have a good surprise when I manage to do it perfectly!

BR- What kind of séance? Trance or physical ones with ectoplasm?

I think we'll start with trance. But there is also that business with ectoplasm, that tacky sticky stuff! That will perhaps be afterwards or at the same time, I am not too sure. It's fun to do as an exercise since one talks about oneself to be recognised! But I have to think really hard and remember my life on Earth. I have the feeling it's been a long time since I was there, yet it's not that long ago?

BR- It will soon be seven years.
Incredible! We are not aware of time here. Anyway, that's what I am doing at the moment. This is to warn you I am doing my very best!

BR- Are you told which medium it will be, so that I don't miss attending that séance?!
Those exercises will take me a long time to do and understand and remember.... so it's not for tomorrow! I still have ever so much to do, so it will no doubt 'take time' but I am sure we shall warn you so that you don't miss me! The worry is I am not sure whether I'll succeed on the day. One is always afraid of failing when one does something new!

BR- You did well with the transfiguration! The other woman spoilt it but I'll be careful now and watch out. You are an excellent pupil, so be positive!
The most pleasant thing will be to hear you speak to me aloud, as if we were together in the same room, or we phoned each other!

BR- Indeed! That will be fantastic!
I am only too happy to do as they say, that way I'll know what to do. It's not as if I had to invent anything myself. So I obey, I listen, I do my best and I practise all that. Those are my activities, Madam! I think that should interest you, shouldn't it?!

BR- You can say that again! Not half! Bravo!
Now I'll let you carry on talking to others, if you wish.

BR- You can stay if you want! Thanks for the news. I give you big kisses. (Suddenly English is spoken, as my Guide steps in!)

Let her go to let others through. Let your Mind wander for a while, then change writing pad. We are here for you. *(So I took the pad used for taking down the dictation of wisdom and knowledge my Spirit Teachers want to compile in their book 'Truths, Lies and Distortions'. The 'Thinker' came through, recommending people should have, weekly, a whole day of quiet and awareness of their inner senses).*

21st April 2006 - 8.50am! *After my Guide helped build up the link, Mum came through.*

It's good to talk to you Sweetheart. I was waiting to be able to join you. As for me, the main thing is I have worked well and still do, to learn to make myself recognisable when I go in a 'dark room'. Apparently one does not always see anybody. I am told one hears people there if they hear you. So I was taught to project my thoughts forward so that they get shaped correctly into words: I must pronounce them clearly in my head so that it reaches your world!

All those exercises are useful indeed as one really must practise for it to work! My fear of not being able to do it properly 'on D day' has diminished a lot now. I have more self-confidence and I do hope I'll succeed on the day when you are present!

I am told I shall also have to show my own face over the medium's face, but that will no doubt be for another time. Practising concentration on oneself is rather difficult at the beginning but it is interesting in a way. One has to think so much about oneself and Earthly details of the life one has lived! It's weird and makes me dig into my memory, which I have regained fortunately! I remember suffering from its loss at one time!

I gather I have to let you go as you have something to do, but I want to give you a big kiss and tell you all is well this side, even though I still miss you all! Yet I have plenty to do and am proud of myself because I am beginning to feel I can do this 'work'. I hope not to disappoint you the day we meet!

BR- Can you manage to cover your whole body with ectoplasm and be able to walk? Or just show your hand for example?

Unfortunately not very well yet but hopefully it will come? It's always a question of practice as usual! Once I have mastered it, it will go smoothly I am sure. The pleasure of speaking to you 'live' will be so great that I train as best as I can nearly all the time, to have you 'online' to me for those short moments. We shall enjoy them indeed, shan't we? Right, I must let you go, sorry to have delayed you. I wanted to be able to kiss you and tell you I am tackling it fervently so that it is a success!

BR- Well done. There are not that many 'physical mediums' around, so I hope you find one I know of!

27 April 2006 - *My Guide starts the dialogue.*

The lady you know here, your mum, is working very hard to help you practise and communicate with her. She wants to be able to talk to you daily, practically, but she really wishes to be in conversation when you are in a room where you'll meet her one day; she is training and learning how to do it as well as she can. An example of practice: She has been talking to strangers on Earth, to make sure you receive her when she does come to you. She's been to groups where there is communication, so that she knows how to give her voice out and make herself felt. This has to be practised, so she is doing well. All around and within her is the desire to succeed. *(Note- This must be taking place in trance séances).*

128

Make sure you connect up well with us. At the moment there is a lovely wave between us, linking us. Let's ride it together, we are on the same wave. It is blue and white, tall and loving too. You stay on that wave and we'll be able to carry on talking. When you hear us it's because we are on the same wavelength and that's what makes the communication possible - but if you switch off or change wave, you can't stay on the same level of frequency. My Mind is reaching yours to try to help you focus quietly and then others can come too... but they'll have more difficulties if you can't stay online with us. Let's try now as there is another personality here who wishes to talk to you. It's a gentleman who has a lot to say if you can listen to him. *(Sudden change of communicator).*

Hello young lady, can you hear me? We have spoken before and I'll talk again, to help you understand some 'mysteries' (as you call them) of life. The life you know is one of many lived by many people on Earth. Not one life is similar to another because each has been chosen to suit the personality embodied in the flesh. If they were all the same you would be 'clones' or carbon copies! *(Then he carries on with dictating swiftly six pages of handwritten material related to profound Knowledge he and my other 'Wisdom Inspirers' had already started dictating to me for their book of 'T, L & D':* **The flesh body is created to fit in with and reflect what the personality wants to learn by choosing that particular life!** *It is better understood if read within the context of the teachings of that book).*

5th June 2006 - *I relax for a long time with gentle panpipes music on. The pen writes flowingly and clearly the first eight words in 'Automatic', in French.*

Léonie Moleux Leclercq here. Do you wish to speak with me? My dear little lady, my dear grandaughter, I was hoping you would want to - as I have waited for ages to be able to join you again! It's been a long time since we last spoke! I have a small story to relate to you. I thought you may like to be aware of the fact that even before I saw you as a baby, I had already been taking care of you. It gives me pleasure to recall it and to let you know. (*She went on with very touching and unexpected details of some very old private family matters. I was very surprised as I'd had no idea she'd been involved in them. This warmed my heart and showed what a wonderful mother and grandma she was and is*).

8th July 2006 - *The pen starts in French.*

I was your father too at one time and I am now your father for spiritual coaching. I have been looking after your spiritual education, my little one, ever since you have come to Earth.

BR- Do you mean this current life?
Yes, the life you are leading at the moment.

BR- (Puzzled) Why speak in French? Are you my 'Silver Arrow'?
(He reverts to speaking in English!) You can call me whatever you like and we can speak any language you like! **The language barrier does not exist here;** you can have any tongue you like; **we all communicate by thoughts.**

My dear friend, you are what I call 'my daughter in spiritual matters'. You and I have been speaking to each other for a long time. You call me 'Silver Arrow' but I thought it might be interesting for you to know that I can communicate in French too, in your Mind, if I trigger the 'French speaking part'!

BR- Oh?! I see... so you are indeed my Guide?
Yes, I am here to tell you that the time you spend with us is always useful. So please make it as often as possible.

130

Now I'll tell you something else if you like, to keep you going and interested in the subject.

There was a gentleman, when on Earth, who used to listen to **our** world when he wanted to make some progress in his work. He only needed to relax and could listen and tune in easily, as you call it. He was a great worker for our world because he taught people some truths about many things. His name was not as important as his deeds. He had so much capacity to absorb our Knowledge and Teachings that he could spend hours listening, then could remember what had been said!

BR- Wow! I wish I could too!

You could if you tried more! When he left the Earth, he promised himself to carry on with his teaching of the world but from this side of life, as he could do it better, having more information at his grasp and more details to delve into. He has been communicating with the Earth for many years now, in various ways and wishes to help you relax and absorb facts in the same way as he did. He wants to teach you to absorb by listening out for the words in your head. He would like to be your guiding teacher for a while, if you let him.

BR- That's very kind. Can I have a name to recognise him more easily?

He'll soon be recognised by his words and his manner, but if you want a 'label', you can call him 'Brother John'.

BR- Did I hear correctly? You said Brother John?

The name is of no importance but the label is correct. You have indeed been told of his approaching activities, his impending coming. He is here now if you wish to be his pupil for a while. He is very patient so you will not be told off as often as with us! You can trust his Knowledge is of the highest and purest we can give you for the time being.

BR- I feel very honoured and humble. (Short silence. Then I hear...)

The pupil listens, the teacher teaches. Perfection comes out of patience and discipline. Aim for perfection, don't be satisfied with second best. The more you want, the more you will get. The more you get, the more you'll want but also will achieve. The more you achieve, the bigger your progress towards perfection. Perfection is the ultimate goal. Truth is the perfect goal to aim for! Truth is what you should have been taught in the world but it has been distorted over the ages! You and I and others are incensed by this, aren't we?! So, we are all here to teach the TRUTH!

Truth is what should be known for the facts one teaches are what things **are** - and not what things people imagine, or decide, or distort to suit their needs and wishes! You and I and others are bent on getting Truth into the world, so that people do not suffer because of untruths or lies. Is that correct?

BR- Yes absolutely. (Most of the following dictation and conversation is now included in their book 'Truths Lies & Distortions' but you, the reader, may be interested to learn or be reminded of some of those facts now).

So, we'll start with simple facts and will build up towards better, higher, deeper, more profound or detailed Knowledge - so that no stone is left unturned if we can avoid it, to help Truth be known in certain areas, certain subjects.

Point one: Simple facts of life are not always known. Just look at the birth of a child, who will be a grown up human of course. Has **anyone wondered what the baby in the womb thinks** of his position, his situation? He is in a strong position, he is 'a Human' in the making. He has just left the world of Spirit he was in, perhaps for a very long time and now he encases his spiritual Energy in a body of flesh, which will have to be his vehicle for possibly a long time!

What does he think of it, as he lies there, being created bigger and strong enough to come out and face the world of Matter? **We** know he is a Spirit but no one (or few) seems to remember he is a 'Spirit' in a vehicle of flesh!

Well, we can tell you the experience can be a torture or a delight, depending on the aims and the goals that particular Soul had set itself before setting off on that trip. So, the torture could be part of the built-in fears the baby or child or adult will have in their life! The personalities come for something to learn or experience but are dreading it at the same time! That is how and why some youngsters are 'tortured within' without even knowing it!

If people could learn to **send healing thoughts to babies** in the womb, it would help them emerge more safely, of course, but also more sane mentally. If the baby needs calming before he is born into the physical world, he'll benefit from the healing vibrations sent to him.

BR- Couldn't those in the Spirit World do it before he is born?

The healing thoughts are to come from those who are going to receive him into the physical world, because they have to be on the same vibrational level as the personality's new Energy level.

BR- Can you explain this a little more please?

Once one is in a flesh body or part of a flesh body, the Energy level, the vibrations of the flesh have a great influence on the way that personality reacts. The fact of being into a 'casing of flesh', so to speak, makes a great difference to the way people react. It has a greater influence then on one's way of thinking. So, the baby needs to be told within himself that he can be healed, he does not need to suffer and dread what is coming - if it is in that 'position', that way of thinking.

BR- But we can't know what he is thinking!

The fact you don't know whether he is thinking that way or not, means you all need to send healing thoughts to babies 'on the go', in the making, to send them strength, determination and encouragement. They have to make a big trip, a hard one for some, as they dive into a new world... once more, possibly! They may be looking forward to it of course, but it is more likely they are dreading a lot of it. Why? Because having to leave the World of Spirit, as you call it, in order to delve into a restricting body of flesh (which no doubt will come with all its problems!) instead of staying in our wonderful World of Mind and Light is a big, big step to take!

All of you should feel sorry for babies who are being born - feel sorry, not happy! That's what we wanted to tell you. That everyone rejoices at the birth of a new Soul in the world is very nice - but **you don't see it from its point of view!**

'Baby' may be very miserable to have had to make the trip and that's what should be set up - a healing minute, or whatever, for babies coming into the world, for their Souls to settle down and their Minds to have more peace within, as they make their way through nine months of pregnancy and the years of babyhood.

To be a baby is very hard work when you have been a free Spirit, a grown up Soul, a knowledgeable personality who has chosen to go back to Earth for whatever purpose. A Soul making that trip has indeed a lot of courage, no doubt (may be mad too, I'd say with a smile!), but is indeed very brave to have left the world it was in - our world - to go to you present one and face many unknown factors.

So will you try and let people think about it? Those who have to be the parents will need healing too; they have a big responsibility and many are not always up to it, even though they have created the little one. It takes a lot of courage

134

and dedication and often basic knowledge of man's Mind to handle the upbringing of a child and future adult!

So, all in all, healing has its value on all levels and scores. You all need to give healing to babies, future ones, or those who have arrived and their family! Because that is what the world of Humans is made of - children and parents. The world cannot be made of unhappy Souls who dread what they are going to live in!

BR- Is it the majority? Some seem to be happy.

Many children are happy indeed but I am talking of the many millions who have chosen to come, knowing they'll probably have a life tougher than most. It makes it even worse for them in the long run, because they arrive dreading what they may be in for!

BR- May I ask a question? Why are poor people born in Africa, for example?

It has been said that a pupil who asks a question is one who is interested, so do not be afraid of asking questions. You wonder why they are born? Because they want to learn something, experience the fact they are poor or starving, to understand better those who are also poor and starving, to help them in turn. If they did not, there would be no one knowing what it is like!

BR- So one can't break the vicious circle?

The vicious circle started when Mankind did not make everyone equal, back in time! It started long ago and still exists! Mankind had forgotten that the trip to Earth was supposed to be an enjoyable experiment, in harmony with fellow travellers. It has turned into a battle or competition between who can be stronger or better than the others. That was NOT the original aim!

So, to come back to what we were saying, the little one being born dreading his trip on Earth has to be helped by sending him (or her) all the possible loving, healing thoughts to fortify him in his endeavours. If you don't, if no one does, then he is really on his own, you see and that could make his adventure much worse than it needs to be.

BR- I had never thought of it like that. Is it the same for Animals then? We would be at it all day long, sending healing thoughts!

Bravery is more what 'Animals' are coming for. They usually come to experience physical life, of course, but also the link with Mankind in some cases, or the freedom of having a flesh body but not linked to Mankind, as in wild Animals. So, in the latter case, it is all a question of being brave enough to risk being on one's own to face the world of flesh with all its demands; the demands of the body of flesh versus the adversity caused by elements and wilderness. They have to be brave and need bravery in their hearts to face the world.

Many will die young, simply because they cannot cope too long in that world and would rather come back to us here. Others will last longer but will still need courage to face the world. All are Souls from our world, on a journey for themselves usually and who, whether Animals or Humans, need badly the help provided by healing, living thoughts!

BR- But that means millions of them needing my healing thoughts!

My dear, you don't have to heal them all now! You can simply help by sending thoughts now and then, but, most of all, also teach people to think that way too! The rest of the world could and should do the same. That would be the ultimate aim, eventually.

BR- Why do Animals chose to be born, say, as cattle, or risking vivisection or being hunted etc?

An Animal accepting the challenge of an Earthly life has been there before.

BR- Really?

Yes, they did have a life on Earth before and do accept or decide to go back, for many reasons or for one, depending on their choice. It has to come from their own desire and choice, otherwise they could not go back, you understand?

BR- Do you mean, for example, the lambs and calves and battery hens know of the horrors ahead or, say, the Muslim ritual of bleeding them to death etc?

All Humans need to learn their lesson too and go back to the Original Plan, which was and still is: Helping each other (and ALL living Beings) on the journey of physical life! If all did it, no problem would ever have been encountered, you see. Never! No disease, no problem! But Mankind created the problems out of laziness, selfishness, greed and lack of consideration.

So you'd need to have a 'plan zero' and start from scratch again to have a perfect world! You can't do it overnight or over centuries. It took longer to become bad, so it will take a long time to become good again! You may say: "Why don't chickens in the making choose **not** be born to battery hens?" If you wiped off the population of chickens before Mankind accepted to let them be free on Earth, it will take so long you'll even forget what a chicken looks like!

BR- Pause please! Am I correct to think there is no life in a body if no Spirit goes into it?

Of course! Millions of times 'of course'! So, you think if all chickens stopped existing now, it would prevent suffering?

137

BR- Them and all Animals!

What would happen? Animals are Souls who wish to come to develop their relationship with the world of Matter, in a way which is different from the way Humans relate to Matter. As you know, Mankind behaves in one way, Animals in others. So, if you wiped off all Animals for a while, by not having Animals of any kind born in situations where they could suffer (your suggestion!), it means it would restrict the scope of the 'Animal' world in ours.

BR- It would only be temporarily, until Mankind learns.

Till Mankind learns?! How long will that take?! Would Mankind not wait for a resurgence of birth and start again killing for that pleasure they had been deprived of for so long?!

BR- There used to be (more?) cannibals.

You have good but impractical ideas, I think! The situation needs to be rectified via Mankind's progression in its thinking and beliefs. It may take longer but it will or should be longer lasting.

If you stop eating Humans because you **do not want to do it** for good, sound reasons, that is the safer bet! If you don't do it now simply because of lack of, or shortage of bodies, you'd soon do it again if and when the bodies reappeared!

BR- Very sad!

So to come back to my topic: When coming into a flesh body on Earth, there is the feeling of dread, of "Shall I be able to cope with it? Shall I suffer?". It is valid even within the Animal Kingdom!

By the time you have absorbed all this and more, your thinking will have expanded to breaking point, possibly! It makes the Mind grow, stretch, screech to overstretching reaches but it will not harm it.

138

BR- It's a good thing our departed beloved pets are there to welcome us when we too pass over!

Of course! Love never disappears! All has been said on that subject for now. Would you like a rest?

BR- Maybe I'd better sleep!

We'll let you sleep and hope to be with you again before long. Yes, I am 'Brother John' if you wish to know, though **the Knowledge comes from higher and wider levels, not just from my own Mind.**

BR- I am most honoured to receive it.

You can call me anytime you wish. I'll be pleased to oblige. (*And he signed off "JOHN"*).

****

CHAPTER 3
Physical Séance: Materialised hand - Mum helps 'departed' children - My first search in French archives - Pets sense Spirits - Amazing dematerialisation - Feeling Mum's Energy

13th July 2006 - *Today I went to my first private guest séance of physical mediumship with genuine and renowned Physical Medium Stewart Alexander in Yorkshire. Of course, over the years I had attended numerous public ones before. But this time it was more special - and it turned out to be so, indeed as I was one of only nine guests, instead of the forty to one hundred in public ones! (For readers interested in finding out more details about Stewart's great gift and dedication to the Spirit World and its scientists, please read his fascinating memoirs as a physical medium - which included independent detailed reports of his séances - in 'An Extraordinary Journey').*

One of the pleasurable aspects of being present at such an event is that I know from experience and without a shadow of a doubt that everything happening there is absolutely genuine; there is no 'trickery' whatsoever! Stewart Alexander's mediumship is well-known and respected for its authenticity and probity.

*Stewart is a non-egotistical medium who has selflessly dedicated over forty years of his life to the work those scientists in the Spirit World wished to carry out. They are advanced and evolved scientists who master the manipulation of matter in such **ways impossible for human scientists to achieve.** What for? To attempt to demonstrate to sceptical Mankind that survival of death is a fact and the World of Mind and Light is a reality. Amazing physical happenings cannot be denied when every single person in the room witnesses them, whereas 'messages' from people on the Other Side passed on via 'mental mediumship', though wonderful and evidential to the recipients, are not tangible or visible to an audience.*

Anyone interested in finding out more about the mind-boggling feats of that very special gift can discover more, as there have been and are scores of absolutely genuine physical mediums helping the Spirit World scientists demonstrate the reality of Survival. The list is huge. Of course, like in all fields and professions, over the recent centuries since records began, there will have been people who may not have been so genuine and have been found out. Sadly those are the ones whom sceptics and detractors quote and enjoy tearing apart, automatically ignoring and tarring with the same brush the numerous genuine and authentic mediums!

Apart from Stewart's, I have also met, attended and even helped organise genuine séances with great physical mediums such as Colin Fry, David Thompson, Bill Meadows and Scott Milligan. I also sat several times during the famous and astounding 'Scole Experiment' (in Norfolk, UK) in the 1990s, so I can vouch for its authenticity too! And so can eminent researchers (from the Society for Psychical Research) such as Professor Archie Roy, Professor David Fontana and journalist and researcher Montague Keen. They investigated thoroughly those happenings personally and wrote their worldwide known, favourable and positive 'Scole Report'.(More detail in 'Witnessing the Impossible' by Robin Foy: The authentic and original diary of all the séances in Scole during which mind-boggling and 1000% genuine phenomena were produced - without the use of ectoplasm - in successful groundbreaking experiments by evolved scientists in the Spirit World).

One way of finding out easily more about the various wonders of physical phenomena, worldwide, over numerous decades and provided by amazing scientists in the Spirit World, is to look up' Zerdin Phenomenal' website and their magazine, which one can subscribe to.

So, back to Yorkshire and my July guest séance with Stewart Alexander: After emptying our pockets and leaving our belongings downstairs, our small group of sitters settles down on our tightly packed seats in the small upstairs séance room. The medium soon goes into a deep trance in his armchair against a corner wall. When in trance he is unaware of anything and anybody in the room. Phosphorescent strips are taped on his arms and legs so that everyone can keep track of his slightest movement! All his limbs are tightly strapped to his armchair (by independent attendees) with secure cable ties, which can only be removed by cutting them with pliers. This is because ectoplasm will be created and used by the Spirit scientists. As it is easily destroyed by light, there is a need for darkness during part of the séance.

The usual Spirit communicators start talking through him using his vocal apparatus. I feel honoured to be recognised by 'Christopher' then by 'Walter' when they greet me by name. As they said, they are by now "acquainted with my Energies" since I had attended many séances in the past.

*As usual, we enjoy the many successful experiments and fascinating demonstrations of objects levitating and flying all over the room at high speed, performing fast intricate patterns or suddenly gliding smoothly millimetres from someone's face. This indicates they are controlled by an intelligence aware of space; Dr Barnett walks round the group, touching individual members to give healing, as well as saying a few relevant words. He can be felt physically because he wraps his current Energy body in a cover of **ectoplasm**, that Living Energy substance mystifying human scientists, as they are unable to reproduce it and analyse it properly, since its components are produced by some special physical mediums' bodies, but also come from the Spirit Realm Energies! Dr Barnett also does experiments to create a 'Spirit light' untouched by Earthly human means.*

Ectoplasm is used by 'invisible' Energy Beings such as Spirit communicators and departed loved ones to make themselves tangible to our physical senses. It resembles 'cheese cloth' or muslin, yet metres of it usually comes out of the (entranced) medium's ears, nose or mouth. It sounds weird indeed but this is what happens. There have been and are scores of photographic records of it and testimonies confirming the authenticity of such astounding phenomena (See 'Zerdin Phenomenal').

Also during Stewart's séances, evidence of survival is always given in the form of personal communications from sitters' departed loved ones talking with them. They can do it through trance (through the medium's vocal chords), or by direct voice (i.e. their voice coming 'out of thin air' or via an ectoplasmic 'voice box'/spirit loudspeaker), or thanks to the intermediary of 'Freda Johnson', a retired school teacher in her Earthly days, who is now a regular communicator from Spirit and passes on their messages and evidential details, if they can't master the other methods.

*And of course (departed) Walter Stinson - brother of famous medium 'Margery' (Mina Crandon) - and his Spirit Team of scientists proudly demonstrate once more their extraordinary and authentic feats of the **passage of matter through matter** and the **materialised hand experiments**, which they can repeat at every séance!*

Unknown to me, a wonderful surprise awaits me this evening. The small, low table is placed as usual in the middle of our tight circle of seats, in front of the medium in trance, whose arms and legs (wearing phosphorescent tabs to show his position) are still tightly strapped to his armchair.

The low table's translucent top (about 40 to 50 centimetres diameter) has an interior red light and its intensity can be controlled and switched on/off by Raymondo, Stewart's circle leader, who obeys Walter's instructions as he speaks through the deep trance state of Stewart. Since the Spirit scientists are using ectoplasm and it is very sensitive to bright light, they must take great care not to risk affecting their medium's health because that 'Living Energy substance' is linked to him, hence their careful use of red light.

A lady sitter is called to sit on the spare chair opposite the medium and asked to put one hand on the lit up table between them. That way the other sitters can see her hand silhouetted against the red light. As the amazing phenomenon (I'll describe it next) takes place successfully for the other lady, I am leaning forward to see better from my seat. Spirit communicator Walter notices and calls out to me: "Can you see enough Brigitte? You are leaning forward". How kind of him!

Once the experiment with that sitter ends, to my great delight Walter calls out to me again and says: "Brigitte, you have not had that particular experience before, have you? You look forlorn. We cannot disappoint you. Please come to the chair at the table!" Delighted, I obey and tell him how honoured I feel, having hoped for years to live this moment. Walter replies with kind words about the Spirit World knowing how much work I have done and still do for Spirit etc. He adds: "We see and know the inside of you, not just the outside". I thank him warmly.

*He then instructs me to keep my hand still on the illuminated table top. I can see (and so can the onlookers) a foggy haze emanating from in front of the medium, which thickens into a darker mass gradually building itself on the glass, a large blob of ectoplasm - at the same time as I feel the low table vibrating! To my amazement that small table gradually tilts up 45° (unaided by Earthly hands or means!) and locks against my knees! Then it lowers itself horizontally as I can clearly see **fingers gradually forming themselves** out of the mass of ectoplasm still on its top! The hand thus formed moves forward towards my own hand, grasps all my fingers*

144

together, squeezing them firmly. It then lifts my hand up, to shake it several times in a firm handshake! It feels normal and warm. A strong man's hand. (Definitely larger than Stewart's in case some readers may wonder). It then lowers and places my hand back on the lit-up table top. His hand shrinks back into the ectoplasmic mass, which then melts away centimetres from me!

Walter, whose hand it was - and which I held when he wrapped it up tangibly in that Energy substance - then jokingly asks me if I enjoyed "shaking hands with a man who has been 'dead' for over ninety years"! Of course I did! He gallantly adds, in his inimitable, deep, voluptuous velvety voice (with a touch of Canadian accent): "Shaking hands with you Ma'am was a pleasure I won't forget". I know he is being pleasant and always is to all the ladies! But those were a few extraordinary and momentous moments I shall never forget!

Stewart's Spirit Scientists have also developed this particular demonstration by adding additional features which I have witnessed and participated in over the years. They want to counteract and block any doubt and claims that it could be the medium's or an accomplice's hand suddenly appearing! For this they call three sitters to squeeze round the table, each with both hands flat on the lit up top, fingertips touching their neighbours'.

*Spirit Scientists then paranormally release entranced Stewart's arms from the straps tying him down and place his hands on the illuminated table, finger tips touching the sitters' fingers adjacent to him. They even call for an extra overhead red light clearly illuminating the four pairs of **immobile** hands flat on the translucent lit-up top, so everyone in the room can witness the situation.*

*Then Walter **creates his materialised 'extra hand'**, which takes shape on the lit up table in the gap between the immobile medium's hands and may even touch some of the* *sitters! This is to show that the new hand is not Stewart's, nor anyone else's, as no one could possibly squeeze themselves in the very tightly packed group!*

Experiencing phenomena with genuine and trustworthy mediums and their teams is wonderful! For more details on the phenomena and experiments in these particular séances, the reader may wish to read Stewart's memoirs and its independent reports.

****

14 July 2006 - *I send thanks to all those in the Spirit World for helping me experience that séance. My Guide pops in:*

What did you gain out of this experience? A lot, we hope! You had the opportunity to talk to us in this world to share Love, Peace, Joy and Upliftment... and also 'wonder-full' experiments! We are pleased you were able to experience your own private touch and experiment with ectoplasm, as it is something really unusual and special! We were delighted Walter did not let you down.

As you know, we are willing to do anything for you and with you, so we hope you can do the same for us. Look forward to more work with us, more time together, more writing... more typing! More of everything, so that you can progress on your path and feel fulfilled. If you want to add more activities you can always try! Lots can be done with a quiet Mind! Get the quiet Mind, we'll do the rest!

11th August 2006 - 07.25hrs! *During all the previous weeks, whenever I tuned in, my highly knowledgeable Friends from Beyond came regularly to dictate more fascinating and mind-boggling facts and knowledge for their book 'T, L & D'. This morning the pen starts in French for a change!*

Slowly but surely your mum is here. Sweetheart, I have not spoken to you for a long time because I wanted to make sure you had some time to type our book *(her diary of conversations with me)*. I am sorry for the work and hassle it causes you, Darling, I do realise it must be an enormous task, but it should really be interesting! We have to get a move on with it and make it a success, hey? It would be a pity to give up halfway, since we've managed up to now. The hardest part is the typing, the preparation for publishing... it will take a lot of time. It will not be easy because there are heaps of things to do for that, but we'll get there, don't worry!

BR- I am sorry for the delay, but I also have to do the translation of all dialogues in French as well! And taking down the dictation of my Spirit Teachers for their own wisdom book... plus deal with my all teaching jobs etc.!

It's very understandable, you can't do everything! But try to have a go at ours as often as you can and prepare what is necessary. As for me, I am involved in lots of things as usual. The most interesting is to look after people who have just arrived as most of them feel lost and unhappy to have left their family behind on the Earth. They have so much to say and feel the shock of having arrived here without having been able to warn them or talk to them! You seem to be in the middle of a war (on Earth) as there are hordes of people coming over in groups, in large batches! There must be heaps of dead people on Earth? I think there must be some bombing or things like that. It's awful because they are always so miserable about their situation.

I try to help them by making them grasp that they've arrived somewhere with no problem, no pain and though their loved ones will be unhappy, they will understand it was better for the departed in the end. Everyone mourns those they have 'abandoned' that way! That's because it was often so sudden, they did not have time to say goodbye, to warn them of their departure. It is always the same thing - the worst is the sudden separation, or even less sudden, but it is the parting. The physical pain one may have suffered disappears once here, but the pain of being parted can last; one cannot cure it so easily.

Children who 'die' have nearly always some parents on Earth and it feels strange and is sad for them, of course, to be far from them, when they were used to be with the family. So, there are people here who look after them, who are 'foster parents'. These people wanted either to have children or love children anyway, or need to learn to be kind to children.

Personally, I had trained as a nursery nurse; I have always liked children, as long as they behave! So, I was given the task to look after those who arrive here without any parents, because I can be kind to them and make them play. I do little fun exercises which keep them busy and show them how to use their power of Thought, which they will need here anyway! It does them good, it helps them feel better and it facilitates their progress with coping here more quickly and easily.

If they were left alone, they would not know what's going on and no doubt would be frightened, because visions and sudden apparitions of objects are bewildering when one does not know they may happen or why they do! When you are warned and have practised, it's a little easier and understandable and less scary. So, I look after the little ones as well as grown-ups; a child is a future adult, so there is no difference! The Soul is the same, it has just a little less practice and experience of Earthly life. The exercises we do are always fun. I enjoy them myself as there is always the child within all of us, isn't there? The children love doing that because it is a distraction for them, a way of spending time pleasantly! It helps them forget their family for a while and teaches them to cope here, as I have already told you.

148

Being able to understand how to function here is ever so important! Too many people don't know it. In fact I reckon no one knows it, because we do not practise that on Earth - to think of an object and see it appear at once! To start with, it would make Earthly life easier - we would not need to go and buy things! Then when we arrive over here it would be normal to do it. Why isn't it taught on Earth, that's an important question?

Anyway, my protégés manage and when they cry I console them; I am their temporary and adoptive mum until they calm down. We give them a lot of love here, so they feel much more comfortable and safer, yet there is the loss of Mummy and Daddy and their dog and their dolls etc. My little ones are not very skilled yet at creating and reproducing things. They think about the object but we have to teach them to keep in Mind only one thing at a time. It is really hard to do, isn't it? Practice is what matters most. Once it becomes 'normal', we don't think about it anymore, I mean we don't have to make any effort any longer, it becomes much easier.

Children always ask questions which I need to answer. That's the most fun, because not only it is pleasant to do but it amuses me to realise I have become a teacher of the Afterlife and not of French or English - like I did on Earth. **It feels good to be of use to others** here and not just do everything for myself. It seems less selfish, because since I arrived here I have spent most of my time enjoying myself, learning for myself. But now I can use my knowledge to help others and I have always helped children with their problems at school, as you will remember. So, 'arriving' here is a much bigger problem to understand and solve! Therefore, I've transformed myself into a Teacher of the Great Beyond! It helps them and I suppose it helps me too, it makes me more useful. I like to be helpful and of some use, as you know. So these are my most recent activities.

You are aware, aren't you, that to speak to you I have not used the 'black corner/wall' for a long time now? That's because I learnt to listen and think in my head, without having to go anywhere in particular, so I hear you and receive you easily, without having to sit at the desk. I no longer need to jot notes down. I can do it but I know what I want to tell you, so I can think it 'towards you' and send it to you that way.

A last little detail: You know cats and dogs who arrive here do not need an adoptive mum to guide them! They know what to do! They seem to be able to adapt much better than Humans do. They get on with their quiet little life, have fun, play with leaves or the other Animals and stroll about. They probably may imagine they eat too, though I don't recall having to do that much with them; it's more important to stroke them and love them, that's what 'feeds' them better I think. They don't have any problem adapting.

I assume they have less links with 'families', i.e. parent cats or dogs. It's more affection for their masters but for them it looks to me to be easier. The youngest children have difficulties understanding what they are told at first, as long as they think like tots. As they get used to being here, they begin to blossom and to become 'Spirits' again (as we all are!) and to remember what they used to know before going to Earth! I suppose it's easier for them because they have not had a long Earthly life blocking their Minds on that subject and filling it with lots of complicated situations, ideas and associations etc!

Here, we live as we think, we think as we live. We think **and** we 'are'. It is really a case of "I think therefore I am" (as Descartes stated with his famous saying) though here, it's rather "I am as I think". A very profound conclusion, isn't it?

150

BR- You are doing an excellent job Mum! (My Guide steps in).

Men have always been cruel to their fellow men, so what's new? You cannot expect them to be kind when all they think of is fighting their opponent to obtain gain and take and steal whatever goods they want for themselves. The past years were 'good' examples of wars in the world, your world and nothing good, really good has come out of it! Lost lives have arrived here, lost in their Souls and Minds, because they could not see why they had to die for nothing. Such lost lives can mean lost Souls and destroyed homes or families. We know we cannot change things from our end. It can only be done from within the hearts of each man and woman on Earth. They all need to want peace at all cost, without giving in to going to war and bashing the adversary into submission because one has superior weapons. Because of that, all these 'lost' Souls feel they have been cheated, yet they did choose to die for the cause, otherwise they would not have chosen to be there.

If even one war made a difference to the world, one could praise it, but no war has ever made a real difference to your world. It may have changed things in as much as a party or a man would not reign, or would reign over others, but it's not what I would call making a difference to the world.

BR- I understand. But some people would say, for example, we would all be Nazis, or there'd be no Jews if there had not been wars and so on!

In a nutshell, whatever you may 'gain' on Earth will not be a 'gain' once back here, because you'd see the folly of your actions, the kindness of some versus the abominable horror of all these killings. You cannot condone wars. It has NO place in our world! No justification. No 'raison d'être'. Whatever reasons Mankind invents to justify a war will not withstand a jury in this world against war! You cannot comprehend the

151

harm it does to a Soul to have to go out killing, or worse, to choose to go out killing others for the sake of a 'cause' or a political party, or some belief ingrained or implanted into his Mind by others!

No baby is born wanting war. He comes from the Spirit World. He would not want war, he would want peace and fun and kindness to himself, that's all! No man can justify war!

****

(On 12th September 2006, I set off alone to cross England and the English Channel, to go and spend a week in Northern France to attempt to search in person for possible paperwork relating to Grandma Léonie's first baby! (See volume 1 of ND-AWB).

The first hurdle was locating the official buildings and getting there. Unfortunately some of the records were disseminated between several towns! This meant umpteen journeys across the region by train and bus or underground in towns I did not know at all. Having found the correct building, by the time I got there I often only had five minutes to choose the files to examine, because of a rigid daily 'deadline time' to register for them! French bureaucracy! I painstakingly ploughed through what was available in archives. Other files had been destroyed in the wars. Most Archives Departments I visited were in the process of getting files onto microfiches and had not yet reached the dates I was interested in! Enough for me to want to bang my head against a wall in sheer frustration.

One of the old maps I was allowed to examine gave me some hope, as there was a little manor which I had not expected to see there and seemed to fit in with the adoptive lady Mme Balduck's faint memories. Then the relevant cemetery which I eventually travelled to and visited appeared as a strong possibility; unfortunately it had been modernised and greatly *expanded, of course. I discovered that bones from graves that had been dug up after one hundred years were put in an ossuary (bone house), but the French authorities do not keep written records of the names **unless** family descendants had kept up paying a fee over the past century ! What a short-sighted and frustrating system! I told them what I thought of it - since we did not know the grave existed, how could we pay? But my complaint did not change 'le règlement' (the rule)!*

*The exhausting week passed too quickly for me to travel further in the region, so I came back to the UK promising myself to explore more, one day. That day has not happened yet so far, because of lack of time and funds. Travelling and staying abroad is quite costly and time consuming. Also, knowing that over a century has passed and records are obviously likely to be scarce or impossible to find if destroyed is a frustrating prospect. I know and have **no doubt whatsoever that baby existed on Earth**, so the search is not for me, but to back up the revelations from Spirit World which surprised even my own mum when, unexpectedly, she was faced with her unknown half-sister, on arriving in the Afterlife!*

I hope to be able to tackle it again somehow, when there is a gap in my work publishing books dictated by my Teachers in the Spirit World. I also hope that the records I need were not the victims of war destruction and that the relevant French microfiches will have at last been updated if and when I find them!)

21st September 2006 - 15.00hrs. *My Guide starts in English.*

About your research for evidence of the baby's existence, we understand the difficulties. You don't need to rush doing it now, but it will be nice for you to succeed in getting it right, then you'll feel you have accomplished something valuable, both for yourself and for the community of Human Beings on Earth.

You can rest assured we want to keep talking. An 'American Indian' would listen to the ground with great attention to hear whether the enemy or the prey was coming his way. You should do the same with listening to us when linking. It is not who is coming which matters but what is being said. We are all the same, in as much as we are and you are so-called 'Spiritual Beings' as opposed to Earthly Beings, yet even they have Spirit Power within them! So, the male entity whom you call 'River Man' *(one of my Spirit Teachers dictating their wisdom book ' T L & D.)* has as much power as all of us - and so have you, when you stay online without disappearing by losing your concentration! He is one of the many who wish to teach you facts which are not always known on Earth, or have been forgotten.

'River Man' is one of those who have already started telling you things, to correct misconceptions brought on by Mankind's misunderstanding or distrust of the truths that were taught. Or simply Mankind's voluntary distortion or, at times, destruction of what had been taught by those in our world to those who should really listen. All those facts are now given to you so that **you** publish them or let them be known, to put more seeds in Mankind's universal brain! Hopefully, the majority of those who would listen to sensible Knowledge may then start paying attention to what is given by those tuned in to the right information.

Now, the next person to talk to you will be your own mother (of this present life of yours), so that she can catch up with your news and you with hers, thus keeping her Mind and heart happy with the link and the reports. We know you have difficulty at times to keep the link up, so we are at hand to help her not to lose you and you her. Here is you mum now...

(Sudden change of communicator and French is spoken!) My little Darling, good morning, or is it good evening? We know you did try hard to find your 'proofs' of my

154

sister's existence. We are all very pleased you made the effort and we hope you are not too disappointed with the result so far. The kind people here who look after you tell me you found some details which are good, but there are more to be found. Even though it is difficult to do, it may still be possible.

So it might be necessary to have another go. We want to help you as much as possible but as far as I am concerned, I can't as I don't have the facts! Your friends here seem to think there'll be a few more details which could help you. The hours spent are not wasted, I assure you, but you'll need lots of them, that's all! You'll always be able to go back another time and look further. Don't worry about it if you have other urgent things to do for the time being.

Last time we spoke, I was telling you I was looking after young children who arrive alone here, as I do feel sorry for them when they look for their parents and do not understand why they are here without them! We have to explain to them and it takes time, but in the end they accept the situation, especially if we give them a lot of love and play with them. As I told you before, the games are always useful and personally I like what is useful, so I enjoy entertaining them by making them do little things that I had to learn when I first arrived as a 'newcomer'.

Children seem to learn faster than adults, even the little tots, because they are more open-minded and everything is more easily fun to them. After all, deep within themselves they are Spirits who went to Earth and came back! So, they have not been too brainwashed by Earthly things compared to adults who had a whole material life of 'facts' imposed on them, either by themselves or by other adults, saying: "One cannot do this" or "That does not exist!".

We do all sorts here, as I've told you before - creating objects or surroundings for the pleasure. They have a great time doing that and even having fun creating new toys for themselves to start with! Then they progress with doing useful things like learning to 'walk in the air', as they call it, which is really the start of travelling without using one's feet. They also love 'dressing up', as they call it, that is showing oneself as if one is someone else! So, they pretend to be all sorts of characters from fairy tales, from books they'd read or heard of, from films seen etc. If they are told they do not need to change back to their 'original' body, they are very pleased to stay as Cinderella or Peter Pan or Sleeping Beauty etc.

The best is that, meanwhile, they forget to cry and ask for their parents! They dive into their new games and put their hearts in it, so the joy thus created and felt gives them 'new wings' (symbolic, not real, hey!) and it heals them little by little: heals the sorrow to be parted from their Earthly family.

When they know more, when they are more mature mentally, we can explain more to them, such as life and death and eternal life. At that level, this heals them even more, of course. There will always be the underlying sadness of not having their real family with them; they won't forget their family, obviously! But it is essential to understand that the most important thing is to give them courage, peace of mind, heal them of the shock of the transition from one life to another. Afterwards, the rest is much easier to do!

So that's my (pleasant!) work at the moment. It took me some time to be able to do this as I too had to learn all this, in the first place! One cannot teach what one is unable to do oneself!

Children of the world are Spirits who **chose** to go on the Earth in order to experience life there, for one reason or another. If they've **left the Earth at a young age it is also for one reason or another.** Perhaps they only wanted to be children and not adults with all the responsibilities that entails? So, they must be considered as Spirit Beings, because sooner or later they **will remember** why they had left our world in order to go 'over there', on the Earth! Then, when they recall why they had departed as 'Human Beings' going towards the Earth, they will remember again having simply been 'Spirits' and not a flesh body with a flesh brain etc! Their spiritual origin will come back to Mind, as it is the true and real origin, because Earthly life was only a temporary passage to another 'country', another world, a school where one does some experiments!

BR- Yes I agree. Do you realise you would have been 98 years old tomorrow and Dad 103?

All a body of flesh does is to give you problems sooner or later! A bit like a car or a boat! That's my opinion! Well, I'll go back to my little kids, who are always so well behaved by the way!

BR- Really? That's amazing since they are newcomers.

No, I do not have any discipline problems with them, that's what is remarkable. They are perhaps here because they are 'good children'. It's 'my level', as you would say. There are perhaps places where children - who are really nasty deep within themselves - find themselves and probably need more care from Spirit psychiatrists or similar! I am lucky to have to deal with well behaved kids, sad at the beginning but well behaved.

19th October 2006 - *2nd anniversary of Dave's passing. I am hoping to get some news. My Guide arrives.*
The needs of your own children have to come first, so we'll say this: Your Dave - and their 'dad' - is in good shape here now. He has progressed well since he arrived. He is deep into learning how to concentrate his own Mind to be of use to all of you, by sending his thoughts more clearly.

He needs to be allowed to speak his words and will look forward to when you all let him close to you. He needs to talk to all of you and is frustrated not to have been able to speak to his children himself, he says. So let them know he wants them to find time to sit quietly and learn to do just that. The idea being he could communicate directly with them and thus feel closer and them feeling him closer, which both he and they need! So the parting will no longer be so strong.

Last night his 'little girl' *(Anne-France)* had an interesting time in her sleep. He met her, they felt together and it was good. She needs to feel he is still as close to her as he was when she was small and even later on... *(Brief silence. Then change of communicator: Dave is now directly on line!)*

My view of your life is distorted by the distance and 'the levels of vibration', they say. We are on the same level when we speak to each other, or near enough. But it's a difficult state to maintain, I've learnt that! So the kids will need a lot of practice to achieve it but must not be put off by the difficulties, because the end result is worth it! I want to be part of your lives as I was before, kiddos! My love for all of you is still as strong as before.

I am in a state of bewilderment and excitement at the same time, because I can't help wondering at the marvels here and yet I love every bit of it, because it is so new! On the other hand this has caused me to be away from you in a physical sense. So I want to feel we can be reunited now and then, often enough. Just as if I'd gone to New Zealand again or something like that. Not really gone but a little apart for a while. That way the gap will be less painful. So you can try, can't you?

Try to link up with me and my friends here will help you, they say. I am not the man in the dreadful bed with the awful pain and agony. I am not there any longer. Please do not recall those days, they were horrendous and not to be remembered because they are over for good now! I am whole, healthy, young and fit! I am not an old man affected by a disease he could not comprehend - so this is not to be thought about anymore! I do not think of it any longer! You must not think of it ever again, as it is non-existent now, do you understand? It has too many terribly sad memories, we cannot dwell on this, neither you or I.

Now I am free, fit, healthy and my usual happy self, jolly and fun, aren't I? So you will remember me like this and I shall always be like this. It is no good whatsoever to think otherwise! You can tell our children to be proud of themselves as they have achieved a lot and will do even more later, I am told. They are both great kids and I am proud of them. I love them deeply, you know that, they know it too, I am sure.

So you say I have been here now for two years? Well, it does not feel like that. It seems much less and perhaps longer too? It's difficult to judge. You have a more accurate perception of time than I have here. We can still travel together through life as if we were not parted, because the link is still possible, as said before.

You mentioned it would be nice for the kiddos to have a word from their dad, so their dad is here, now but also always! That's why I came to say hello to all of you. Me, healthy me, happier me (though I would not say happy to be away from you!). You can tell them I am here and not far away from their thoughts. If they reach me, I'll reach them. An example? I can send thoughts to their Minds to inspire them to do well, just like when they asked me for advice when I was there amongst you. So it's not very different, is it kids? You listen, Dad speaks! That's it. Like at Xmas! I spoke and sang wildly and you thought I was mad and merry! I am happy to know you are doing well on Earth... *(Unfortunately I lost my concentration as I dozed off! It may be hard to believe, but focusing on listening while relaxing in an altered state can make me slip into sleep!)*

(28 October 2006 - Evening. I found my cat Princess lying at home, with the lower half of her body paralysed! I rushed her to the emergency vet and had to leave her there. He called later to say she was declining fast and advised to put her to sleep to prevent her to feel more distress. I had to accept, sobbing my heart out as I could not be there to hold her in my arms. She is now resting in my back garden near little 'Timmy', her adopted brother, whom she loved to play with).

30th October 2006 - 20.30hrs - *My Guide comes to explain the situation.*

An 'Animal' has its own point of reference. It lives on emotions and sensations. It is an 'Animal' mentally even though it is obviously a Spirit', which means it can only do and feel what it used to. Your cat has of course arrived safely here and she's been looked after by those who love cats - my friend, your mother is of course amongst them! The cat has lots of other playmates around her, she is not feeling miserable; she has freed herself from a frightening body which was not responding as she was expecting. She could be in your house if you wanted her to be. If you wish her to be there, your thoughts will attract her and she'll see herself in that familiar environment, but she can feel free to roam wherever her Mind takes her to.

BR- By familiar environment, do you mean my house and garden?

The environment she was used to was of course your home, but she can adapt easily. This is why we say not to put 'Animals' to sleep too early, because they need to have seen where they will arrive and that way won't be confused. If they 'die' before they have had time to roam around here mentally, they could be confused. But if you felt they would be suffering more by staying alive longer, we understand your concern and

160

your love: it will be possible for us here to make them feel at ease and adapt easily, by welcoming them lovingly.

The reason some people sense their cat in the house is because the cat wanted to be there as if it was still alive. You cannot 'judge or blame yourself' by whether the cat wants to be there or not! It is not like that. It is a question of mental attitude. If she likes roaming, discovering and adapts easily to new situations, then she'll go where she likes when arriving here and will make new friends. If she was pining for home, she'd be able to see her (your) 'old' house and she'll see you, or think she does, even if you are not there. She'll live a pretend life there. Yes, she'll imagine she sleeps there, eats, runs around, meets her usual friends and that will happen in her Mind as if it was true in 'real life'. So there is no need to fret. She can be there near you and be happy, even if she does not really see you or you actually don't see her! There is always the love between the two of you and that will never disappear!

BR- Can you also tell me about, say, a pet sensing a Spirit Being in a room? Is it as a light or as people?

When a 'Spirit' Being meets another Spirit Being, they know and recognise each other as such, i.e. an Energy of various individual colours (as you would see them) - vibrations and ranges of vibrations is more how we would term them, if we had to use words.

So if your cat sees one of us in the room, he will sense a big light moving about. If he wanted to 'recognise' that light as someone he knew before during this, or one of his lifetimes, he may see it as that 'man' or 'cat' or 'dog'. But if he is only aware of the Energy, then he may only see that large or small blob, or trail, or sparkle of Energy. That may fascinate him, of course, as it is always interesting to look at something moving, glistening and attracting your attention, which is different from your everyday mundane life. So we'll say the cat sees what he wants to see as far as the 'exterior' appearance is concerned.

Yet he will also have the **inner knowing**. He will know instinctively and inwardly, i.e. with his own Spirit Knowledge that the person or 'Animal' he sees in the room is not 'bad' for him. Unless of course he sees one he did not want there - he may be scared to see a huge dog or elephant taking over his lounge or bedroom! But that is more a rare case than a regular or constant occurrence.

If the cat sees a light he likes to play with, he'll be fascinated, but he will sense from his inner knowing the attitude and intention of the Being showing itself. So the cat will know whether the man/woman/child, or other cat or dog, will be a friendly or not presence towards him, the cat. He may not want that company in his room or house! He may think that person or 'Animal' is taking his favourite food or place etc. But he may also understand the 'visitor' is not nasty towards him, so he may accept to have to share his building with the newcomer and may get used to it. As usual, it's all to do with wavelengths of communications, inner links, Minds to Minds, hearts to hearts, Spirit to Spirit - not flesh body to flesh body.

4th November 2006 - *09.15hrs for a change! My Guide joins me.*

If you like, we'll tell you the following: The day you were born to this Earthly world of yours, was a **sad day** for us, because we knew you would no doubt have some ups and downs which would make you unhappy! But we also knew that if you followed the way you had chosen to go, the reason why you went there in the first place, it would be very satisfying both for you and for us. We are pleased to say you have done very well so far and we are happy you are still on that path.

(Unfortunately, just then the electrician rings to announce he is free to come round now to do the required work! I feel terrible to be obliged to cut off my conversation with my dear Guide. Later on, in the evening, I attempt to link

162

up again at 20.40pm. Having been told during our home séance that I should try to sense and see a lady helper in Spirit World, I send a thought about it to my Guide).

The name of the lady you wish to feel and sense is not known to you. It is a lady who had lived nearby for a long time but now wishes to make herself known to you for reasons of her own. She desires to work with you.

BR- Work with me? How?

Yes, work with you in as much as you can help her link to Humans and 'Animals' who need help with their health. You link to her and she'll send Energy through you into them, as it is important to be able to heal people and 'Animals' who are suffering. Look out for a little noise here and there, or a movement of air around you, or anything which is unusual for that time or place. Her Energy will affect your surroundings so it may take various shapes or be different occurrences.

A Human Being or an 'Animal' should not have to suffer if everything within him/it is balanced. The Energy of Healing is of a high vibration which rebalances those out of line. It only takes a few minutes to do some good, so please try to find opportunities to help others.

BR- I feel 'rusty' at the moment...I may not be a good 100% channel!

Look out for signs within you which show you have a link with Higher Energies. Higher Energies reflect themselves in your body and Soul as fine sensations - lots of heat possibly or a little tingling or waves of hot and cold. All sorts could happen but that's when you'll feel the differences, when you try to link up with us and us with you for Healing. Yes, it feels different. When not for Healing it's more like now. Let us look at something different now. When you last wrote down what your Friends told you.

BR- Are you referring to the Inspirers I affectionately call my 'Three Musketeers'?

Yes, but you need to call them 'Friends from Beyond' as that's what they are! So you then wrote down some very important information which will also need typing into a book form. It is of the utmost importance you get that done do you understand? It is part of a scheme to bring Knowledge to the Earth from different angles and if you fail doing your side it will lopside the rest, somehow! You need to type this as well, so all that is a coherent piece of work, with good knowledge and information.

All it takes is a little discipline, organisation and a mighty focus of the Mind. After that, it will be plain sailing. Lots more things are to be given to you as you go along, so there is really no time to waste. You cannot let that drop now that it has been started so successfully!

Your mother's book will be brilliant and your Friends from Beyond's book will be as much if not more, though it will have more controversial material in it! But that is what it is meant to have! **So that the world opens its eyes to all the untruths given over the centuries.** Then we may all be able to rebalance the level of thinking in order that Spirituality and Truth survive and overcome the debasing of real facts. We'll win, you'll see, we'll win. It might take a long time, but better long than never!

BR- (Jokingly) I might get burnt at the stake or guillotined because of it!

You can rest assured you will be in no danger whatsoever for it. It is just a question of standing up for your beliefs and your Knowledge. There will be criticism, no doubt, but the other books on the go will back it up. The one dictated to you is meant to be part of a whole, you see. The 'whole' being a **'many facet single book' written or produced across**

164

the world in various forms, so that the Truth emerges through each of its 'pages'. Look at it as a team effort of like-minded people, linking not only between the two worlds but among themselves over the continents and oceans, yet not knowing each other! A mighty but successful operation, we are proud of it!

BR- I am honoured yet a bit scared, as I don't want to let you down!

We want to say thank you for your efforts. It is always hard to fit things in in a material life, but with care, willingness and dedication, you will definitely succeed. So all is said now. Many thanks for your efforts and good luck with your daily life reorganisation. We hope those around you will understand the importance of this task! We cannot say anymore. Good work now!

9th November 2006 - *I was lucky to have successfully booked another place at a Stewart Alexander private guest physical séance. So many people wish to attend the small group! Throughout the day and on my way there, I was visualising myself called to take part in experiments which I have not yet directly experienced myself - and I sent thoughts to 'Freda' to try and bring Mum or Dave to talk to me. Who knows when I may be able to go again?! It is such an exhilarating personal experience to witness at close range all the exciting authentic phenomena in that trustworthy environment.*

*The séance: After great displays of the astounding skills of the Spirit Scientists, Walter announces he wants to demonstrate 'the passage of matter through matter', carried out by Spirit Scientists. This is when Walter, the Spirit communicator in charge of this **well-tested 'feat' of superior physics,** actually **DEMATERIALISES** one of the securely locked looped cable ties securing the medium's wrists and legs to his armchair. (Anyone familiar with cable ties will know it* *would be impossible for the tied up medium to free himself to open them up. They have to be cut with pliers. This is NO conjurer's trick. It is Advanced Spirit Physics! After every séance the only way to release the medium from his chair is to cut off those tight secure ties from round his wrists and legs).*

Walter repeats this mind-boggling demonstration several times in the evening - so I am thrilled when he calls me and asks me to come and sit as close as possible to the right of the entranced medium (through whom Walter speaks). Both Stewart's arms and legs (with phosphorescent tabs stuck on) are always tightly and securely strapped to his armchair with cable ties.

Walter asks me to put my left hand gently but firmly on Stewart's right hand and keep it there, not letting go and confirm what I feel. I can assure everyone in the room that the cable tie is firmly in place, thus binding the medium's wrist to the armchair. Walter then asks me to constantly hold the medium's hand and not let go. As I do that, I suddenly feel Stewart's right hand and arm rising off the armrest (with my hand hanging on to his!) as his arm is raised above his head!

I excitedly confirm this to everyone. The arm is quite free of the cable tie which (I check with my other hand) had remained securely strapped to the armrest of the chair! And the medium's other arm/hand is still safely bound to the other armrest too. Walter requests that the red light is briefly put on, so that all can witness that Stewart's arm is free from the cable tie (with my hand and his interlocked in the air). Seconds after the light is turned off, the arm comes down (with me still glued to it!) and hey presto, it is instantly paranormally strapped again by the cable tie firmly round the wrist! And the medium is still totally entranced, of course! Mind-bogglingly exciting! There is no doubt whatsoever that entranced Stewart (or any other human) is not involved in doing anything in this demonstration, which is under the direct control of Walter!

As I continue to keep a firm hold of the medium's hand still bound to the armchair, Walter then asks me whether I would like to have that very strap as "a small memento of our encounter and a token of the Spirit World recognition of my hard work for them". How kind! Of course I accept! He instructs me to keep holding the medium's hand with my left hand as I hold the cable tie (looped on his wrist) with my right hand. Immediately our linked hands go up in the air, I feel the strap - still looped - pushed firmly in my hand, as Stewart's arm drops down, unbound, on the chair armrest!

As the medium's right arm is free, Walter tells us he will secure again Stewart's arm to the chair by using one of the spare straps on the table. At once we can hear one of those straps being pulled by Walter (no one else in the room has moved!) across the table top, then the clear sound of the cable tie being clicked into a loop around the wrist and the armrest!.

*Walter tells me to keep as a souvenir the strap I was holding, adding that I have just witnessed the **passage of matter-through–matter** at extremely close range. (Close indeed. I am sitting millimetres from the medium's body and chair and centimetres from the small table!) An experiment which took him and his Spirit Team decades to polish!*

I ask him whether he dematerialises the medium's arm or the strap. He replies the Spirit Team had tried, years ago, to affect the arm but it risked being 'burned' by the manipulations of the Energies, so dematerialising and re-materialising the strap was safer for the medium! I return to my original seat in the tight circle clutching my precious possession. It is still looped. It cannot be straightened up with bare hands. And I would certainly not want to!

Later on in that same séance, after various phenomena, as usual, 'Freda Johnson' (as she was known at one time on Earth) facilitates many communications between sitters in the room and 'departed' loved ones. Suddenly, out of the blue, she

167

calls out to me, asking me to come and sit near her, i.e. near the entranced medium whose vocal apparatus she uses to communicate. She states she has a lady with her who belongs to me, who is very impatient to come near me!

*"I understand she is your mother, my dear. She says she had a lot of leg troubles when she was on the Earth but now she wants to tell you she is fine. She wants me to tell you she is doing high kicks and dancing all over the place to show you she is fine! She is also very close to her father. She is so thrilled to see you here! She wants to come near". (Even **before** Freda said that, I was already aware of a sudden tingling Energy all around my head, face and shoulders. Also, mum was a ballroom dancing champion). "She says she is kissing you as she used to do, especially when you were a child, with both hands on each side of the head, kissing the top of your head and forehead". That is what I was feeling! I had completely forgotten that's how Mum used to kiss us children (As she thought it was "more hygienic" for us, rather than lips coming on our faces and near our mouths!). I feel emotional, just as if I was in Mum's arms as a child. There is a brief silence...*

Freda says "Just a minute, my dear...". This is followed by a few muffled sounds via the medium, as if someone was struggling to use him to talk. Then Freda comes back: "Your mother was trying to talk directly to you through the medium - because she thought it was as easy as when you receive her (clairaudiently), but she did not manage it. No doubt she'll try at some other opportunity. She loves you very much, she is ever so happy you are here!"

There are evidently other Spirit communicators keen to talk to the families in the room, so I return to my original seat, delighted to have heard from Mum that way and to have felt her kiss. As I sit down, I suddenly realise I unexpectedly feel absolutely showered with and filled with the most wonderful and overwhelming loving and tingling Energy;

stronger and lovelier than I have ever felt before or since! For a short while, I have the elating feeling that I am scintillating from head to toes and can 'see' and sense the sparkles in my mind's eye! Mum must have followed me and is definitely close to me with her loving Energy and kissing me again! I'll never forget those special moments.

10th November 2006 - 08.35 hrs! *I hear English spoken. My Guide is online!*

The séance was a wonderful success for your mum to be able to talk to you, even though it was for a short moment! She was so happy to have been recognised and you felt her kissing and hugging you! She has been talking of nothing else since! We are proud of her and you can be proud too, as she also tried hard to communicate through the medium but could not understand the mechanism this time. It will probably be possible another time, don't worry, it's all to do with practice as usual!

The lady in charge ('Freda') had met your mum beforehand to make sure who she will be dealing with and said this time it would be wiser to content herself with a go-between, but another time it might be possible to do otherwise. Lots of people in our world queue to have a chance to do it, so you were 'lucky' to be chosen! But you know it was not luck, it was us deciding you could be treated to this occasion, so that you know we do not ignore your requests and also your mum's, who had been waiting for a long time to talk to you.

BR- Could she see me?

The 'light' was not exactly good since you don't have any but we do not request nor need one from here! We see you if we want to. It is not so much a question of seeing you physically as a body, as seeing you with our Minds and hearts. **You appear** but **as a Spirit, with all your beautiful Inner Light,** more than the flesh aspect. It is possible to sense you as a person that way, in fact even better because we sense the personality and characteristics and emotions, rather than just an outer physical casing.

You were as emotional as she was and that blended you two even more! We had her dad there too, who helps her when she does difficult experiments. She succeeds every time she tries hard because she has the will power, dedication and love in her inner heart.

Altogether a great success, as well as the 'exchange of rings' (Ha ha!) with the dematerialisation of the bind holding the medium! You had wished you could be called up there to do all these. **We fulfilled your wishes so that you had a memorable day,** my dear, to thank you for all your efforts in various directions. You have had a sad time lately with your little cat going away from you physically and we wanted to console you one way or the other.

She is with us now of course but she is also with you when her Mind reminds her of 'home', as she saw it. She'll be close to you if you think of her, but don't worry if you cannot see her. She'll think you can and will 'pretend' in her heart that you are doing with her what you always used to do. So she won't be lost or feeling rejected!

We could talk longer but it may be wiser to let you go since you have something to attend to. Try to come back to talk to us and perhaps your mum will talk directly to you. We came first to make sure the link was strong and faster, so that you were not delayed. You can rely on us for not trying to delay you more! We love you far too much for that. (*I could feel he was smiling as he said that*).

170

23rd November 2006 - 12 noon. *English is spoken. My Guide starts the conversation.*

The level of attunement is very important. We are now ready to talk to you if you feel you can do so without interruption. We have a lady here wanting to speak to you. She's been waiting for quite a while now. We have your mum online, all set to share her experiences! Make sure you don't interrupt her.

BR- All right, thanks.

Mum here Sweetheart. Don't forget I love you forever! I wanted to talk to you to tell you how happy I was when I felt you near me when I went to attend your séance that evening! It was an incredible opportunity that was different for me and I did not want to miss it, as you can guess! I approached the tall lady *(Freda)* who was talking to all of you. She gave me permission to speak to you, but I didn't really know what to do to talk to you directly through the medium; I haven't actually practised enough to do that. On the other hand, she told me to simply tell her what I wanted to let you know and she would repeat it. I was so glad to feel your presence! I did not see you truly 'solid', it was more like a shadowy body of Energy, or something like that. Yet **I knew it was you, I could feel it was you! I could actually recognise you**, though I don't know how I did! So I wanted to grasp the opportunity to kiss you as I had been unable to do for such a long time! I was ever so delighted and happy to be able to embrace you and tell you I love you and I am close to you... it felt ever so good!

I was not able to stay very long because there was a queue of people waiting behind me! But I wanted you to know I feel ever so well nowadays and so free and young and in good shape; I showed her I was still able to dance if I wanted to! I no longer have pains in my legs and hips and back etc. It's so good, isn't it? I ran and danced around like a mad woman in

171

high spirits to show her I was in great shape and very fit, so that she could tell you! I am ever so happy we were able to be close to each other. It's been such a long time we've been parted physically!

But this is not the last time! I do intend to try and learn to communicate even better and more clearly another time. My friends will help me practise. One has to learn to do all those things. So don't worry, I'll be helped and I'll know better another day and I shall come back. But you need to be very patient, as I have no idea how long (in your timescale) this will take me to be able to do it so that it works well in a proper 'séance', as you call it. I'll come back one of these days, don't you worry!

I have other things to tell you to bring you up to date with my activities recently. As usual, my friends are always ready to help me learn more and me to understand more, so they and I are indeed on the same wavelength!

I keep practising going places in a blink; all I have to do is think of or look at somewhere I want to go to immediately and I find myself there much more quickly than I did before. As usual, it has to do with more concentration. Concentration is hard, isn't it? Like you, I have to work at it! Yet it is really worth practising, you know! I have done it before but I have a go as often as possible and find that the more one does it, the better it gets. It's just like learning to drive or ride a bicycle; one gets down to it and one learns better. On the other hand, 'travelling' here is done with the Mind, therefore it is quite different from having to move using one's legs. Legs here exist in a way, as I vaguely feel I have a kind of 'body'. Yet I do not really pay attention to it or think of it, so the 'body' which moves is, in fact, following my Mind rather than my Mind moving the 'body', if you see what I mean! Doing all this is very interesting, like everything else we do here. As you know, I always have heaps of activities - I am never bored!

172

Something else I'd like to tell you: Some years ago you said you were able to see **music in colours.** Well, I realise I can do that too now! I saw colours and when I delved into them I could sense music, can you imagine? It reminded me of what you used to say when you were young, that you 'saw' the notes in colours when you played the piano. *(Note- This is part of what is called 'synaesthesia'. I discovered years later that my son Jim - a musician - has the same ability. At times I also feel that some names or words 'have a colour' too).*

Now it's me who is beginning to do it; it's good fun and also very pretty! Notes appear as blobs or lines of colours if I listen to some music. When I look at some colours, the sounds coming from them are truly magical! It's like a conjurer's trick, showing music which becomes colours! I've tried it many times just for fun and also to make sure I could do it properly. It is not essential to life here, yet it is ever so pleasant when you realise you can do it and can use it.

It's of course a question of 'vibrations', 'frequencies' - physics as usual! Always physics...but it is feasible without knowing all the scientific details! I wish I could understand them better to be able to explain them to you, but I think it will be far too complicated and I only like easy things, or at least not too complicated! So that's my 'cinema' of 'music in colour' or 'colours in music'!

I also did some other experiment with my dad as he is always ready to teach me more! It's as if I was at school; he always wants to make me do something different or new! He's known for a long time how to **transform a sound into light** and he wanted me to learn to do it.

BR- Did I hear correctly? Learn to transform sound into light?

Yes, a sound becoming light. He knows how to do it! It's like music in colours but this is a particular sound and he can make it turn into a 'note', let's say. He did it in front of me and wondered why I was not doing it too. "It's so easy", he kept saying. Yeah... easy for him! But hard for me!

BR- What do you have to do?

I am not exactly sure! I had to kind of hum a note and hold on to it for a long time, then try to 'lighten' it (I think that's what he was saying) to make it lighter and higher and more vibrant...but I really had difficulties doing that!

BR- Isn't it the same as when you did 'music into colours' and vice versa?

Music transforming itself into colours - it was not me who was actually doing it all - it was done in front of me and for me. The note, it was me who had to do it. For notes into light I have to lighten myself, lighten the note, transform everything into lightness, 'light' flimsy vibrations etc! It is so complicated in my opinion that I reckon I am going to 'fail my exam' (if there was one!). It's fun but a little too hard for the time being.

BR- I thought you had learnt before to turn yourself into a point of light?

A point of light was my Mind, my Spirit body, my Real Me. So it was easier as all I had to do was think of myself as a 'Body of Light' and tell myself: "Off I go, I am shrinking, I am a point of light!" But that trick of transforming an external or exterior note into a point of light is much more difficult I reckon, at least for now! I hope to manage it soon. My dear dad will be pleased to see me succeed after my having failed several times and feeling sad not to have managed it!

I have something else to tell you: Your children are little darlings, you know! *(Unexpected and unprompted remark!)* I have sensed them near me, many a time, during your Earthly 'nights'. They come to see me and probably do not realise they do. I saw their presence near me and kissed them like I kissed you the other day. It gives me great pleasure to receive you here when you come and see me during your bodily sleep. It's a pity sometimes you are all so tired that you appear sleepy - but it is still good to feel you close, or as if I saw you from a distance, a little hazy.

All this is incredible, isn't it? To feel close, to see each other, to kiss, to speak to one another, especially you and me! I would never have imagined one could do all that after our 'death'. But of course you knew it... I had to learn to understand it. Well, I have now learnt it, at my cost; **I had to 'die' in order to be able to discover all those wonderful things**...but it was worth it!

I think your children are well. I am so pleased. I would have liked to have seen them more often when on Earth, but never mind, we shall all meet again one day! I wish I could kiss them for real but at least we've seen each other, it's already something! I want to kiss you too Darling, from the bottom of my heart, I feel you near me though it is more your thoughts than your whole presence. I assure you we all love you here.

BR- You were right to tell us as children: "Do not waste time as it cannot be found again"! I have to type your book and my Spirit Teachers' book of hidden truths! It is taking longer than I thought!

Thank you for all you do and try to do, we are aware of it and are grateful. We know it is not easy to find time to achieve all that! Lots of kisses and thanks for coming to talk to me.

28th November 2006 - 11.10hrs. After doodling first, the pen starts in English. My Teachers dictated the following short extract for their 'T, L & D' book, which is shared here to make sure more people are aware of those facts.

'Animals' are a subject you always like to talk about, aren't they?! Well, we love 'Animals' too here, as they definitely are special Souls who can do so much good on Earth and even here, as they heal people and other Beings by simply being there. They have a particularly strong power in as much as they love to be loved if possible and they give out one hundred times more than they receive! This is why they are so great.

BR- Why do they give out so much?
They can empathise with people and other Beings and **they have this built-in mechanism to magnify their own power.** They don't even know they are doing it.

BR- But isn't everyone 'Spirit'?
Yes, all 'Spirits' are 'Spirits', as you call us, i.e. Energy from the universal, eternal 'Energy pond', so to speak - but these Spirits who come as 'Animals' have a quality within themselves, which allows them to magnify what they are and how they give it out. That's why an 'Animal' as a pet is a soothing, loving creature who makes other people feel better!

If it has been hurt, it will feel it even more, because it is so sensitive to feelings in any direction. It can **suffer more emotionally** than a person, because of that extreme, intense sensitivity and power of love and compassion built in itself. It is not usually known, but we thought we may like to learn this so that you understand even better those you love on Earth this time round.

BR- I feel guilty about my Princess' passing. She was alone when the stroke hit her and I could not get there on time when the vet put her to sleep. He had an urgent call to go to and would not wait for me!

176

You cannot blame yourself for a cat leaving the Earth. She had her time chosen and has left because there was a reason for her to want to leave. A presence near you has to be felt for you to know she is around you often. You are surrounded by the love of your cats, both the ones near you now and those who have been with you before, because you have loved them so much! You cannot realise how much **your love for them has helped them progress** to a heightened sense of love and compassion.

BR- Can you explain that please?
Their Soul was and is good, of course. Each one of them was a healing Soul but coming to Earth to help you too. They increased their awareness of the touch, the physical contact and therefore the exchange of vibrations between Beings at a closer ranger on Earth. That has helped them understand the need for closeness and the need to give out even more. You would give to them without thinking, you loved them 'full range', that's it! So they love you back full range and are around you whenever you think of them, of course - but even if you don't, because they sense your vibrations and they like it. They enjoy being close to your 'cat loving vibrations'; the love one gives only when one has that sort of love for them. Make your senses more aware and you'll feel them close.

BR- How can I sense them more?
Sensitivity has to be worked on, my dear. A sensitivity which needs to be heightened needs to be worked on by simply feeling around oneself, letting outside influences come close. As they are of the high vibration range, they need to be felt in a very different way, because the feel of material impressions are on the skin and five senses, whereas the sensitivity required for outside range vibrations has more to do with your inner senses than your outer physical senses.

To do what is needed is the most important for any job. Do what's needed in your everyday life but also what's needed for the books. You have to publish. You know or will have to know the rules of publishing, so that Earthly matters are seen to in that field. But you can rely on our support as far as inspiring you to say or do the right thing is concerned.

You seem to be tired now, so you can leave if you like and come back at a later time.

14th December 2006 - 20.00hrs. *I tune in as I listen to some lovely music. The pen starts in English.*

There is a glow of light all around. You are so uplifted by this music that you feel so much lighter and you look lighter. It takes so little to make you feel good and able to link up, you see? We'd love you to feel like that more often; it would make our work so much easier. We have your mum here for you.

(Swift change of communicators). The 'door opened' so that Mum and her daughter can talk to each other! It's been a long time since we did, hasn't it?! Well, recently I got down to doing some music too. I had never really learnt to play properly except the piano, a little. So I've started learning better in order to play well. I wanted to study it to grasp the different sounds, the levels of vibrations, as my friends say.

It's not so much playing with my fingers than extending my knowledge of sounds. I do play them a little, yes, but it's mainly to recognise them better. There are wonderful sounds which are beyond what we hear on the Earth; nothing on Earth can reproduce them! So I am beginning to learn to distinguish them. It is incredibly pretty and beautiful; it's so marvellous that I can see them in colours too! It's not just music, it is 'musical paint' as well! So I love watching those gorgeous pictures of music and hearing those beautiful sounds of colours! It's really weird but also intriguing and exciting!

BR- Hasn't my dad mentioned it too?

Yes, my dad and yours too had already done so. They took me somewhere where we can see that easily. It's a kind of place where sounds are played by other people, but we can enjoy the beauty of notes by seeing them float in front of us as 'multicoloured colours'! It's impossible to describe them as they are beyond words and hues we know of on Earth. You will have that pleasure when you too come here - **seeing music in the air and hearing colours** reverberating around you! It's a very special experience!

By the way, my parents' children met once more to get to know each other!

BR- (Puzzled) - Do you mean your half-sister and you? You have a funny way of saying it!

Yes, my sister and I. We've spoken more than we had done previously because we did not know each other and the little one had only had a short stay on Earth. She had come back here because the Earthly situation was not favourable for everything to be normal. *(All explained in volume 1 of 'Not Dead: Alive without a body').* So she remained there for a short period of time then did the return journey very quickly. There were tears, lots of tears, on both sides, because she was loved, even though she had hardly seen her real mother. But things went back to normal once both met here, as they got together a lot.

On the other hand, I had not really seen her much here because I was far too busy trying to sort myself out and settle down! Now I know more (ha ha!), I told myself it would be silly not to try to get better acquainted with my half-sister. She will have more knowledge than me anyway, after all the time she's been in this world. She could teach me some things!

So we met and we chatted as if we'd always known each other! Very strange, considering we had hardly seen one another... but that's what happens here! She showed me what she has created and why she did. I told her of my funny experiences but also and mainly of the fact that my own daughter talks to me from the Earth! I said: "I hear her and we are writing down this book together, so that the world of Humans learns what they have forgotten. That **we are alive indeed and we can communicate**!"

It seemed to impress her, though obviously she knew about it already and also we had spoken of her with Mum and the kind lady (*who had adopted her as a baby*). Therefore, with all that, we have at last something in common and we had fun chatting happily!

****

CHAPTER 4
**Progress: New way of thinking - Focused thought creates -
Illness and inner turmoil - Transfiguration - Mum's lives -
Wingless Angels - Dave's update - My 'fatal' fall**

25th December 2006 - 18.00hrs. *My Guide starts the
conversation in English.*

Learn from our 'lesson' to you and to the world.
Communication between our two worlds is a very delicate
operation, which needs to be handled with respect, attention
and dedication. We love communicating with you, so let's
begin with the latest news this end.

You have a mother who has not stopped working and
learning ever since she's arrived here! And a father who has
learnt so much now, he can teach it to you as he is improving
'day by day', as you would say. Also a Dave who is both your
husband and your best friend here, in a way. He'll defend you
and protect you because he loves you deeply and wants to
make things right for you. You can rest assured your Dave is
not far from you all. He has your love for him and his for you
all, to keep him going. He is also very much helped by those
around him who look after his interests and do not let him
struggle and cope on his own. He's had help since he arrived
and even before, of course!

Now he's on a kind of 'course' whereby we help him
learn to open his Mind more to the realities here. **He has to
shed the Earth way of thinking** and accept that all can be
done by Mind Power and thoughts here. He is learning well,
but it has to become second nature for him to be more settled.

Examples would be of the kind your mum told you.
Little exercises or fun or simple activities which help open the
Minds of new arrivals, so that they lose the restricted way of
thinking which binds people's Minds when they arrive here.
We can do it easily. They can't.

He has been surrounded by his family all along, so he is not lonely and feels all right now. Of course, he feels grief within for being parted from the children of his life just gone. But he is not grieving like he used to do, because he's understood the law here is: What you use your Mind for, you surround yourself with! Make yourself understand that too...as on Earth not many people know how to use this fundamental tool!

Let's approach another topic: The three most important people you speak to and who speak to you to dictate their book *(my Evolved Teachers)* have more revelations to make to you. You can listen to them quietly now? All right, here they are:

Not to be ignored: One of the most vital things we have to talk about is the concentration of thoughts in one place and the harm and good it can and will do! If one person thinks of something, it is obvious others will feel the influence of his or her Thought Power. But it is **one hundred times more powerful when many people gather** in the same place, **to send thoughts in one single direction.**

That is what was understood in the olden days of the churches and it is why so many places of worship and temples were built over the centuries. As churches and temples (or huts at first) were built to maintain the power within the building, some priests of the time took the opportunity to use the power for their own good and did not let others use it!

So if the church needed repairs they asked the crowd to pray for the money. The funds would start coming, because there are always people who want to help others, **but also** because money is an object from the material world which can be created out of matter by sheer intense Thought Power! Yet people did not realise that the great intensity of the prayers would help coins to be materialised in their coffers, or wherever they might be able to store money. It had to be from an outside source and it was, but what brought it in was the great **intensity** of the concentration!

If the Thought Power was concentrated on a building to make it be created or grow or even be repaired, it would have the same effect! Lots of people will think you are mad talking about this, but those who understand will grasp it. It has simply to do with the intense concentration of Thought Power on one goal, in one direction and the good it will bring will benefit Mankind.

If it was for 'doing harm' the hatred power would be successful too because it is Thought Power, sadly... but the results will have consequences; they'll bounce back on whoever made them because the Universal Law of justice and kindness has never been revoked! It has been said many a time: "What you do to others, you do onto you!" So make it work for you rather than against....

(Unfortunately the room is very warm and I am tired, so concentrating on listening made me doze off! My poor Inspirers are very patient with me!)

26th December 2006 - *As my Spirit Artist practised psychic art 'through me', a quick sketch of the face of a sad looking man was drawn. I asked who he is, wondering whether it may be either just a 'practice drawing' or someone else's relative. My Guide replies.*

Latent sadness caused by illness, stress, worries, poor food. All these contribute to bad health. The man in this picture has been your helper and by your side for a long time. He is your 'Silver Arrow' whom you have been wondering about for so long! *(Note- This is the name my Guide gives himself as a 'label').*

Lots of years ago, in fact centuries ago, you and I were together. We then made a pact that we would reappear eventually on Earth together, but you there and me here (in the world of Mind and Light). So in this sketch you have my recollection (rather vague I must admit!) of my appearance at that time, when we were together as father and son!

In that life we roamed the Earth - well, not quite the Earth but the country! My little friend, you now have a picture of me and it took a while to build up because I do not have a very good recall of my looks in those days, of course! But you could imagine what a hounded man, suffering from ill health at times, would look like. They were hard times and we were poor, but we struggled well and lived all right. You had to have your lady friends but I did not, because we could not stay for too long in one place, so we kept moving on. Lots of sad memories of those days, not needed now!

We couldn't afford a lot and we could not reside in the same area for long, because of the hunt for civilians who backed the bad king John *(in 12th century)*. We supported him at first, because we thought he was right. Then we left his side because we realised he double-crossed everyone! So we ran away. But we could not hide forever and eventually we died by the hands of our foes. It was quick... and we survived anyway since we came here where I am now!

Then you eventually returned to the Earth to try to right some wrongs - and that's where we are now! Make the most of your life, my 'son'. You need to do your utmost to achieve what you came for. You learnt even during what you call your 'wasting time period', so it was not all wasted. *(Note- During this current life)*. Put all our notes for the book together, make sure it is as should be for publishing. Pace yourself, allow time for all this. This is what has to come first, after your most urgent and essential Earthly activities. Get these great works of spiritual art on the way to Mankind for them to benefit from what we have been telling you for years of your time!

(Throughout the following weeks my Friends from Beyond used my linking up time to dictate more of their fascinating book of knowledge and rectified misconceptions. This is why there are no dialogues with my family for months!)

16th April 2007 - 15.15hrs. *My Guide comes close as he has a message for everybody.*

The sun in your life is not shining enough for your Soul to feel uplifted. You can rely on good weather in our world; here it's always great and therefore we feel good! You need to have more sunshine in your life; the 'real' sun, as you call it, and the joy of being able to do what you want on your spiritual pathway, which is or should be very clear by now!

It's only a question of listening within yourself to feel even more uplifted by what we tell you and because we tell you things you did not know or needed to know. It is essential to listen within now and then to plug into the Eternal and Universal Energy which you and we are all made of. You can rest assured we only tell you things you or others need to know and be explained to you.

So this is what we'll say now: If ever you feel down, all you have to do is look within yourself. **Analyse** why you feel down. Could you find the cause or causes? Has someone said something that upset you? If you cannot pinpoint the actual cause of the 'down feeling', **look at yourself**. Why are you feeling like that? Has your life not been what you wanted it to be? Are you frustrated by ineptitude, failures, lack of success, lack of a feeling of achievement which we all want to like to feel?

It's as simple as that. Usually you'll find that it always boils down to oneself, because if you feel down because someone said something to you, it is often because they have 'touched a nerve', touched upon one particular aspect of yourself you don't like.

It can be of course that they have been dishonest, untrustworthy or disloyal to you and that will indeed hurt you badly. But is it the only reason? Are you made to feel smaller because of it? Do you not like being made smaller or unworthy? Why not? And so on...

185

So what we come to is that people should look within, no matter what their problems are, because the answer will be there, either to solve a problem or to solve a feeling of inadequacy, which might trigger many a symptom in the physical body as **the body of flesh is a reflection of the Soul's body.**

A Soul is a Being who has chosen to be on Earth for a period of time and needs to be able to move about in the physical world, so it needs a physical body like all do.

If a Soul is unhappy in its physical body, at times, it **may decide it wants to leave** it! You call it 'dying'. It is not wise to do so without first having a 'good think' about one's aims and directions, as leaving the flesh body means you won't be able to function there anymore as a human person, obviously!

It is more desirable to analyse oneself, so as not to make the mistake to shorten one's journey (by taking one's life) in this experiment on Earth which one started so many years ago. It's not as if you could just pop back into it after you changed your mind, is it?! You'd have to be reborn as a baby! It's not done overnight! So it's most important that the advice above is followed to ensure a good trip on this Earth you have chosen to come to!

(Over the following weeks, whenever I tuned in, my 'Friends from Beyond' kept dictating more information for their own book 'T, L & D').

27th May 2007 - 09.45hrs. *After receiving more advice and encouragement about my spiritual work from my Guide, I asked whether I could get some news about my husband Dave.*

The man you speak of has his hands full, so to speak. He is very busy and wishes to concentrate his Mind at a slower pace, so that he can control his thoughts and therefore stop creating all sorts around him! He has little exercises to do to help him achieve this, but he also wishes to send his love to all of you left behind. He cannot come to talk to you now as it would take his Mind off what he is doing at the moment, that is very specific exercises to guide and keep his Mind on one direction, while the rest of his life goes on around him.

BR- Could you explain more please?

You can rest assured he is looked after. He has little (or 'big' he would say!) exercises which are practices for him to concentrate the Mind in one direction, on one single focus point. This means he has more discipline in what he does, instead of letting his Mind roam around and finding himself constantly looking at something different! He has to build his environment as a steadier 'place', so to speak.

BR- I thought he had already done so!

He did concentrate before and saw himself in a garden-like place, etc. But that was not enough, it was not steady enough for him to last in.

BR- What do you mean?

What he needs is something much more profound in one way and steadier in another.

BR- Is he still grieving?

He has learnt a lot since he's arrived here and knows there is no point crying over those he can't be with physically. But he now has the understanding that since he communicated with you, it meant he could indeed link with the Earth plane, therefore he was not really cut off. The physical closeness will be missed, of course, but that feeling will be found again one day when you are all here.

All is well now, so don't fret about him. He is all right and knows you all love him. He is doing what he has to do but he enjoys it! Nothing is a chore here, remember. Just things one chooses to do for the pleasure of one's Mind improvement and inner satisfaction. Lots of people have to do those sorts of activities to settle in, so please do not be concerned. It is quite normal, he is doing well.

1st June 2007 - *I had attended a two-day workshop during which we sat individually for transfiguration for a short while. (**Transfiguration** occurs if the medium's face changes to reflect somebody else's features - usually a recognisable 'departed'. The medium is NOT 'possessed' or 'taken over', as explained below! It is more like a thin 'mask' of Energies superimposed on his face, reflecting someone else's face.*

*It can first be sensed clairvoyantly by onlookers, but when the phenomenon is well developed, everybody in the room can see those **temporary changes** physically. It is one more way of giving evidence of survival).*

During the workshop, the tutor and some other students could apparently see changes occurring over my face, making me look like a bearded man! As for me, my lips and eyes 'felt different'. I now ask my Guide about this form of mediumship. It should interest readers wondering about this phenomenon or about developing this gift.

If you sit quietly often enough, it gives a chance to people in the 'Spirit World' to practise. All you need is to sit quietly for half an hour every day. You'll be at peace for your own sake and we'll be working on it for speed. You can look in a mirror if you like, but you may be bored staring at yourself! You may not even see it at first, as some work has to be done from within outward.

BR- Can you explain more please?
The matter your face is made of has atoms, of course and they can be manipulated so that the desired result is achieved. So we'll work on those to prepare them for the day

when they need to be fast reacting to the procedure. Then it will give a quicker result for the person (watching you) to recognise the loved one. You cannot have results overnight! But you cannot doubt the possibilities; you can't stop us doing something we can start if you are willing. If you can practise the sitting, we can start the shaping. If that works successfully, you'll be on the road to success for others to see for themselves. You cannot time this, it all depends how well it works once we've started.

BR- Any advice? Is drinking water helpful?
Water? Yes, of course, always, always lots of water. Plenty of healthy food, of course. But it is not necessary to avoid eating beforehand. Avoid greasy and unhealthy food, hard to digest, but you do not eat that way, so you are all right! Just sit, drink, listen to lovely music.

BR- Did you say lovely or lively?
Lovely, lively music will do!

BR- You mean not relaxing music?
No need for deep relaxation there, as what is involved is the atomic structure of the matter you are made of. So if we activate that structure, **you'll provide a texture we can manipulate at will, to make it suitable for forming another face with features different to yours**. You try. We try. We see. You'll see results. You'll trust. You'll then do even better in everything else too, as the confidence will grow even more.

BR- Would it be possible to do transfiguration and at the same time get messages to give out?
What do you think we do this work for? Isn't it to prove we exist? So, why shouldn't we be able to show our faces and "give messages" as you call it?! Of course, you'll have to use

calming sessions for the Mind too as the lively music for the face will not be lively relaxation... but if you know how to tune in to us for 'messages' without the need for quiet music, then you'll be all right.

BR- Can't you work at it when am dozing off or asleep and without music?

What music does is uplifts the vibrations around you. So, if you have music it does speed things up a bit. But I did not say we could not do it without it. Some of the work certainly can be done at night or other similar relaxing times. So, we know you seem interested. We don't mind you trying different ways because we may thus find another way to work with you which fits in with your busy life! You can try anything you like and if it works and you feel you can devote some time to help it progress to a finish and success, we are more than happy to help you work at it with us and us work at it with you!

BR- Can you work at transfiguration any time?
My little friend, the face changes come with relaxation.

BR- Why? I thought you said there was no need for relaxation music?

We cannot work on **a 'disturbed' Mind which will be reflected on the body** at once, one way or the other. So if you are tensed, not relaxed, we won't be able to make the flesh change or, at least, manipulate the atoms. So you have to be peaceful enough. We did say it is **not using** the Mind, but it still means you have to be relaxed all over, in the sense of not feeling disturbed! (*Note- Essential to know that your state of Mind always affects and is mirrored in your flesh body sooner or later. That is the real CAUSE of diseases. More explanations on illnesses by my Spirit Teachers in their book T, L & D*).

190

BR- I understand. How is Mum?

Your mum is well and happy, learning more and more and enjoying it. She has her hands full too, as she is tackling a new way of thinking that has repercussions on her way of making life work for her.

BR- Can you explain this please?

She has many ways of thinking open to her. The one she's chosen at the moment opens doors to her that she had not realised existed! So she'll be excited next time she'll tell you about it, as it is exhilarating for her. A bit difficult to explain yet still very interesting. All in all, a busy family 'up here'! You have them all working hard at improving their comprehension and understanding of their new world. Very commendable, we could say! All is said now, if you need to stop.

26th June 2007 - *11.10hrs - Eight years today without Mum on Earth. My Guide wants to explain something.*

Plans of evolution are always hard to grasp. It is important to understand what a Soul has to go through step by step, to **progress to higher levels** of intuition and inspiration of inner Knowledge. All Beings are different. Each one has his/her own pace and details to experience, their own readjustment and most of all, understanding capacity. So it is with your dear mother.

You have understood it is not easy or wise at the moment to let her know you would like to speak to her if possible on the anniversary of her passing to this world. This is because **to her it is a joyful event in a way**, even though she lost physical contact with you all on Earth. She has learnt and progressed so much! It is a pleasure to see her beam with new Knowledge of Self and of all other aspects she had encountered and 'studied'.

191

BR- Could you give me some details about this please?

The little lady has been so keen to find out about her Self and her other lives that she travelled in 'time' in a way - and yet not really of course - to see aspects of her Whole Self as she's never known herself to be before!

It has to be done gradually, to encounter one aspect at a time, so that the rest blends with it gently and smoothly. It cannot be done in a sudden surge of all sides of one's personality without drowning and crowding one's Mind! One facet at a time, to find out some detail relevant to what one wanted to learn at that particular 'period', as you would call it.

Yet those are not all as 'separate' as it seems to be when on Earth. It is like being at the centre of a big ball while you look at those facets. They surround you, they are all around you. You can only grasp, look at, scrutinize, feel and think about one at a time, as **you cannot focus on all** in one go! Yet they are there present and waiting! Do you see what I mean*? (Like a 'snow scene shaker'?)*

The 'present' is always present. The 'past' is always present. The 'future' is always more present than either of the others, because it is hovering as strong or weaker possibilities. So **the focus you give them** individually is what you **will experience** 'at the time'. But it is not to say none of the others exist then too! All are there waiting and yet not happening as far as **your** narrow conception of time allows it - or rather does not allow it! It is very strange and subtle for an Earthly Being's Mind, but comprehensible once you are here in this world!

So your mum is happy to be doing what she is doing! She is concentrating on all those different aspects of her own Self, which had evidently always been a mystery to her before! That's because she had not really considered those possibilities as even remotely possible! It was all vague and foggy in her Mind; not really possible or 'graspable'. Now she is clearer in her Mind and feels those 'mental journeys' are so much more

192

worth it than journeys on land, as she had loved to do at one time of her lives! She is happy within and that's what you want to know.

BR- Will she be able to tell me about those adventures, what she was in various lives, just out of interest?

As she comes back from these inner trips, she will be able to explain some of it to you, do not despair, because she'll be full of exciting and 'excited' information! She'll be thrilled to talk about all those details which, no doubt, will amuse her and you too. So, be prepared to wait for a little while, then she'll come and tell you more. No need to fret, she is in good hands, as you know. She is having a great time, discovering what she needs to discover - that is what we call 'Progress'. So Mum is progressing fine. That's all we can say for now.

BR- Do you have anything else to talk about or shall I do some book typing?

An Angel of Mercy is not a winged Being. It is a peace-loving Being who loves to come close to those wanting peace in their Mind. It is a Thought Power with a caring, compassionate attitude as a Being who wants to help those on Earth.

No Angels float around with wings and feathers on them! It is a figment of Mankind's imagination but we find it hard to make some people understand that! It has been invented by Mankind and some will see such 'feathered Beings' simply because that is what they want to see, or expect, or hope to see, or subconsciously would be amazed to see! Therefore, this happens! As you think, so it appears!

But a fish tail on an 'angel' may not look as nice as wings, so wings are what those people see!! It is not important really; it does not make that much difference. But it is sad to see people engrossed in their beliefs and visions which they'd fight to their death for and yet they are not correct!

193

No Being floats around with wings here, first of all because that would make them 'Earthly matter objects"; **a wing** is an **object made of matter since it's made of feathers!** So it is illogical to want to see them like that! An 'Angel' has **no gender** (it is not a 'he' or a 'she'), has no wings, no flowing dress nor long golden hair or whatever! **It has nothing human!**

What is possibly perceived by some people is the 'aura' or **Energy of loving Beings who may not have ever come to Earth,** but who want to help those who do go there. It is a kind of Being who cares, as we all do here if we are at the 'right level', (That means excluding, for example, those so Earthbound who can't think beyond their old Earthly activities). If the right amount of compassion and caring is felt towards others who are not here, it is quite normal to want to help them by going closer to them and supporting them with one's own Energy. That's what 'Angels' are.

Statues of marble won't do justice to the beauty of Love and Compassions emanating from these Beings who want to help or teach Mankind better ways to go back to the original plan. Make people understand no matter how many statues they build, it will **not** make Mankind better. It has to come from the inside of every man and Being on Earth, so that the Will has found its way to the right path again. Once **the Will to do good only** is set, then the rest will follow.

No Angel with or without wings can change the state of the Earth or of Mankind! *(Note- That was a very unexpected and unrequested topic!)*

16th July 2007 - Midnight. *The pen started drawing concentric circles, and 'spokes' shooting out from the nucleus-like centre of the **dome** this formed.*

Which one is first or last when you stand in the centre and look up above you? It all depends on what you are looking at and whether you see them all in one go, or whether you look at them one by one. All depends on the observer; it's seen from his point of view! The man in **the centre has no sense of linear time but instead of 'everything at the same time',** as all these little blobs could represent events or years or centuries. It is all in the perspective and Mind of the beholder.

So when you look at 'Time' from this point of view, you can understand that 'past events' are close to 'future probabilities' in the same way as there are **'past probabilities'** which have not materialised as such in your world, because they have **not been focused on enough!**

24th July 2007 - 11.00hrs. *I first give my Spirit Artist friend a chance to practise his 'psychic art'. The pencil sketches very quickly an Eastern looking man's face! So I then ask who that person is.*

All drawings at the moment are of helpers. This gentleman has been with you for a very long time. He has the privilege to talk to you of profound subjects to make you and others think of the nature of Life on both sides of the Earthly world. He has no particular 'name' but you know him as 'the man by the river'.

BR- Oh! That's him! I simply call him 'River Man'! He looks as if he is from the Far East?

Looks means nothing, dear. The look is only an appearance to give you something to concentrate on, if that's what you want. He has no 'name', no 'country' - he is himself. But at one time he has been a monk in the Eastern countries. He likes to remember those days as days of Knowledge and Learning, so he showed himself to you as such. He has been with you elsewhere 'before' and 'after', but that is his picture of himself to you; a meditating profound thinker, who liked the Eastern way of looking within oneself to find the Truth.

That is what you are looking for, so that is what he shows himself as - looking for the Truth within. He can show himself as anything you like, but this is what **he** wanted to portray himself as, to make you think you need to do what he does. Look within and 'meditate' more, so that the truths you are looking for come up to the surface and float in your Mind for others to share too.

One man, one Mind, all Minds link, you know! No need to feel separate, we and you are all One Mind linking at various points or degrees of intensity, to make up the One Whole Mind that is 'All Knowledge'. We are all part of it, one way or another!

25th July 2007 - *The pen starts with two energetically drawn concentric circles and lines linking them as if forming an '8'.*

The world spins round and also revolves around the sun. It is so in your own Mind, all of you Humans - if you don't listen to your own thoughts, you listen to others! You are always churning words round and round in your Mind, that's why there is that constant chatter! If only you could keep that down to practically nothing, it would really make life quieter and communication much easier between our two worlds. As we speak we have to 'avoid' your odd incoming thought wanting to intrude!

It is a question of discipline of the Mind and it is not easy to do if one has not trained to do so. Lots of people have tried and succeeded in quietening their Minds to such a degree that they can control it. It would really be great if you could **all** do so! The passage of 'Time' is non-existent. Whether one has been here one year or one hundred, it makes no difference. What matters are the experiences one goes through within one's Mind at this point. That's what your parents and other family are all doing, sooner or later, at a more or less advanced stage.

The latest news of your husband, my dear, is that he has suffered such a shock at finding himself here rather suddenly (because he did not know what to expect) that he has needed a lot of counselling, explaining, 'proving' and disproving on his part. He could not quite grasp the 'how and why' of what he saw or thought he saw! That way it took much 'time', you might say, for him to really grasp what his Mind was making him do.

BR- Please explain in more detail?
He would go on a mental trip round his neighbourhood, let's say and find himself somewhere so unexpectedly different and out of the ordinary that his conscious thinking could not accept it. He would not believe or grasp at first, that the reaction of seeing something different would **trigger other thoughts**, which in turn would create more puzzles to solve! This is why he had to play with his thinking for what may seem to you a 'long time'! To our world, 'time' does not exist, is not considered and cannot be taken into consideration. **All that matters here are the states of Mind** of each and everyone and everything.

If someone has not got a happy, settled Mind it will reverberate on all others, sooner or later, because the vibrations will get most confused all around him or her. This is why we advise to leave such a person 'in peace' for a while, so to speak, not to deprive them of your company, but because they have got to **come to terms with their own way of thinking!** That is all it takes but it is a huge task at times and that's what your Dave is doing.

BR- I thought he seemed more settled and understanding his Mind had an effect on what he saw. He'd do some gardening, knowing he could just 'think of rain' to make it rain, or plants could grow indeed without being cared for.

197

The plants would grow indeed without having to be looked after, but he enjoyed having a say and giving them a loving, helping hand, because he still loves them, like he did when on Earth. So when he came here that took his Mind a little away from the sadness to have left you all behind. But he could not help rejoicing because he had no more pain, no more worries or duties or impositions on his wishes! He could desire what he wanted as long as it was within this realm, of course.

Yet the fact remained **he still had not really grasped the scope of Mind Power**! Mind Power is so powerful no one can really comprehend it! Not until they look at it from all angles and have a go at using it in ways that are different from how they'd used it before. So Mind Power is a very great mystery indeed!

BR- Is he still struggling with his grief? What has he been able to do so far?

The poor man has had to cope with his grief because he was very upset at first, but we all helped him. He has done well here.

BR- He's asked me to talk to him often.

The question of 'often' or 'not often' is not really relevant here, because it will feel as often or not according to the state of Mind of the person! If one is down and depressed and in need of a talk - and one does not get it 'at once' - one will feel as if a century or two have passed! But if one is busy, happily constructing a new life in an 'orderly way', so that one can find one's way round the patterns created by the thoughts coming to one's Mind, then it will be ever so quick!

The feeling of 'time' or 'duration' depends on the mental and emotional attitude. That way 'time' will be practically non-existent in an emotional way. But Dave has done well since his early 'days' here. He had to learn a lot in one go but it had been staged down gradually, so that he could grasp one part at a time. Now he seems to have come to terms with the fact that Mind and thoughts 'happening into Reality' are a 'fait accompli', i.e. that's how it is here so he may as well accept it!

He was struggling at first, as most people do, but he's gained a lot of ground now and is a dab hand at it in certain fields. So, we are pleased to say he has learnt a lot and is still learning - but this is more enjoyable for him now than it was at the beginning, because he was so bewildered at first by what was happening around him. All is well. Don't worry.

6th August 2007 - *Tuning in during a quiet train journey.*
The little lady you love in our world has done and is still doing a lot of learning and is really excited by it all. She wants to say hello to you as you have not been talking to each other for a long time. *(Immediate change of communicator as French is spoken!)* Mum is here, Sweetheart. Yes, it feels it's been a long time!

BR-Please tell me what you've been up to?
I've been making lots of trips within my Mind. It's amazing! I saw loads of people I did not know before, yet as I met them I had the impression of having seen them previously. Well, I discovered that these persons were either 'facets of Me' sometimes, or friends of mine from 'before', i.e. before my recent life with you in Algiers and Nice! Me reincarnated! I can't get over all this.

I had to really think about 'me', I had to want to see the 'Whole of Me', if you understand that? After my friends explained it to me, I grasped that we all have aspects of our personality which we do not know unless we try to uncover them. So I said: "Ok. I'll try to!" I am very willing to discover more, as you know! Therefore, I made those inner trips.

199

BR- What happened exactly?

I had to relax and think of myself, go within myself. I asked myself: "Where is the 'real Whole Me'?" Then I saw pictures unfurl in front of me, others superimposed over them and I realised there were many different 'Me' aspects I was unaware of and did not know until now! It's exciting, you know, to see yourself as someone you did not know!

I observed myself as a person living in Canada in the days of the bisons and beavers. I used to live in a forest like a kind of recluse, a hermit! I liked it because I was very close to Nature. I loved having 'Animals' around me, even if some were dangerous at times.

BR- Did you learn something from that?

That life had its good points. No problems like I had in that last life with you! But in Canada I was a man, so I had more strength and courage. I wanted to know what it was like to live alone in the middle of Nature. And that's what Pierre did too! *(My eldest brother).* Isn't it strange that he repeated the same scenario?

Then I looked at myself elsewhere, just by thinking. I saw a woman travelling a lot, in practically all the countries. Once more I was still close to Nature but seeing it from different angles here and there. It was my time as a woman explorer; I wanted to see the whole Earth and its splendour as much as I could. That was really smashing and I am truly pleased about it! This is no doubt why Nature, geography and countries have always interested me... *(Sudden interruption as passengers board the train).*

BR- Sorry for breaking off our link Mum. Have you seen some other lives?

The pleasure to talk to you again is enormous, Darling. Please do not apologise, it's normal, you've got a life to live.

As I was telling you, there were so many lives I had no idea about! The best of it is that I used not to believe in that reincarnation business! So it's been giving me quite a lot of strange surprises to see myself with all those 'dressing-up clothes', I could say. I have been various people yet I don't feel any different. It was an interesting and amusing experience to see myself 'disguised' without knowing I had done it! The 'lesson' you talked about is not so much a lesson than a quenched desire; a life right and left, here and there, but each one had a theme that was repeated - for example, being in Nature.

The time I saw myself as a man, I reckon, I seemed to be really brave to find myself alone in the woods without any other protection than what I had around me! It was a very long time ago and I had very few weapons, the best of it being that I would not have wanted to use them! They were just to protect myself in case of great emergency. I loved those beasts around me, they were beautiful. I used to watch them; I enjoyed seeing what they were eating, where they were going, how they behaved. It was a real life lesson in natural history, it was a good life!

You see, we can indeed keep busy here and find out such weird things. It was a shock for me to discover myself as another woman and as a man, yet my inner characteristics were not so different! *(Passengers were getting much noisier, it disturbed me. I had difficulties in keeping my link, then I dozed off. What a pity!)*

7th August 2007 - *I try again the next day. My Guide opens the proceedings.*

All is well, we are here. The mum you want is here too, so please listen to her. You can rest assured she would like to talk non-stop if only you could let her! She wants to tell you lots of things, we'll help her if she struggles. We'll let her in now. *(Suddenly I hear French spoken).* Mum is here now,

Darling. You see, we've managed it after all. It's not always easy, but we are coping.

As I told you, I saw lots of lives. There were others during the Middle Ages! I was a lady who appeared quite dignified, I think, as she was walking about looking self-important and wanted people to look at and listen to her! She was perhaps a 'bigwig' but what really mattered is what she wanted to do. She yearned for people to listen and pay attention to all the things she felt she had to tell them! She was more strolling around than strutting about, yet she enjoyed when people asked for her opinion on topics more serious than those about everyday life.

Therefore, I reckon it was a seed of what I did with you and during that life you knew me, when I was teaching you and my boys and also others whom I helped with their school work. *(Note- The only similarity is the 'teaching' side, as my mum never strutted about and was certainly not bigheaded!)*

I saw that this woman had very strong opinions and noticed everything happening around her, she did not miss anything! She needed to learn not to feel so 'self-important', even though what she used to talk about was valuable and useful. She had to become able to lessen her pride or self-esteem, yet what she did and said was quite good indeed! She had to put a brake on her ego so that it did not go to her head. She must have managed it because 'after that', I could say (yet I **don't see lives as successive but as if at the same time**!), she had lives including various travels and different interests, yet of some importance. She never wanted to deal with stupid things. It was always intelligent and useful.

During my inner travels, I see myself in front of 'me', if you grasp what I mean? I am in front of me, or rather, the 'Other Me' of that period stands in front of me and looks at, or explains to me, or simply lives her life and I watch! It is 'me' yet it's not completely 'me' as I see myself and feel now, not the 'me' that you know.

It has taken me some time to get used to the idea of 'reincarnation', as I had never really understood how we could all reincarnate and come back to Earth and have been all those possible people! I thought it would mean too many people to reincarnate, too many millions of people at the same time and it was bothering me! But now I can see it does not work like 'a box within another box' - but is in fact all lives together, 'at the same time', so to speak! To me, that seems much more logical and comprehensible.

That way, I can now tell myself: "I went to a given country, did such and such things, came back from it and decided to do other things elsewhere. That is why my Soul knows so much and I have to discover what I learnt during those various trips and experiences of life on Earth".

My recent life with you had nothing to do with the travels on Earth (as I had done that before) but with journeys of Knowledge of facts. I had to accumulate and gather useful facts, anecdotes, information. It used to give me great pleasure to be able to collect all those and pass it on to other people if possible and of course to the four of you. So, I have had and am having fun once more with those experiences. It is always very useful to know oneself well and deeply. This is why we do those 'tasks', as my friends call them, but I label them 'my little homework' or even 'my games'! That's how I spend my time, Sweetheart.

BR- Very intriguing! Did you see more other lives?

The lives mentioned above are the ones I remember more easily because they were clearer. There are some for which I only saw some periods of a particular life, but I did not always get all the details of the whole life. It was more like a glimpse, a summary of what really mattered as an experience in that life.

It must always be useful. We do not go to the Earth to do 'nothing'. We must always live for something. Therefore, it means one must not waste one's time with idiocies because that's not what we go on the Earth for! Getting on board a flesh body then starting to waste one's time with stupid trivia - or totally useless or dangerous things - could mean the result will be that the Soul will no longer want to stay in that flesh body and will decide to leave it! So making the effort to come on Earth may as well be worth it!

BR- Thanks. Anything else? They gave me a lot of work with typing their profound 'T, L & D' book!

The aim of a book of 'Spiritual Knowledge', as they call it, is to open once more people's eyes. It's for those who do not realise they were apparently taught or brainwashed with rubbish or wrong 'facts' or lies! I would not have quite realised it myself, but now I am here, I can see all that from a different point of view. It's much more interesting and very often also amusing. This is why I am having so much fun in this world!

I see it and I see yours (on the Earth) in such a different way now! It makes me wonder why we were made to waste so much time by obliging us to 'swallow' Earthly man-made teachings that are either crooked or illogical or stupid! Personally **I now feel whole and complete without a body of flesh**. Yet so many people believe all that we Humans are is a body of mortal flesh and not a body of Light!

When the little baby, my sister, came here her mother was not present, of course, but there were people here who knew her, loved her and taught her who she was. After all, she had only been a baby for a very short time so she could forget it quite easily and go back to what she was 'before' going to the Earth. This is what we constantly do here - going and coming back! *(That was an unexpected and unrequested comment. Unfortunately, concentrating so much at this late hour made me doze off once more!)*.

15 August 2007 - *My Guide comes for a chat.*

Last time we spoke, we mentioned the fact your mum had made trips within her Mind to discover who she really is. That is valid for all of you and all of us! We all have to go within to discover the vastness of what each one of us is as a multidimensional personality!

Our 'persona' on Earth is only a pale reflection and only one facet of our many-sided Being, who is the Whole Being of 'You' or 'Me'! We all have that journey to make, many times, to find out where we are coming from and have gone, where the 'Real I' is and what motivates it. When that is found, there will still be more to discover, because it is a never ending quest! The 'You' others know is not the 'You ' that you will uncover gradually 'page by page', or leaf by leaf, as if you were a giant bush to 'unpluck'. So we'll say: Look forward to finding out more about yourself when you come over here!

The largest mammal on Earth sleeps too, so you'll need yours and you are not a large mammal either! You can rest assured we are only joking. Your mum is always concerned you don't sleep enough. We know you tried to go to bed a little earlier those past days or so. The concentration needed is essential to all good communication, so do what you can now and we'll pick it up again later.

Topic no.1: What is an Earth dweller? A Being of flesh outwardly, a Spirit Being inwardly. So, the Inner Being is always more important and real than the Outer Being, of course. Being an Inner Being, or 'Spirit' as you call it, implies eternity as **eternity is what Energy is made of**. Eternal Energy does not disappear, whereas flesh matter does, since it is only designed to be a temporary experiment! As an eternal Being, one has certain responsibilities. One has eternity to find out what one has not done 'right' over the centuries of various lives. Also one has to try to make amends for the hurt one may have caused then. It may not always be possible but it is worth trying to do somehow. So, the eternal Being who comes back here has always a phase of his stay in our world taken up with looking at his recent life on Earth, or wherever! This is to reflect on what he may or may not have achieved, as far as the Law of our world is concerned.

The fact every one of you is a Being of flesh does not mean the flesh body is right! It means the flesh body may make demands on you, but the 'You' is not that flesh body! So, you cannot be a slave to its ideas and exactions if it goes against what has been set as the primary Law of Nature and of our world - you shall **not hurt others on purpose**. You can and shall progress and create but not by being harmful to others. This is why one must always consider other people before oneself! *(My concentration gave way to the need to sleep).*

13th September 2007 - *Midnight but I feel quite awake. I hear English spoken.*

Make sure you understand how important peace of Mind is!

BR- I do... any news about Dave?

Now he is training for recognition of his Self. He is analysing and discovering his 'Higher Self', as you call it. So it would be wiser not to tear him away from that task for the time being, as he is deeply involved in discovering his own Self, as said before. You can rest assured he is well, mentally and emotionally. He is all right. He has had his sad time, not because he could not talk to you but because he had to accept he was 'away' from the Earth life. He has now settled well in his new world. His family have been around him and he's been guided step by step all through those times. He is now at the inquisitive stage, trying to grasp why he did, liked or disliked things. He is having fun, he is learning about 'himself on a bigger scale'. That is always very useful to do, so do not worry about him. He has what he needs for the time being!

BR- Would my sending thoughts to him distract him? Does he get our news?

A man who does not know or receive his family's thoughts is not a man in this world! Of course he has your news, as you all progress on your path. We tell him and let him know what happens so that he is kept up to date.

BR- He had asked me to keep in touch.

You are in touch more that you think! **You've been here!** (*During body sleep time*). He has seen you and loves you for it! He is grateful for the support, the thoughts and the news too. You cannot worry about him because he has nothing wrong with him. He is all right now! We all love him and help him.

22nd September 2007 - *Mum's 99th birthday anniversary. My Guide starts the dialogue.*

The last time we spoke, we discussed the need for Mankind to rely more on its Inner Knowledge than outside input, as the inside one is safe and secure - the outside one could very probably be distorted or simply misinformation.

The need for inner guidance is that once you are here, you cannot physically go back to undo what you have done 'wrong', when on Earth. So you may as well try to get it right, or as right as you can, the first time! When you have a problem facing you and you can't decide the outcome, simply **listen** quietly within yourself and do not think - just listen, feel, sense. Work out what those feelings are, relate them to previous experiences in similar conditions of having to make a choice, a decision.

You can be sure you've got it right when the inner feeling is decisive - fulfilment, utter peace, instead of churning. That's how you learn to recognise what is right or wrong, what's good for you, or not. Listen within! When Mankind manages to do that in all occasions, for all decisions, then there will be peace because **no Inner Self would advise war!** No one wants war, not even your enemy at the bottom of themselves, but they may have been pushed or brainwashed into that kind of action.

When Mankind realises there is more to life on Earth than what money can buy, then they'll take a bigger step forward than those taken by technology, because technology does not always bring peace of Mind! It might be handy and convenient at times, but there are too many cases when it is not good for Mankind in the long run! All is said with love and integrity. We know some people will have already talked of and taught this, but it is important to restate it, because this is the fundamental line all should take. **Look within and the answers are there.** That's all.

Not everyone knows how to do it, not everyone is even thinking of doing it. We just wanted to make a point regarding the necessity to mention this material again, even if others have already done so. The aim of all these books is to open the eyes of Mankind and most of its heart and Soul!

When a 'Soul is lost' on Earth, it is when they don't know how to reach within to find the answer. If they knew, they would not be 'lost'! It is important to guide them whenever one can and that is one way. Likewise, when Souls arrive here and feel 'lost' because they still think they are one Earth, they have to be guided, encouraged, prompted and supported until they find their feet again and realise where they are. We are well acquainted with the process, as we've had to do it many millions (no doubt!) of times. So we'd say: Let's stick to that programme to help those lost in their Mind and not realising **they ARE a Soul**, not just 'have' one or 'not have' one as the case may be!

It is also urgent to understand the law of the land has no

jurisdiction over the way you think within! They cannot say certain things to certain people and it's supposed to be correct. No Human on Earth can tell you how to feel and think within! That's why you have to let yourself be guided by those who can reach you and your own inner guidance, as mentioned before. Those who do not listen within will have a much harder time both on Earth and in the world after, when they come back to it after their Earthly stay! It cannot be denied, it cannot be rejected. It just IS a fact. So why not try to put everything in your favour by acting accordingly to make your (and others') life easier?

Just when people think they've found a way to be 'happy' by earning or winning more money, they'll find other things will go wrong! Why? Because the Soul is not looking for money but for its own fulfilment. Unless the money was really put to greater use for the relief of others' pains and troubles there will not be deep-seated satisfaction in having material pastimes and extra goods which have no aim but make life more 'modern' or more wealthy-looking!

This is why we say: **Look within and be rich as soon as you delve into the treasure chest of Inner Knowledge**, the bottom of which can never be reached. It has that magic asset of never appearing or even existing, as Inner Knowledge grows deeper and better the more you use it! That's why it is so exciting, uplifting and valuable to have constant use of it; a constant replenishment of one's Soul and its source. That's the way it was meant when the Earth was first created as one had a Soul to drive the flesh, but the flesh did not and was not meant to drive the Soul! But 'times have changed', as you say - or rather attitudes, sadly, have changed, giving priority to the physical needs. Now is the time to work at straightening up the balance, so that all is not lost in a world meant to be happy, as has been said many times before!

BR- May I ask you about Psychic Art? I've started receiving some lovely portraits. Some I could place whom it's for, others I can't or I don't seem to get details about the 'sitters'. Why? Could you explain how it works and what's needed?

Practice! Practice! What is happening is this: Your Mind is receptive to the **drawings sent by someone in my world.** You have the ability to receive the 'impulses', let's say, which create the drawing as is. It is possibly not always a hundred per cent correct but it will be a very good likeness. Unfortunately, that comes as a drawing because the Soul who is drawn is a Being of Energy. So the Energy is used to draw that person as she/he **thinks** of her/himself. It cannot be the same Energy used for giving information.

BR- Why not?

The Thought Energy sent to guide your hand is not the same as the thoughts sent about facts, dates, names etc. It is a different type of work which we are working on at the moment.

BR- I thought 'Thought' is 'Thought'!

Thought is a power, a creative Energy. As it is driven in one direction to create a drawing - which is a reflection of one's thoughts and memory of an 'ex-physical' self - it is not concentrating on the life nor the details of that life. So there will have to be a switch, a different type of Energy to join you, to add details to what the pen drew after receiving the influence from your Mind and brain, which in turn have been influenced by the Mind of the 'sitter', the person sending it from our world. The two are really very different... just as you cannot 'talk' and 'sing' at the same time. It's one or the other.

BR- Where does the Spirit Artist come in?

The Artist is definitely there! It is an essential part of

210

your work. The Artist here looks at, senses, reads the 'Spirit'personality who wants to be drawn. Then she/he sends the thoughts and guides you. She/he knows how to draw as she/he has expertise and experience in that subject. But you have to be receptive to both their Minds. The Mind of the sitter here is blending with the Mind of the Artist, who is blending with your Mind too. So your Mind is receiving both influences!

BR- What's the solution? How can I get more precise info, who it is for etc?

The thoughts sent by your Artist will be made even more precise for you to pick up more correctly. That's one thing we can do from here.

BR- Are you talking about the actual drawing?

The thought sent as to where the pen should go will be made even more precise. It is not difficult to do, that's fine. The direction and destination is another problem, separate from the first.

BR- What about getting more facts about the person?

An Artist in our world is an Energy Mind, who draws with their Mind, into your Mind, having received from someone else's Mind the information their Mind remembers relating to their shape, size and looks! Do you see the problem?

The details of the personality, the person on Earth, whether passed over or still there, are more difficult to give you at the same time. You'll need a time lapse and a changeover of Spirit inspirers or 'guide' to help you receive the facts. It can be done and is done with other mediums.

We have started with you and are still working on you. You'll do a drawing, we'll change over here and we'll bring someone else to tell you who it is, why or whom it is for.

It might take quite a lot of practice but it will be worth it! You are getting there anyway; you are beginning to receive information about people, so we'll work more on that side if you want to. But remember an Artist can be there, yet no sitter. If you sit to receive drawings, an Artist can also be there to give you some practice drawing, it does not have to be of a specific' real' person. All that is needed is practice and patience. If you put those two together, you'll get great results!

Mind your Mind! Keep it calm, quiet, peaceful, rested. Even. Not up and down and churned. That way you'll be much more receptive and aware. You'll win on all scores and levels.

6th October 2007 - *09.20hrs for a change!*
Your mum is here. Do you want to speak to her?

BR- What a question! Of course!
We'll let her through. *(Swift change of communicators).* Sweetheart, at last! It seems to me it's been a long time.

BR- Lovely to talk to you, Darling Mum. So, what have you been doing?
Last time we spoke, I think I was telling you I was doing some research within, in my Mind. Well, I am still at it; it's ever so interesting and intriguing! I have made lots of discoveries regarding the psychological side which is in all of us. We are both 'Spirit' and a Mind. But a Mind with lots of ramifications which can discover itself by exploring within!

This is how I found out that the experiences I had on Earth during several lives transformed my point of view on the 'human condition', as Balzac *(Famous 19th c. French author)* called it. My view point as a 'woman' but as a 'man' too changed over the centuries.

BR- You remembered being a man?

I have been a man indeed, but I only saw a small portion of that life, in the same way as for the other lives. Only what is important comes back to the surface to make itself known, and to demonstrate or remind us what we learnt and found out in that particular life. I was impressed to see that sometimes as a man, I didn't used to think very differently from me being a woman after all! Me who believed they saw things in another way. In the end we are not so dissimilar!

What matters in every life is to do one's best with what one has and who one is. That's it! If women cry more than men, it's possibly because they show their emotions a little more, but it does not mean men don't have any. A man will bottle them up more perhaps, that's all. If they are together in the same accident, one of them has to show himself as the 'tough one' to give courage to the other one. That task has often rested on the man. So that's my small inner adventures in little bits of 'films' without a full story - just extracts, flashbacks in my lives.

What about you, is everything ok? I know that Dave has a sister who came to visit you recently. You went together to his grave, yet he is not really in it since he is here with us all, happy to be in this world instead of suffering on Earth!

We see each other now and then. I think of him and he appears to me. Usually he is very busy with one thing or the other. That's because he is in the middle of learning what it's like to be here! It means lots of discoveries! Especially for him who didn't know much before arriving here! But he looks much more serene and less worried and sad. He has understood it does not do any good, whether to oneself or to others, to fret about the past or the future. The best is to live for one's own present and build it solidly and usefully. This is what one must do on Earth too!

When you arrive here, it's a terrible shock, you know! It's so frightening in a way to feel cut off from your family and everything you are used to. It gives you an awful blow even though you feel well, are free from pain and are with people you had not seen for a long time. **It takes a while to begin to make a life for oneself in this new system of thinking**! It can be whether because one does not need to eat etc. or because everything one thinks appears if you think it strongly, with intensity and continuity. Yet the pleasure to **be free** dominates everything! Free to do anything, free to say anything. No hassle. The only problem we could have is regrets. That can spoil your stay here as it gnaws at you inwardly and is not advisable! Yet somehow we cope one way or the other - we manage to get rid of it or explain it, or understand how and why.

Anyway, I wanted to know how you and yours are feeling. Everything ok? It seems to me there is no big problem. Jim seems fairly settled from what I was told. Anne-France too and I don't feel you have any real problems. You've worked at our books; there is a lot to do, I know and I understand! But you'll make it. It's a pity it was not possible to publish it earlier, but don't worry too much about that.

BR- What about your parents and my dad?

Your dad is fine, we are all well here, of course! He is deep into things which really interest him and is very busy. He hasn't always time to explain everything to me but I reckon he is having a lot of fun. You'll know about it when he can let you know, if he comes to talk to you. As for my parents, I haven't seen them for some time.

BR- (Surprised) - Did I hear that correctly?

I have not spent much time with my parents 'lately' because I was making my little journeys within. I put a lot of 'time' and effort into this, in order to be able to discover my own Self. It seems strange, you know, to realise I am far more than I thought I was during my last Earthly life! I used to see myself as a mother of four children, then I discovered I had unknown 'facets' shaping me, which are part of and complement me! It's terribly weird but extremely interesting too!

So there we are. After playing with my thoughts to create vases and gold walls, hover over water and come to Earth to see your home etc. *(See Vol.1)*, I now go within towards the 'inner Me' that I am - and have always been without knowing it - in order to analyse the unknown aspects and their 'raison d'être' (reason for existing). Saying this does sound profound, doesn't it?

Therefore, to sum up; one must always try to do well, so as not to have any regrets which one constantly carries within oneself and brings over here, because they spoil one's 'paradise'. After all, why bring that baggage here, hey? It's like taking your dustbin with you on holiday, isn't it? There is enough to transport without lumbering oneself with that too! There is so much to do to enjoy ourselves and keep busy here, we have too much to choose from!

BR- Are you still looking after children who arrive feeling lost?

There are always children coming here without their parents. I do love them, poor little things. They feel rather lost at the beginning, but we entertain them, distract them and cuddle them and explain things as best as possible. *(Unfortunately the phone rings suddenly and I have to take the important call)*.

21st October 2007 - 15.30 hrs. *French is spoken at once.*
Now we are all here, we are not going to miss the opportunity to talk to you, are we? As I don't have anything urgent to do, I'd better spend some time with you for once now you are free!

BR- We are all fine here. How are things with you Mum?

Everything ok too, of course. We don't have any worries here! So, what have I been doing? Well, as usual I have been doing little a 'homework' like a good pupil, as well as my journeys in thoughts to make me discover who I am.

BR- Are you still doing those then?

Oh yes indeed, as you could guess! There are heaps of things to do and see; it's not achieved overnight! There are lots of possibilities when one examines oneself that way. I have to observe myself as I am now but also as I was in the past. Moreover, I need to see how things could have turned out if I carried on this way or that way and how it could be improved! That is the hardest but also the most interesting in a way, because I ask myself how I could become better if I thought or acted differently. Then one sees heaps of **possibilities displayed on the screen** of one's Mind and one 'dives into it' in a way and act a game of choices and results! The stakes are always the same - to succeed in improving what one is and was. That is progress, this is what matters. The rest is not as important.

The child I have been in the life you knew me grew up in 'that' direction and did 'this'. If she had grown up in 'another direction', what would she have done and why and what would the results have been? It gives lots of different scenarios and makes everything ever so interesting. Unfortunately, when there were mistakes, it is sad because one sees the results from the errors. It's a pity because it spoilt the picture, the life of that particular time. Yet everything can be repaired and one can change things to make them exist for the best, which seems to me absolutely incredible! But if one does it and 'repairs' it, it allows possibilities ensuing from this to exist and to create more positive futures, without any clouds!

216

That is the ideal but, of course, one cannot always spend one's time repairing everything! There are things one wants to see at closer range and go more deeply into, so it takes 'time' and leads you towards another track!

BR- Have you seen any particular or interesting lives? (Unfortunately, my rescued and wandering ex-stray wild cat 'Marroo' appears, wanting to eat and begs by giving me a tap on the hand! As this is progress since I managed to gradually tame him, out of sheer love, I can't ignore him! So I quickly put some food down and link up again, apologising to Mum).

What matters is that we can link up together again, Darling. Don't worry about interruptions. I want to tell you that I am told to let you know it looks as if there will 'soon' be some good changes in your direction. **Predictions are difficult** to make, as you know, since anything and everything can change at any moment! Yet they would not bother telling me this if it was unlikely to happen in the very near future, in your world! I also would like to say that Dad is deep into his little researches and discoveries and has great fun with all that. He's found 'solutions' to questions he was asking himself. No doubt he'll tell you about it before long!

BR- Do you know whether Pierre (my eldest brother) is still on Earth or somewhere in your world? I haven't heard from him for a while.

No, I don't see him here, I don't know where he is but I think I would have been told if he had arrived. The main thing is that he is well, amongst you the 'terrestrial people', though he must be quite old after all this time! I must say it's not a disaster if he (or all of you) dies, because he'll come straight here and there is nowhere better, you know! I do hope you are all happy or at least quite content. Here it's so easy to feel happy if one has not done anything wrong!

28th October 2007 - *In the evening. After a Spiritualist Service, during which I was able to go on platform and give 'spot on' messages from their loved ones in Spirit World to strangers in the congregation. Now the pen moves and I hear English spoken.*

Pass on our congratulations to yourself! You've done well to have heard us and given the messages sent. We tried hard indeed on our side but we are delighted to have been successful and glad you are happy. It is important for you to be noticed as a genuine medium and to be seen by your peers to be able to do it too. It is understandable as you cannot be ignored after all the work you've put into it! We are very pleased to have been of service, both to yourself and to the people you spoke to.

Now, the lady here who wishes to speak to you was interrupted the other day. Would you like to talk to her again?

BR- Of course! I always love talking to my mum!

(Suddenly French is spoken). Mum here, Sweetheart. Happy birthday to you my Darling! It must be quite an 'old one' after all this time? *(I tell her my age).* Oh! Well, not that old after all! There are lots of them still to come, I am told! I see you've done what you could to get rid of your cold and cough. I was told you had been suffering lately and we had to send you healing thoughts and wishes to speed up the process.

My life has not changed much since the 'other day' but I have a little detail to tell you about. The day you asked me whether Pierre was here, I looked all around me and I saw nothing. But I had to do some research more deeply to find out what the situation was. He has not made the 'big leap' yet so far, but he has aged recently according to what I was told. He had some health problems which weakened him and he's understood he has to take more care of himself. I think he had an attack of malaria or something like that. He must have been

218

shattered since he lives in such a hot climate! So we hope he will recover. That's what I wanted to tell you. He was not in pain to the extent of dying, but he was in a bad state. that's what made me think I should check. He is better now.

You'll have some news from him as soon as you write to him, so get down to it! He and I have not spoken to each other for a long time, what a pity! Anyway, we'll see each other again one day, that will rectify the situation!

BR- By the way, thank you again for giving birth to me! It's never much fun!

Your birth was no problem Darling, you know that. I was very happy to give your dad a baby as he wanted so much to have one! He adored you, you have no idea how much! He was so proud of you, **his** own daughter!

Something else I wanted to tell you in passing: My life has not changed overall, but there is a little detail which intrigued me. As I told you, I made some trips within my Mind and I saw lots of interesting and (to me) extraordinary things! But the best was a glimpse of one of my 'fleeting' lives, I could say. Perhaps not very long but intriguing! I had been a courtesan in the days of the Romans! I was being served by slaves (unfortunately, I must say now!) yet I was quite kind to them. But my main occupation was to... provide for the desires of my masters, the men! It seems I did not mind as I had my youth and my beauty, I think! But there was a time when I had to choose between two men, because one was jealous of the other one and they fought about it. It was sad, though I suppose flattering in a way! That choice was difficult because I was fond of both of them. I had to choose one or none. So, I decided to go away and leave them alone...to fight for nothing since I was not there anymore!

I went a long way away, but I learnt later than one of them died of his wounds. I never knew why he was injured but the main point was that I had to make an important decision regarding life and death, we can say, because if I had chosen one, the other would have probably tried to kill him! Life was not very nice on those days! Well, I did not want to have a death on my conscience!

So I left them both, thus depriving myself of many a pleasure and much wealth... but I scored 'good marks' here, would you believe? Because I did my best so that no one died because of me - at least as long as I could prevent it. Therefore, it was worth it in the end, wasn't it?

BR- You've always 'done your best' as far as I know and remember!

Well, at least I have always tried to. Now I'll let you sleep after this old little story of ancient history, since that interests you too!

BR- (Teasingly) - You see, I did tell you one reincarnates! So there!

The most interesting points are not so much the life one had or who one was but more **why** one had chosen it then **how** one coped with it, what good one did, or perhaps less good! Because that is what matters in the end: Why did we go there and was it worth going? After that, we come back here, so we may as well make a trip which was worth it.

So that's all for now Darling, because I know you are staying up late. If you continue, you will be unwell again. Go and rest and sleep well. We all kiss you and your children from the bottom of our hearts. Good night Sweetheart.

10th November 2007 - *I first let my Spirit Artist practise 'sending' me a drawing. It was that of an unknown young girl. Then I tuned in just in case someone wanted to talk to me. My Guide esponded.*

'Man' has only one object in his life: To live the life on Earth he has chosen to go to. If he does not live it to its full capacity, he will regret it of course, but he will be able to have another go if he wishes to. There is no limit to what he can do on this Earth he chose to go to as a training ground.

The little girl you drew with our help is one of those people **you** have been at one time! You have been a young girl too in a different 'life' as you call it - we call it an experience. This one was to teach you the love of a family. You'd never had a warm, loving family 'before' that life, as you'd say. It was important for you to know the feelings of a pleasant and loving environment where you felt loved and supported. It was a young life, it did not last long, you just wanted to know what it was like to have an affectionate home and be a child there. There was **no need for a longer life with adulthood responsibilities**, so you left it when you thought you had experienced enough.

You as that little girl lived in England too. It was 'a long time ago', as you'd call it. Somewhere towards the end of...possibly the 19th century, I think? It was not essential to recall the dates, the times were not of importance. The environment was a family of several children with parents who cared. Not terribly wealthy, but well off enough to give you all a comfortable and suitable home. As we look at it thorough your Energy field, we see the little girl had her heart set on 'Animals' too. She loved them in those days as you do now. It was one of her built-in feelings she kept since, a praiseworthy one. The love of her 'Animals' and the love of her parents, brothers and sisters made her feel good.

That is what she had come on Earth to experience, as it had been lacking in other lives for some reason or other. It had to be built into her Soul, as the lack of it would have been detrimental.

BR- How could you 'see' her face then?

The impression of the physical appearance has remained engraved at some point in your own aspects, your multi-facets. All we had to do was to look for it and at it, then project it to your Mind and your drawing hand. It has not come out badly at all - a young, fairish girl with big eyes and a love for Animals, who wanted peace within to find peace 'without' her too. We didn't do badly, did we? *(I can feel as if he is winking).*

BR- I am most surprised and impressed!

An example of what can be done if you relax enough to give us time to work with you.

BR- Am sure it could be even better if I could improve my sensing your guidance with the pencil, as well as accurate information about the person. No doubt more practice will help!

An accurate drawing can only be produced when the recipient's Mind is absolutely clear to receive it and them. The sender (in our world) needs to send his thought on wave lines of pure intensity, not jumbled up. It is **up to you to produce the clear channel**. We can only do our bit here regarding the information. You try and we'll give you more, you'll see.

1st December 2007 - *Started to tune in at 20.45hrs but dozed off till 00.15! I then got up to have a wash and get ready for bed, which really woke me up! So I tried tuning in around 1.00am. By 1.15am the link came. In English, so it was at least my own Guide. As it turns out, there was a surprise to come too!*

There is a gentleman here who wants to speak to you with a great desire in his heart to do so. We'll let him in. He's been waiting for a long time; he's been wanting so much to link up because it's been 'ages' in his Mind and he feels lonely without doing so. *(Swift change of communicator).*

Hi there, my little W—-, it's me, Dave. I am so pleased I can at last talk with you! Yes, it's me. I hope you are all ok. We are informed of what goes on in your world, so I know you've had your share of problems, but the kids are all right and you too.

I have got to tell you what I have been up to, haven't I? We have a really incredible world here. There is so much to do and discover. I've been learning more about my Mind Power, would you believe? I did not realise how much one can do with one's thoughts and if it's a consolation to you, I'll say you were so right when you spoke of it long ago as it seems new to me!

I've looked at what I did when on Earth and saw my life as a dad and husband and teacher etc. It was not too bad over all, I dare say, but it could have been better here and there. You've been a great help you know, without realising it, as you told me things (about the Afterlife) which I'd ignored or rejected, but now that I see it is true, it's easier for me to accept, rather than having to meet them for the first time! We (My dad, mum and I) have been working at piecing together a lot of things so that I can understand them. Now I feel more at ease with it all and know it's all a question of keeping one's Mind focused in the right direction, so that it makes sense and it makes things happen consistently.

There were those longs walks here I went on at first. That's because I needed the freedom of thought and body. I had been trapped in hospital for so long I could not bear it. Now I feel freer and that's what's important. When you knew me I was a little man in his corner of the world. Now I can go where I like if I feel like it, that's what is so wonderful! An example: I left Russian and all that behind. I've forgotten about teaching it, I am through with it! Instead I have travelled all over the world to see other places I had not been to and looked at what they've got there. It's just a question of thinking: "I want to be there" and it happens! It's amazingly easy and wonderful.

When I went to the Pacific Ocean to see what they have got, it was all islands of a rare beauty, which I would have liked to live on if I'd still been there. But there is even more beauty here, so there is nothing lost! I did look out for your brother in New Caledonia *(Note- Comment out of the blue! I had not asked him to do it! Kind of him)*, but I could not quite see him. I may have not been focused enough on him.

You might wonder why I did all this. It is because the freedom we have here is incredible and wonderful. You can actually do anything you like and it can happen, if you see it plainly in your Mind and your heart, so to speak. You have to think of it so clearly for it to happen. I mean your intention and wish have to be clearly defined.

When you first arrive it's all a jumble in your head; it's all regrets and sadness and desire to go back and longings! And confusion too, as there is also the pleasure to be free from pain and hassle and of seeing again in this world all those you'd lost and loved. But all that settles eventually, in a way.

I still miss you all, I still wish I could see you all and hug my kiddos, but I can't and had to accept it for the time being. The garden, where I used to work in at one time in this world, is still here but really it can grow itself - it does not need me at all! If I want to be there I can, but the plants will survive without me as I am only a tool which is not essential. It is not necessary to feed the plants and water them. So I have my plants around, yes, but they are more for decoration and the pleasure to see them than having to work at growing them now! That's the difference. There are also lots of birds and flowers I'd never seen before and it's fun to feel surrounded by beautiful creatures and landscapes.

It can change any time, you know! I can be at the seaside one moment and decide I want to be on a mountain and it changes at once. It's amazing and fun too! (*Brief silence*)... Ah, that's better, I had lost you! Now, as I was saying, I had fun looking at all these different sceneries and did a lot of 'mental walking', so to speak, because it is neither painful nor hard work, it's simple really! But the lack of gravity means you don't dread a fall like one does on Earth; being on a mountain is always dicey on Earth, you could fall a long way down - like I nearly did once! But here you need not fear anything, just enjoy the beauty and the wonderful feelings one has when one is free from any hassle and pain.

That's what I have been doing most of the time here. My mum and dad came sometimes. At others I went on my own to clear my Mind of the stuff which clogged it. I had to sort out my thoughts and I feel better for it now. It was a long walk which clinched it. I had to have a long stroll to see where I was heading for. I was going to a new world in my head but I had to accept it and to accept it was hard at first, as I wanted to go back to help the children, see them and hug them and love them.

Yet it is so difficult to figure out why one is so churned inside; it is a big muddle and you have to think of one thing at a time, weigh it and sort of discard it to one side, like 'solve it' in a way; it had its days. But I won't be able to explain that well as it's all to do with feelings and impressions.

Finally, after my long Soul-searching walk I felt so much better, because I had come to terms with myself here and myself as a person which I didn't always know. I looked at myself bit by bit and saw I had sides I had not thought about before or known about. So I went on walking, sorting them out. That's what I have done for a long while, I think! Now the main part left to do is to understand how everything here works. It's so incredible to think just **Minds and thoughts make this world exist**! I can't quite get my head round this point.

There is a light you can see but which has no source! There are waves of beautiful colours appearing in the 'air', so to speak, but there are no reasons for this to happen! There are sounds you hear but no source for them and so on! It's incredible! I've asked people around and they are beginning to explain to me what causes all this, but it's hard to grasp as a Human from Earth. It's as if there are magic tricks all around and someone is laughing because you don't know who does it or how it is done. No one is laughing really, but it feels as if I should know why it's there and I don't always. It has, no doubt, to do with Mind and thoughts and other people etc...(*Brief silence*)... The link between us got broken again. It's a pity as it makes it laborious to get going again.

What I was trying to tell you is that it's constantly changing around me, in the sense that if I think of something it will happen. That's why I've learnt and am learning not to think of several things one after the other, otherwise there is like a 'traffic jam' of thoughts and happenings. You can't believe what a shambles it can create! So it is a constant lesson in Mind control to make sure nothing overlaps something else! But it is fun too and it is very interesting, I must say. All I have to do is know what I am thinking about, instead of letting my thoughts wander and them creating havoc around me. Can't think of much more to say on that!

I have made progress in many areas and am learning to constantly send you all thoughts of love and good luck. That is something important you need to know because I don't want you to think I have forgotten you lot! I am still 'Dad' and Dave to you and I am not going away anywhere you could not reach me. So it's important that you know this. I have not gone out of your lives as it may seem. **I am still within reach,** even though it's not as easy as on the phone or a visit. But we have our thoughts for each other to link us: you think of me and I think of you all! That's all I'd like to say on that, because it has so much emotion in itself and it's painful if one starts thinking what could have been if only I'd stayed on Earth etc. But you will be all right, I know, you'll be looked after and I can only stay here and wait for you to come over one day. So that's fine, just like my mum and dad waited for me to arrive here - to my great surprise!

BR- What do your mum and dad do?
They have their own occupations, so to speak. We all have our own pastimes, therefore it's all different for everyone. We do what feels right at the time; there is no obligation to do anything or go anywhere! It's freedom, holiday time here but no bills to pay, no flights to catch, just do what you want all the time. Then you look back and think: "Oh! I've learnt something new! That's fun!"

When we meet we exchange 'notes', we share with each other our adventures or happenings. It's all in the learning of new experiences. Nothing is boring, everything is useful or interesting and not stale, that's what makes it great. I could not do with repeat programmes on TV, it was so boring! But here nothing is repeated like that. It's always fresh and new and interesting. That's why I am happy to go along with the experience and live it to the full, to know what's next and what it leads to. That's all one can say about life here. As I walk along I see things I'd never seen before and I examine them.

BR- Can you give me an example?
For example, birds of a new kind, or flowers and trees. Also, people I had never met before who tell me of their own experiences, both on Earth and here, how long they have been there, but not in the sense of 'Time', more an extent of their Knowledge. Some of them have a lot to say and they explain things very well to make it easy to understand, or easier!

But I have my own old friends too whom I meet sometimes. Those I knew on Earth, whether at school, college or neighbours etc. - and my family of course. Uncle Alfred is still at it with flowers now and then, but like me he has learnt to do other things. I know it is difficult to explain in words what we do, because we do more with our Minds and thoughts and emotions than with our arms and legs (which we don't really have after all, do we?).

So this is only a general 'report', if you like, of how I fare here, to let you know all is well in a way. I have not got lost! I think of you but carefully... because I have to make sure I don't let the emotion of being parted swamp all over me again. I miss you and still love you all, as always and I hope you think of me too, so that we don't lose our link. We can rest assured it won't get broken because I'll never forget any of you, so I'll keep it going anyway!

It's a strange world to be here but it is all worth it in the end, all the more since it is a real world, not an airy-fairy affair! We know we are here, you know I am here, so I won't go far... and I'll see you all again one day. You can be sure of that now because **I** am telling you from this side!

(2.30am. I then give Dave latest news of our children, me, his sister Marion and her husband Keith. It is important to understand that long conversation above [or most of it being a 'monologue'!] was at a constant flow. Dave passed from one subject to the other as he was thinking aloud! He was trying to let us know what he's been up to and how he felt and feels, because he knew that's what we wanted to know and also he is full of his amazing new experience, evidently! Who would not be? I did not interrupt him. A couple of times either he or I lost our concentration (he has to concentrate his thoughts hard in my direction for me to receive them) but I never knew what he would say next!

1st January 2008 - 14.40 hrs. *After a few doodles, the pen starts in English. My Guide is there.*

'Last year', in your terms, was quite a good one for you in many ways; you've achieved much more! You are not to fear the new one to come now, it's going to be even better! It has a lot of potential as always, it's up to you to make things happen. Focus on what you want to do and achieve, tell yourself that's what you wish to be able to do, as it makes you feel fulfilled. All is up to you, in your hands, as we cannot impose anything on you - you have your Free Will. You decide, we guide, then the light will be an inner light of knowing it is 'right' for you. That way you'll be on the right path. It's so easy when you know how to understand your own Self, so simple indeed! Just focus within, that's all.

BR- Why was I born with such an active Mind, since it causes me trouble for this work?!

We see the Mind like very thick, multiple layers of thoughts. They intermingle with each other, jump from one layer to the next and it means one cannot track them down easily! So, at times, we have problems reaching you. The choice of personality was and is yours! **You** decided it would be so! It could not be anyone else's decision; you had to make the choice! It could only be good for you to learn to pass from one state of Mind to another. It's simply a question of learning to adjust the volume, intensity and direction of your thoughts. You had to learn that it was 'meant to be', as you'd say.

When you want to receive 'messages' for someone, you've learnt to listen intently and ignore the rest around you. That way we can talk to you better, in a more precise way, with more information for the person you speak to. You know everyone is always keen to communicate, you can rely on that! We love to link up with you all, as it is a good learning experience for us and a way to help you all whenever we can. It is a special experience, believe me, we do not treat it lightly!

229

There is someone here close to you, who is always ready to speak - your mum. She is always so keen, we cannot stop her, even if we wanted to! It is not unusual to have that inner excitement; it is in fact very natural! There she is! (*Swift change and French is spoken*). Mum here, Sweetheart! You've made progress with all your manuscript typing! I was told you worked hard at it!

BR- Indeed. I had to translate all the French conversations into English, type and check them! Now tell me about yourself please?

I made some progress too in my new 'kingdom'. I've tackled loads of other experiments and exercises. I moved forward at each step. The hardest things to do are the ones when one has to think in a different way and not forget to sense impressions one receives at the same time. It's very important to pay attention to our own impressions and emotions as they provide us with lots of information.

So, this is what I have been concentrating recently. It is much easier to make an object I think about appear than to analyse and sort out my volatile thoughts and impressions! But it is also there that experience shows up and where the pleasure of a job well done stands out more and more as it is done successfully! (*This is followed by a discussion on private matters*).

(*During the night of January 8th, I had a very lucid dream of meeting Mum. We hugged and I had a wonderful feeling we were 'melting into each other'. Obviously our Energies were blending through our loving closeness. It felt very real. Throughout January, whenever I tuned in, my special Friends from Beyond dictated even more knowledge they want included in their book 'T, L & D'. So I had little time for any other communications*).

230

20th February 2008 - *My Guide comes unexpectedly to give me some reassuring news.*

You will be starting a 'new venture', if you want to call it that, as soon as you are free and able to sustain the pace. You are on the right road to a new way of living. You won't be teaching French for too long now, you'll see!

BR- I hope it's not my 'subconscious' just saying this!

We are not your subconscious my dear! You know that! You have been wishing so much to activate the final stage of your action plan for Earth life linked to 'Spirit World work', as you call it, that we wanted to let you know you are on the right path and will be doing so before long, for a long time.

You desire to get rid of the language teaching because you want to work for us and with us. This **will trigger a series of happenings,** which will bring you what you want deep down. We can only tell you the way things look at the moment: You are on the road to doing a little French teaching for a short while but it will come to an end because you will want to put a stop to it! That's how it should be, as always, from desire to reality, from wish to happening on Earth. You can see it happen if you keep the desire alive, the fire burning and the result in Mind, as that is the secret of success!!

Look after your health, you have to catch up with your lack of sleep. Your eyes will rest and your Mind will feel better. Be of cheer, the new life you wish for is just round the corner!

*(Throughout March and the weeks after, the few times I managed to tune in my Evolved Teachers and Friends from Beyond took over as they carried on with the dictation of their book of knowledge. On **11th May**, I tripped over some steps in the Spiritualist Centre's car park and literally dived forward head first, crashing down full body length on the tarmac further down! As I scrambled to my feet, I was amazed my*

231

legs and arms were not smashed, especially at my age! As my head had hit the ground, all I could think was to check [in a car side mirror!] to see whether I still had a face! Surprisingly I did, even though my cheekbone had hit the tarmac with force. Apart from skin scratches, a swollen big toe with a sore blackened nail for some weeks and an arm aching for a few days (but not broken!), I was astonished my cheekbones, nose and jaw were undamaged. In fact, I was flabbergasted to be in one piece and to walk away from this incredible collision with solid tarmac! People kept saying to me: "You've been so lucky!").

14th May 2008 - 14.20 hrs. *Sitting in a park. English is spoken first.*

Lots of people here, as usual, ready and prepared to talk to you. We are all willing! The main person today will be your mum as she's been waiting for a long time to have a chance to chat and tell you what she's been doing. You can talk to her now. *(Swift change of communicators as French is spoken).*

My Darling! At last! How happy I am, once more! You see, I always try to speak with you if I can!

BR- I love you, Mum.

I love you too, Sweetheart. I await your arrival here (a long time ahead!) by keeping myself busy learning lots of new things! I have made an inventory of my Earthly occupations throughout various lives, including the one when you have known me. I realise I spent a lot of time teaching myself new things, over centuries I suppose. Perhaps that's why I used to say to you all: "Do not waste your time! Learn something!"

The last life I have been looking at closely was one spent in Asia, in Japan, I think. I was there as an explorer and was interested in Japanese art, sculpture and buildings. I don't know why I wanted to do that, as now it feels rather weird, but I must admit it was interesting in those days.

I had no idea the Japanese would become our enemy one day. As happens with all wars: people like each other then hate each other, fight, then make up or at least are on speaking terms again! There is so much to say about the horrors of wars and similar 'lawful murders'! It's ever so awful and sad.

I discovered something else when I was a man in that country and that life: I wanted to do things 'my way', as your Dad used to say. Well, 'my way' was to find out what people liked doing which was different from what was done elsewhere. So I would explore, going from country to country. I would watch, take notes and I thus learnt quite a lot that way. I have always had a taste for adventures with journeys and discoveries ever since, but that life was really very special as I was able to observe the whole world, or at least a good part of it. I learnt ever so much! Now I only see the main points which help me understand myself to know what I like doing, what I learnt and why I wanted to do it.

BR- It seemed to be enjoyable!

Oh yes, I did enjoy it at the time and I can now see I loved it through the impressions I am left with. The actual facts I learnt are not as important as the impressions, the extension and opening of Mind it helped and allowed me to have! I could see the world bigger than it was from the point of view of someone who lives in his little village and never gets out of it! So this is why I had chosen that traveller's life, as an explorer of human lives and also of unknown lands! It is really indelible and cannot be erased from my memory and the 'subconscious of my Spirit'!

We have to become aware of what we love doing, why and how it may have affected other lives and people with whom we have lived. There have been many other lives 'before' and 'after', of course, but I must analyse them as to their 'psychological and spiritual interest', if you see what I

233

mean? There are always reasons for choosing one life or the other, you understand? It is not a lottery; **we have chosen it in order to learn or practise something, to enrich one's Spirit and Soul**. Not just to have temporary human pleasures. That is why I am doing this at the moment.

BR- This is fascinating Mum. Unfortunately I'll have to stop listening for now as I need to leave. I am very sorry. I'll try again later if you can come back. (Later on that evening, I tried to link up again. Mum was there like a shot!)

The little interruption was not terrible, Darling. I knew you had to leave therefore it was not a problem. So, as I was telling you, I had quite a lot of 'adventures'! We study and analyse ourselves to see why we chose those particular lives and what we did which was of interest to our Soul and Spirit. In fact, it's a kind of self-examination - examining one's conscience to see whether we did some good or harm and how it was of use 'later on', one could say.

I saw I really had to learn to live alone and not depend on other people, yet at times other people interested me as far as cultures and customs were concerned. Therefore, that is what made me take an interest in history later on, I mean during my life with you, because I wanted to see how facts and events linked up, were transformed into causes and consequences.

It's good to analyse oneself like this, it does help you understand yourself! I could say the most interesting thing is the fact that there is no time to feel sorry for one's fate, either now (for having left you all behind), or 'before', when one sees lives which really have nothing to do with what one is or how one feels at present! So one cannot think: "Oh, poor me!" In fact it's amusing to watch all this like films in one's head and to gradually understand the development of one's own interests and attitudes!

You'll see, when you to come over here, you'll have to do this at one time or the other. You'll notice how strange it feels to perceive oneself as another person, totally different and yet you know her, without knowing why, at the beginning! It's sometimes nearly comical: "That woman over there was me? Yuk!" Well yes, there are times when one does not like what one sees in some cases. Yet it has not often been the case for me up to now, fortunately!

I also intended to tell you there have been some discussions about you and your books. They realised they gave you some very difficult work which took you a long time and gave you a lot of work. They are sorry in a way. They realised they had to pay attention to how they presented it to facilitate things for you. So they promised themselves to dictate the rest into chapters more defined and coherent, as they say. It's nice to have guides helping you to do things as well as possible! They are very keen for it to be published as soon as possible. That's why they don't want you to be fed up or lose patience or courage!

BR- I still have yours to carry on typing and translating too!

There is indeed so much to do. It sounds more like chores than pleasure doesn't it?!

BR- No! The knowledge and information are so fascinating! Can you ask about my stopping my teaching job? Will it cause me financial problems?

They tell me the answer does not come easily: "There is a question of division of loyalties".

BR- What do they mean by that?

The reply they give me is: The lady you work for has problems and will probably be annoyed you are abandoning her, but she will have a solution soon. You must therefore make her understand that it's not just the work at the college which makes you unhappy and that **you also need to have some peace and quiet in your life.**

BR- Why do they talk of "division of loyalty"?

The division is within yourself. You had to make efforts to calm yourself down, to see Earthly life from a new perspective recently. You had to come to understand that work with money as a goal is not always the work one has to put up with if it does not bring peace of Mind. Therefore, one must undergo an 'inner examination' and see what is worth it. You have finally made the decision yourself, instead of being told. You had to do it yourself so as not to have any doubts within.

BR- I still have some, in case I am making a 'financial mistake'!

One cannot live just to earn money 'in case one may need some'. **One must live to have peace of Mind and Soul,** so that it is worth living and to keep oneself in good health! There is no other solution!

If the Soul is unhappy, physical health will deteriorate. So why bother, hey?

BR- Please sum up their reply then?

The result that **you** have chosen is the one which will bring you more peace of Mind, rather than staying and doing something which makes you unhappy and delays you with your work for the books.

Those books are **very important** to us and to all of you on Earth. So they say the reply is: "Bravo for having at last had the courage to make the choice!" You did worry and torture your Mind, didn't you, to know what to do for the best? Yet the answer was and is obvious: One must always do what seems to be the best for the Mind, the mental and emotional well-being, so that the final result does some good rather than the opposite. *(I had recently taken the plunge and retired from teaching local adult education classes after doing it for many decades. But I still have my teaching position at York St John University).*

So, I hope this will help you, won't it? As for me, I no longer need to worry of such things. I am really glad as they can become a nightmare!

BR- Thanks Darling Mum. Anything else to say about your 'new' life?

The anniversary of my death is coming soon, I gather. I must have been here for quite a long time?

BR- Nine years next month. I feel ashamed your book is not ready to publish yet.

I am talking about it because I can see that since my arrival I have really been doing heaps of new and interesting things. I have not only discovered a new world but also aspects of previous lives (and probably of 'future' lives, one day!) which I had never imagined could exist! I would never have believed that some day I'd come and talk to you from my world of 'deceased people' to you on Earth, to tell you I saw myself reincarnated in what I'd call 'previous' lives - and that I am learning extraordinary things! It was worth 'dying' to be able to do that!

Now Sweetheart, you should get some rest. You will be or have been staying up far too long. You must sleep to catch up and recover from all the stress you've had lately. We know what goes on where you are - we see it in what you call your 'aura', I would say, in the light given out by your Soul. So I hug and kiss you with all my love, my little Darling. Be very careful and look after your body, my dearest!

BR- Actually I fell down the other day.

Yes! I know. I was told you had a **nearly fatal fall**! But we did not let that happen because you need to finish your work on Earth, therefore everyone here had to protect you! You were extremely 'lucky'! **You have no idea to what extent they helped you!**

BR- Wow! Thanks! What did they do?!

The only way I can explain it from here is by saying they wrapped you in a 'cushion' or 'envelope' of Love to protect you. You landed **within** a cocoon of 'cotton wool' made of Love...the love of your 'guide' and helpers, your family and all those who love you and look after you. They saw it 'happen' and protected you, covered you and enveloped you in a kind of thick, cosy duvet. I learnt about it afterwards. I would not have wanted to see it occur as I would have been far too scared of what could have happened to you.

BR- Millions of thanks to everybody from the bottom of my heart! I feel humble and honoured. Another incentive to tackle my Spirit 'book work'!

Now please go to sleep my little Darling, or you'll look tired tomorrow!

BR- Lots of kisses to you, darling Mum. I hope my Mind won't be too tired to join you during my sleep.

Loving kisses to you too. Do come over if you can.

24th May 2008 - *On the train from London, my Guide pops in (without a train ticket!). I have just had a weekend at my daughter's where I was unexpectedly offered a health check and food sensitivity tests.*

We are going to say something which may or may not surprise you. You have been inspired during the times and days

238

of your trip so that you could do just that - find out what you need for your physical health, so that your mental and emotional health can improve, which is essential to your work with us and for your well-being all around. We knew we had to guide you to do something positive to help yourself. Hopefully you'll now see the great need for quiet, peace of Mind and less rushing around.

If you had been told by us:"Give up your job", you may have thought we were telling you what to do and ruling your life.

BR- No! Just wondering about possible money problems if I do.

We cannot tell people what to do but we can inspire them, to help them find out what the best thing would be for them for the time being, for their well-being. It is not essential to give up that job, but because to you it is stressful at the best of times, then it would be wiser to get rid of it, for the sanity of your Mind and its own inner peace!

BR- Now I need the courage to tell my University boss the bad news!

Let's start again then: Once you have done all you need to tidy up your 'loose ends', you'll feel much lighter and freer! You'll be able to open up more often to our world and we'll be able to speak to you more frequently, we hope, to find out what else you may want to learn, as well as what else we can teach you to educate the world!

There is a great need to rest, you see. **You have to rest.** You have been silly to push yourself too much, be too stressed. Then you wonder why you have health problems now, which acknowledge the very fact that your Soul and Spirit are shaken and necessarily have a repercussion on the flesh body!

239

When the body of Matter has to reflect the real body of Light, what do you think will look dark or dulled up if the Light inside has trouble shining? Of course, the body of Matter, since it is a reflection of what is going on in the Real You. When you have a decision to make, you cannot make it if there is a tear or a pull between the two bodies - it is unsettling. When the tear or pull is removed or reduced, then the match fits better and the road looks straightforward and the decision is made more easily.

You'll find you'll have to take more care of your body, but these details are only on the physical level. You can and must work on your emotional level, as this is where all the stress is from and lies. It is essential to release pent-up emotions and seek a peaceful way of doing things and facing facts or people or situations! You have to learn to be more at peace within and we'll all win in the process! So that's where you are now. Let's hope you'll get good results out of it.

We now need to tell you there is someone who's been waiting to talk to you for quite a while, very patiently it seems, but also very impatiently because she wants to have a word or two with you. She is your own mum of course! There she is. *(Silence follows for quite a while, then French is spoken).*

Hello Dearest, we had some trouble linking up, didn't we? But I am here and so are you, all is fine. Let's try not to get cut off. I was told you had quite a few 'happenings' lately.

BR- What do you mean?
You made trips and met people. You also seem to have faced facts that we knew about for a long time! You must, absolutely must, rest more and not waste time in between! That way you'll be able to achieve much more than you've done up to now! If you rest more, you will be less easily irritated and you'll see the results will be worth it. We'll have more conversations together and you'll talk to Dad too, no doubt,

240

and to your Dave... and your guides, who have plenty to tell you and teach you! So your books will 'go great guns', all will be well and your life plan (as you call it) will finally be completed one day!

I wanted to tell you that you did well to want to stop work, as it will be the beginning of a series of useful events. Useful to your development on Earth, you'll see. When you have finished my book, you'll have others coming! This is what you have to do - teaching other people the truths you are learning from our world over here. You will be very pleased to be able to do all that!

BR- Does that include giving people 'messages' from their loved ones?

Messages are always very useful of course, you'll be able to do that, but you must first work at our books, so that they are all finished in time with the rest...(*The train compartment becomes noisy with new arrivals, I lose the link for a moment. But Mum comes back on line*).... We'll have other opportunities to talk if you have problems now. It is indeed a distracting and noisy environment from what I feel via you.

We can tell you that the work you will do for other people, thanks to our friends here, will be extremely useful and you will be proud of the results when you get them! They are telling me all this because they wish everything to happen as planned. Get on with the work as you receive it so that you are not late for the flow which will come! It is important to be constantly up to date. Otherwise it's a big batch to catch up with each time and it causes stress. You see, we can feel what you do and how you feel! So, it's essential to organise yourself well so as not to delay yourself. That's it.

BR- Any news from your side?

My own mum is still very busy with her work with the young children she helps. Yes, with those who arrive here feeling rather lost as they don't know where their parents are. But we have ways of making them understand they are still alive and they will see their parents again one day, if they want to. Mum has always liked children, so she is good at that.

As for me, I still have a lot of work to do on myself. I must 'discover' myself more, I am told! That means I understand myself to a greater extent or better and better, by seeing what I did or have been during various eras. People around me had or have had similar experiences, so we compare them and help each other. It is interesting to discover oneself and also make new friends by getting to know others better and better. Japan was only one of the countries I went to long ago...

(Unfortunately my train arrived at my destination, so I had to stop and hurry to get off! Then over the next fortnight my tuning was taking over by my Evolved Teachers dictating more of their book of Knowledge. I also gathered my courage and retired completely from all teaching of French!)

****

My mum Suzanne – 16 years old

Mum at 30

Mum
in her
thirties

My mum & dad – Suzanne & Nicolas

Mum 90 years old – April 1999 –
8 weeks before her passing

My grandma's mother Elenore Moleux

My grandma's father
Edmond Moleux

My grandma Léonie Moleux Leclercq

My grandpa Léon Leclercq & pets

My husband Dave Rix

Our children Jim & Anne-France

The Rix family (left to right): my son Jim, me (Brigitte),
my daughter Anne-France and my husband Dave

My eldest brother Pierre (passed away in 2009) and me in Nice.

Alex Brown

My younger brothers (left to right), Michel 'Mich', myself and Jean-Nicolas 'Touky'.

CHAPTER 5

Dad's mysterious sound - Our Oversoul/Higher Self decides - Baggage of regrets - A robin for Love - A thread through one's lives - No real feeling of 'Time'

2nd July 2008 - 11.40 hrs. *My Guide started in English, to introduce someone.*

You are more rested now. We are online to speak to you if you wish. You asked a question about your father. He's busy but here. He'll talk to you if you desire. It's been a 'long time' since he last did, he says, though 'time' is really meaningless to us. You've been waiting a long while for this. You have his words coming after mine. Here he is... *(French is spoken shortly afterwards)*. Dad here now! Yes it's me indeed! I give you a big kiss too my darling daughter of one of my lives! It's terrible to have all those lives: we end up nearly losing our bearings, with all those different personalities! Yet it is extremely interesting! I made lots of trips in Time and space too, as I saw myself in diverse countries through various eras.

But it's not what I wanted to talk to you about this time. I want to tell you something completely different: You are going to do slightly new things, not just writing books for us here. You need more time to yourself, peaceful and quiet time in order to listen better to what comes to your Mind! It is very important to be able to listen and answer people who come and talk to you of my new world here. It is very imperative. So you must have some quiet much more often and get used to hearing the voices more quickly. It's not that difficult if you practise more, that's all!

BR- What do they want to do?

They say the first thing is for you to be in silence and open to receive. You must have an increasingly better reception so that they can come much closer to you. You will then see there will be changes, additions to what you can do up to now.

247

There will be someone who wants to talk to you personally to teach you more facts. There'll also be another person who will come to make you talk on his behalf, that is to say, so that he can speak 'through' you, by using you *(Note- In an altered state of consciousness for Overshadowing/Inspired speaking)*.

It would be really good if you could carry on with practising this. It's vital to concentrate in silence, to let the communicator speak via you, without being interrupted so he can talk in one constant flow about a topic he chooses. It's very good practice to let him do what he wants as he wishes, because he has ideas in Mind which he needs to communicate without being interrupted. You'll see that the flow will be much better and eloquent, with well sustained and defendable ideas, without any errors or doubt, because he knows what he wants to talk about.

There are so many topics they can discuss, so much Knowledge they can and want to pass on, it's incredible and wonderful! There'll be so many exciting topics which you have no idea of at the moment. **That** is what will be your future - yes, your future, to make time to let those who want to talk to you do their work! All you'll have to do is let them do it! You'll see that you'll find all that extremely interesting, intriguing and fascinating - so well that you'll feel like doing it all day long practically, just to obtain even more Knowledge! Then you'll be able to pass it on to other people who in turn will be interested and fascinated. So, you see, if you want it, of course, you will have your work cut out and it will increase as much as you want it to.

BR- It sounds promising, I hope I can live up to it! What about your life Dad?

There is so much I could tell you! What I do here are always very interesting experiences and experiments. I see people whom I did not recognise and who remind me I used to be acquainted with them 'before'. Because I used to know them, there is a link between us. Many of them are in fact very close and some of them were 'Me' in another period. It's quite fun to see ourselves as someone else we didn't know existed, yet it's very useful too as we discover facets we weren't aware we had. There are also and always my experiments in physics as that will never stop! There will always be heaps of things to rediscover, I must say, as I knew them 'before', I think and it seems to me I had forgotten them. Yet if teaches me so much that I shall never stop extending my Knowledge.

BR- Can you give me some examples?
There still is the light from here which fascinates me, but it's a bit clearer now as I know that what creates it comes from those who reside here, so it's more apparent and more logical. I understand it. *(Note- See Vol.1. The ambient Light at that level is the Light of Kindness and Compassion emanating from all the 'residents' there).* But there are other puzzles, other questions, appearing unfathomable to solve at first, yet which get solved gradually as one delves into them carefully.

BR- For instance?
There was a **sound** which I could not comprehend. A sound coming from around me, which was happening every time I went outside. I was wondering what it was! In fact it was a sound in my 'head'! Not that I have a physical head of course but within me. That's what I did not understand at the beginning. It's a sound of happiness, a sound of joy, a sound of satisfaction and well-being! That's what I had not grasped before.

BR- Why did you feel it?
I heard it and felt it because I was happy to go out into

this gorgeous nature we have here, with the most beautiful plants and kinds of animals and ambience you could imagine and even better! One needs to be here to understand it. So, when I was bathing in this atmosphere of happiness, **the sound of joy resounded within me**. That is why I had it in me and it was not outside as I thought at the beginning. Of course they are vibrations, any sound is vibration. But these are vibrations created within the Soul itself, within one's own Self, instead of outside it. One really needs to be here to live it and grasp this!

BR- That's brand new for me. The first time I've heard of this! Any other discoveries?

The friendship you get here is incomparable. You'd never know that on Earth because people there are usually very selfish, or at least think more about themselves than about you. This is why it seems so extraordinary to have people here helping you and making efforts for you, without you asking. It comes from the bottom of their good heart, that's all. Yet that does warm up your Soul! It is not like having 'a good friend' on Earth, not at all like that, it's much, much better!

BR- Good, I am glad for you! Anything else in physics?

There is something I would like to talk to you about. It's your mum's book *(Vol.1 of 'I'm Not Dead')*... It saddens her it is not already published! You know what I mean?

BR- Yes, but on top of that my Teachers insisted on my preparing their own book for publication first!

Yes, we know there is the other one too! But you must get her book done as soon as you can. She wants so much to see it printed and on the shelves of bookshops! It has been one of her great desires ever since she arrived here! So you'll have to work at it more, please!

BR- Yes, I do know how important it is!

Good, that's all I wanted to tell you and remind you. You must do as much as you can, so that it's achieved quickly. Do not waste too much time with earthly activities of no importance. Of course, you must do anything essential or urgent, but don't bother with what is not important, give priority to Mum's and the other book. These are the most urgent. That's what I wanted to remind you to give you the courage to tackle it as soon as possible!

20th August 2008 - 14.40hrs. *I had a question. My Guide came to reply.*

BR- So that readers grasp it better, could you expand on why and when people leave their body?

The Soul of someone who has just passed away is not always aware of why (and even how at times) it has come over 'back home'. It is always a shock to leave one place to go to another. So it is not surprising some say: "They've passed before their time". But: what do they know about their 'right' time?! It is impossible for them to know at that stage!

However, when the Soul has had time to study itself, its aims and goals and desires for that particular life plan, then you'll see it will come round to understanding **why** it has gone from where it was, to come back then, at that particular time, at that period of its life.

As you well know, indeed no one, whether Human or Animal (yes Animals too!), goes out of their own chosen body to leave for the World of Light, as we call it, **unless the Spirit of that Soul was ready**. This is so, even though the personality on Earth may not feel ready and would deny strongly and even vehemently it/she/he wanted to leave others behind! It is usually **impossible for Earthly Beings to admit they were ready to leave their family and loved ones behind.**

251

But on the greater scale of things, when a Soul sees on the horizon of its 'plan' that it has achieved what it had chosen to do, or it had had enough of that place for whatever reason, it has no choice but to want to come back to where it came from.

Overall, a Soul has usually no advance knowledge of its exact time or day of passing, but the degree of the inner desire, the pull from within by its Spirit/its 'Higher Self' wanting to leave that flesh instrument, that Earthly vehicle, will indeed be very strong! That's why the person on Earth will find himself going to a certain place, doing a certain thing or whatever, which will lead him to leave the flesh.

BR- So, if one hundred people are killed in a crash, all wanted to leave their body?

Yes. All wanted to leave their flesh body for their Spirit to be released, to come back fully aware of its goal. All came back because their own individual Spirits had a goal, many goals no doubt and had finished their journey there. The Spirit, the 'Higher Self', wanted to get back to where it came from. So you may also have one thousand or one hundred thousand - it will be the same. All have or had a reason for going out of their body! There may be many reasons for choosing one or another particular way of going. The person may want to make an impact in people's Minds and say: "I have gone as I believed things should be done" or to help others, or to protest against such and such - or just "disappear from your sight so that you do not have me as a burden".

There may be so many different reasons why someone 'dies' in any particular way, but you have to remember the bottom line of it all is: You cannot die at all! No one 'dies', as he is still alive the split thousandth of a second after he has left his flesh body! **He has NOT died. He has changed consistency and appearance** to your Earthly eyes, but he is not dead! Nor is your cat or dog or donkey or snail.

BR- Could you explain about people in a coma for years?

If we told you they are in 'no man's land' it may upset a lot of people. Yet it is true. They have chosen to be in 'suspended animation'. A person who, say, had an accident and stopped living as a Human on Earth - just staying as a body alive but not reacting as a personality - is a very traumatic experience for those around 'him' and even for himself. This is because he is no longer aware of anything as such, since **his Mind and Soul chose** to be in 'no man's land' for a while.

Such people choose it, so their **Minds create it**. They see themselves as nothing in a way, yet it's not quite correct. They do not actually think they are 'nothing', they just stop thinking for a while. They have taken a break from anything and everything. They have suspended all activities. Possibly because their Minds were overworked, or over burdened, or even confused with their lives overall. It's hard to know why a person does it - it's their own Mind creating it!

The accident or incident which caused the rupture of a normal life was **not** 'unplanned'! It will have been **subconsciously craved for,** to give the person a breathing space, a moment of non-committal, a suspension of activities. It was no doubt needed by the Mind and Soul, even if others cannot see it like that! No one can really see within anyone's Soul and thinking. So 'he' will have taken the opportunity to escape, to refresh his batteries and take a breather. That's what it's for. Since his body had not died, it may be possible to **bring him back** to normal activities, if his Soul and his Mind accept to do so.

If the brain has been so damaged that the man won't be able to function, then it is very unlikely he will recover or come out of his blank state. He will just slip out of the whole body and will be at rest where he was meant to be in the first place: The World of Mind and Light. He may have wanted to know that experience, or his family and friends may have chosen to be part of that sad 'experiment' too. All are their own, private decisions. *(Note- All Humans choose to experience various conditions as part of their various life plans. If we only knew 'daylight' we would never grasp what 'nightime' is!)* Any attempts to bring him back will **fail if the Soul has decided** to leave the body under the guidance and directions of his Higher Self.

But it may be possible to bring him back if the solution has been found by the Soul; if he has regained his inner balance and appreciated or gained from the mental break, the self-imposed 'suspension. He will then react to memories or calls from those around him, who encourage him to wake-up. But that's always a personal decision, only taken by the person involved as he lies there in his bed or wherever. It is not to be worried about as such.

All that can be done from your side on Earth is to send him a lot of Healing, to give his Soul and therefore Mind the calm needed to make the right decision for him. And also send Healing to the family and close ones who may be suffering from that unsettling state of affairs. All Healing given works, as it always has an effect on the inner personality before you can possibly see any results physically on the flesh.

If he slips out of his flesh body and 'dies' even though Healing has been given, that shows that the **Healing Energies gave the personality the strength and courage to make the right decision for himself**, for his plans in that particular life.

**15th September 2008 - ** *14hrs. Mum had told me she had met and seen my Guide as a 'very knowledgeable young looking sage'. Her impression was he may have been from ancient Roman or Greek days. I questioned him about that.*

About your question to do with my possible appearance as an 'ancient person', as your mother said. I have been 'visible'

254

as many different people because I have lived many different lives as 'time went by', as you would say. You have to understand the 'appearance' is only superficial and also is possibly in the Mind of the beholder. So, if **she felt** I was a 'knowledgeable sage of olden days', by her reckoning I might have 'appeared' to her as such. It is not necessary to have a physical appearance of any kind (in my world), as you know well! It's only a convenience for those who need to 'see' something to make their surroundings more 'real' and 'solid'. But this is not essential, so we are back to what I was saying: If you want to see or sense me as a young or old 'sage', you are welcome. But you had not known me as that! In our days together you had the same garb and situation as me - we were poor and even destitute in our Earthly goods, but not so poor in our mental and even spiritual outlook! We could have learnt more but that was extra to what we had to do. So we could not really be labelled as 'sages' for that particular period.

BR- Have you ever been a 'Roman/Greek etc. 'sage', or even not a sage?

There have been so many lives and that's to talk the way you do (as an Earthling!) as all lives still exist now, as you know. But as I am not concentrating on or experiencing them as such, we could call them 'in the past'. There have been periods in a lot of periods, so I would not worry about having to trace them or think about them.

It is what is emanating from you as an individual that matters. Not what you have been or not been. It is the **lesson learnt,** the results achieved, which count, not the whereabouts of the teaching time!

The main point of our conversation, my dear, is to tell you that you need not worry about who I have been or could have been 'before' or 'after', because what matters is what you are getting now (as far as 'now' is concerned for you!). We are

255

together because you need to have some kind of guidance now and then in this particular Earth life you've chosen. We cannot do much with 'past' and 'future' lives since **your 'now' is what matters to both of us**. So we both live it for that! You'll have plenty of 'time' later on, when you are back here, should you wish to do so, to explore what you and I have been elsewhere, if we have done so.

You can only concentrate on what is of importance to your development now, my dear, because you have ever so much to do and see to, you could not digress from your line of thought and work. You cannot waste time on other 'pursuits' because they would lead you away from or delay your present and essential work! We can only follow the path of a straight arrow to be on the right track, to achieve anything. That is why I am here as an 'Inspirer', if you care to listen to my suggestions!

28th September 2008 - *At a workshop on 'Mediumistic Development' somebody (on Earth) declared that our "Guide comes to the right side of the brain and we should breathe in through each chakra (Energy centre) from the front and visualise the Energy being breathed out of the back of the chakra etc..." So I decided to check what my evolved Spirit Teachers thought of all this.*

Let's start with the common knowledge that we are all Spirits, you and I! So we can blend with each other simply because we are a 'light' and you too are a 'light', to use Earthly words. If you wish to think we come from one side or the other or whatever it will be fine because it makes no difference in the end! What happens is that our (respective) thoughts blend. For our thoughts to blend we have to be on the same wavelength. That means you have to send to us thoughts which reflect our 'wave of thinking' and this wave of yours will link up with ours and there will be a bond, a blending.

BR- Could you clarify a bit more please?

Our thoughts are the ones 'coming down' to you while you try to reach us and our level or wavelength of thinking. If you try to link with us, we need you to focus hard on what you are trying to achieve, that means reaching us. So you need to be on the same wave length as us, which is a more refined and precise level of vibrations. When you have elevated and refined your own wavelength so that you can reach us, we in turn, but at the same time, try to 'lower' ours, so that it is not too hard for you to reach us. We make efforts too to find a suitable level where we can both meet.

That way your 'wave of thinking' reaches our 'wave of thinking'- or wavelength- and we can both blend with each other and communicate. It is just a question of focusing your Mind on what you are trying to achieve as we do the same. Our wave reaches yours. If yours has got fairly similar vibrations and refinement, we'll both have contact with each other and succeed in exchanging thoughts. We have to blend with each other. Is that clearer?

When the blending occurs, no matter where you are or what you are doing, as long as the concentration is on us and on that wavelength, you'll be able to sense us, whether hearing, seeing or whatever! So the diverse 'methods' of blending can suit various individuals in different ways, but we have to say - **it does not matter to us how you do it!** What matters is that you do it. You do it in order to blend with us (not to think of something else) and THAT is what causes and creates the link to occur, as your Mind settles in our direction, at our level!

(Note- So all those man-made ways of 'tuning in' are not to be taken as infallible, rigid 'rules'! They are only there as tips to help you focus).

We send Energies towards you so that you can blend with them more easily and ours with yours. But the result will totally depend on your quiet Mind and receptivity, on your willingness and desire to be at one with us. We need your total inner and outer attention for this to work well. If you divert your attention, your Mind and brain will come in with their own ideas and memories and create a muddle if you don't watch it! That's all you need to know for this.

BR- It must be frustrating for you when we Earthlings lose our concentration when tuning in!

All that is needed is to stay mentally with us. The link to your world is a series of fine vibrations from our Minds to yours. So if you put other vibrations in it, i.e. other thoughts, they chase ours out! Then you always find it difficult to linkup again and we do too, because the link to us is a very fine line between various moments of your (current) life and your other lives! We constantly need to check where we are, to keep in touch with the 'you' you are 'now' compared to the 'you' in some other 'times', or more exactly, some **other levels of focus**!

You can stay in yours more easily if you listen constantly on the same frequency. To know which frequency you are at, you simply need to say to yourself: "I am in my 'here and now' and want to stay in this here and now for the time being".

We can decipher your signals according to your emissions and volume or intensity. If we have to keep looking for you, it weakens the link and the flow of knowledge or information given to you. It would be much easier if it could always stay on the same level. We know it is hard for you, but it is hard for us too.

(Over the following weeks, whenever I tuned in, my usual Inspirers carried on dictating even more of their book of Wisdom and Knowledge).

26th October 2008 - 11.20 hrs. *Starts in English.*

The lady in this world who loves you so much wishes to be the first one to talk as she wants to celebrate your birthday! She'll come now... *(Amusing that she's somehow aware of it - probably because I had it two days ago - Sudden change over and French is spoken).*

Mum here, Sweetheart. I want to say: "Happy Birthday" to you in person! After all, it is **me** who gave birth to you, isn't it? So I hope you had a good day in spite of all your activities. We watched what you did and you spent your time doing things for Animals.

BR- I was involved in a fundraising day for the Cats Protection & Adoption Centre.

That's good, though it can be hard work! The main thing is that you are not too tired. You need your strength to do what you need to do on Earth as well as your work for us, which is not all rest unfortunately, we do know that! Do you want me to tell you what I have been doing recently?

BR- Of course!

I saw lots of people from 'before' my life with you on Earth, during lives I lived here and there. I had looked at some others before observing these, but it's always so fascinating and fun to discover I had been 'someone else' several times! Reincarnation and all that stuff is true indeed! How I regret not to have really believed you when you spoke about it. This is because I could not understand how one could have been several persons! Anyway, I've experienced it and grasp it now! I can see that I have indeed been a bit everywhere to teach myself many a thing.

The first one I analysed was when the lady I was did not have many 'spiritual ideas', I would say! She knew nothing about the Great Beyond or any concept of a 'God' etc. Of

259

course, she knew one died but did not believe one would go to 'somewhere better'. She thought life stopped after the death of the flesh body! So it must have given her a shock when she arrived here!

That woman did not actually do any harm when she was alive; she lived for her family and her activities - but I reckon she didn't do anything extraordinary. She wanted to be on the Earth to experience what it was like to be a woman, instead of a man as she'd been before, but nothing fantastic came out of it. I think I saw her to remind me we don't know everything and not always what there is to learn about one's 'spiritual origins'. It's difficult to grasp that someone who was a' Spirit' goes off to live on Earth and forgets he was a 'Spirit' Being and no longer believes in any Afterlife and the Great Beyond!

This is why I was shown that particular life, to make me understand that I too had done the same thing at one time. I wanted to grasp why one could not recall that aspect so easily! My helpers replied: "The Soul **wanted to know what it's like to rediscover those truths,** whereas when one is here one knows about it all and takes it for granted. She had learnt it at one church or the other, but did not agree with what she was told. She preferred to keep her own ideas and not accept what others told her, because she saw no logic whatsoever in their arguments or rather in the ideas they were imposing! But she learnt what she wanted out of that life and subsequently she came back here".

I then saw another life. Only one aspect as usual, as seeing a whole life would probably be boring or useless sometimes! The person I was 'introduced to' in a way (it's always done with the help of other people who guide me during those inner journeys) was an old man. I saw him in his advanced years because that is where the lesson was, or is, if you prefer.

That man had lived to a ripe old age, upset not to have achieved anything sensational! He had brought up a large family and wondered why he spent all his time earning some pennies, very few sometimes, to look after and support a family who was not always grateful after all! He had done his best but could not see why and what it was for, in a way. He would have liked to create or invent something, but all he did was his family duties. Then, when he grew older, he was too exhausted to do anything 'worthwhile', as he said.

So that's another facet of my personality. I have perhaps seen it to make me understand that to bring up **a family is not a waste of time,** but an extension and enlargement of qualities which one may not have developed enough previously, without realising it. *(Note- Mum used to think she'd done nothing special in her recent life with me, as she had "only been a mother at home"!)*

The main points of the lessons learnt throughout our Earthly lives are displayed in front of us, as what I could call 'teaching lights'. It's difficult to explain! As everything is impressions, feelings, lights or shadows, by looking at them we understand there was, or is, a lesson, an explanation and some teaching to extract from it. This is why, from time to time, we examine our various lives which have something to do with what we are doing at the moment, or what we are thinking of ourselves at present. What matters is that **lessons learnt long ago, must now be reflected** in your way of thinking.

If we have not learnt anything out of all those other lives, we have really wasted our time! Yet I reckon it does not quite happen like this, as surely we must have learnt something (else?) from at least one or the other of our trips on Earth! This is what I wanted to let you know, since I am aware the topic of reincarnation used to interest you. It's a way of telling you more on the subject. I am being shown **snippets** of my own lives, when I was not, or not yet, your mum like I was this time round. We must have met before that and liked each other enough to want to be together once more, I reckon!

I want to tell you something else! My 'old lady in the past', I mean the old lady I was in another era, showed herself in a different way. She had children but she did not look after them as much as I did with you all. She had other activities which preoccupied her more. This is what I was shown from a different angle. I had always been concerned in case I was not doing enough for the four of you this time round! But I was shown **she** did not behave that way, she did not really care about it, compared to my 'devotion' towards you (as my friends here call it). So, this reassured me. I probably was not such a bad mother after all!

BR- Of course not! On the contrary! You were and still are wonderful!

Perhaps I needed reassurance or confirmation? I am not too sure. Anyway, I did it, I was told so and it made me feel better! That's what matters in the end. Because if one feels uncomfortable, guilty or full of regrets, one does not progress - that's what I am told. We need to move on and progress to be happier here. As far as I am concerned, I feel quite happy, except for the fact you are not here, of course. But the rest is fine, in fact it's marvellous! My friends do have their own ideas and I am aware they know much more than me, so their advice is always welcome!

I have also made 'Earthly trips' round the world, as I have already told you. Places which interested me, where I had been unable to go. This proves that what we do here is for our own good. We have to get rid of any regrets, if possible, or **we quench our 'thirst' and desires** in order not to carry them 'round our neck' like a heavy weight! We have fun developing as a Spirit Being rather than a Being of flesh. Since the flesh body slows us down for many a thing, whether because of the action of gravity or because of illnesses, it's a good thing to get rid of such 'nuisance' as we feel so much freer when we've done it! We feel lighter, more 'floating', instead of being weighed down by memories or fears etc. This is why it is Paradise here! Being totally free and light is a wonderful feeling! I do enjoy it here. I wish all of you could too, you poor darlings struggling on the Earth!

Anyway, to come back to and sum up what I was saying: I made journeys into the 'past'(and who knows, perhaps to the future, but I don't think I have seen that yet) in order to get to know myself better and to 'value' myself, as they call it. But also to appreciate what my other lives taught me. **This is why we go and live on the Earth - to learn things that help our Higher Self.** The Higher Self is the 'Real You', who is made up of many personalities who lived and will live elsewhere than here, in our beautiful world of Love and Light.

So now you'll perhaps be able to understand a bit better the reasons for reincarnation, if you did not already know them! It was new for me and is very interesting. I shall no doubt see and find out even more, if they make me take more inner trips! You see we don't get bored over here - no need to play the harp with 'angels'! There are plenty of other activities even more useful and fascinating!

The most important is to do one's best, so as not to have too many regrets when one arrives here. You can see how essential it is to get rid of all those heavy weights and emotional baggage when we are on Earth! One must **shed them before** coming here, therefore not burden oneself with them when one is on the Earth - not easy to do, I know! But it is vital to think about it as one goes through life and tries to rectify situations as much as possible. Because it is much harder to do it once here, without a flesh body and real links with people we used to be with 'down there'.

That's my 'lesson' for you today Sweetheart. I know you try your best. It must be hard sometimes but don't worry too much. Do what you can, so that what matters is done. Do it quickly or soon, so as not to regret anything later on! We all love you here so believe me, you are not alone!

30th November 2008 - *My Guide starts the conversation.*
We are here to encourage you with the work you are and will be doing. You must understand we are not here to push you for our pleasure, but to help you do what you have to do because that is what you chose to come and do as part of your life trip and experiment! It is no good us saying: "Do this and that", unless it is what you wanted to do but have partly forgotten it is and was your aim, your plan!

You have someone here who wants to talk to you. We'll let him in so listen carefully and do not interrupt if you can help it please. *(Change of communicator).*

Now it's my turn, Darling! I am your Dave of course. I have been waiting for a long time to talk to you directly. I have now managed it well, I think, as you are receiving me ok. You can rest assured I am still the same as before. I have not changed as far as loving you is concerned but it is strange how changed things look from here. We see them from a different perspective. I have now understood better what happened between us two and the strain and stress that you could not cope with - and the wishes you had that I could not quite grasp before, I suppose. Now I'd like to tell you that I have learnt quite a lot, because I wanted to get to grips with this new life here! It is so important to know what we are doing with our Minds when we are here, isn't it? That's why I kept myself to myself for a while, to sort out what I had to do and how I was going to do it. There was and is help at hand, of course, but they don't push. They help when asked or needed.

They told me you have a lot to do for this world, for the proofs you want to give to people on Earth, people like me who could not get round to believing it was possible to communicate! So, I wish you good luck and courage as it seems quite hard to do. You'll have to have a lot of patience, won't you, as it isn't that easy to publish things? You published some languages courses, like I did, but those were commissioned, asked for, so you didn't have the bother of convincing publishers. "We are all behind you", they say here, all those who look after you and care for you. My own friends say you've done very well over the years to keep the writing going and the link.

The way I need to look at things here is so different from before! I used to analyse so much! Now I need to feel and think in a precise way with lots of intensity to make things I want happen. The little exercises I learn are very useful, that's why I have to do them. No doubt your mum will have told you of similar experiments. We must concentrate our thoughts on what we do and think positively, so that things take place, which will not occur if the Mind wanders away from its focus!

The main things I see around me are landscapes, countryside, gardens. I love Nature so I am in Nature. My activities have to do with painting, walking, surrounding myself with beauty: beautiful flowers and plants. There are lots of nice people around me whom I love, except that you and the kids are not here. I don't want to talk about them too much as I know they are all right. You look after them whenever you can - but if I start talking about them, I'll bring back the longing to have them with me and it hurts too much! So tell them I still love them a lot, will never stop but can't discuss it too much! That's the sad memory of the Big Parting. So I'll have plenty of practice at sending good thoughts in your direction, all of you, and hope you are doing well and progressing in what you are all doing. They must be quite grown up now, though

I suppose it can't be that long since I left *(Note- four years)*. They have their lives to live and that's what makes the difference between us, as I finished mine and have this one to see to and discover here. Anyway, we'll be together one day, 'they' (my friends here) keep saying. We'll have to go off this subject as I feel the longing coming back and I don't want to start down the sad road of sadness!

Now I'll say look for the cheerful Dave and remember him as he was! I am still that and even young again, as you said one could be. I have decided to feel and look young like I was at one time. I did not like getting or feeling old, so that's the new me! I have read many useful books here which have taught me a lot to do with our new world. It is amazing that people on Earth are not taught what I am learning! Why are we so closed-minded when we are down there, I wonder?!

My parents are still near me, quite often, but not all the time. I need to have some time on my own to ponder and practise what I am shown. I had to learn to talk to you directly, that's why I've come today, to be proud of myself! I am, because I can do it without giving information to someone else to put it in your Mind. No intermediary. I can reach your Mind directly by sending thoughts to you and you getting them at once! That's very good, isn't it?!

There is something else I want to say: It's important not to have any regrets! It's hard not to build them up while on Earth. So do not have any if you can avoid it. You can live your life, you know, **you must not live in the past.**

I must also tell you more about my life here, so that you feel you have learnt something new about me. There is a little shed I go to now and then. I sit there and look at the scenery around, which I can change if I wish it to! It has to be my little den - my retirement place, in the sense of away from others. As I sit there and ponder and try things and experiments, I realise what wonders there are, both on Earth and here, which is not the Earth anymore yet can look like it if one wishes to have it. I choose to look at life here as a new trip, a new experience and let things happen as they develop.

I have met your mum and dad again. Not often, but we did talk and share views. Your mum helped me a lot with the acclimatisation to this new place, most of all with the longings and sadness, as she felt and feels it too. So we joined forces, sending good thoughts to help you all in your respective lives!

I also have to say this: There is a little **robin** here, who has been **put in my coffin** for love and good luck with my new trip. I have it with me but it has taken a life of its own in a way! I know it was a little object, beautifully filled with love. Well, you'll never believe **that love has given it some kind of 'life'**! So I have it by my side, often following me! It is **not** a bird from here, it is **that** bird Jim-Bo gave me from the bottom of his heart and his sorrow! I would never have believed that could happen, but it has! So please tell him, if he can get solace and support and love from knowing I have a part of him with me in a way. "Not forgotten you Jim-Bo lad! Keep up with the music! Your Dad loves you."

But Anne-France is in my heart too. Tell her she is not forgotten! I am kept informed of their progress and ups and downs and life in general. We have good informers here, you know! They keep an eye on the proceedings on Earth. We have no need for TV or telephone. They do the job as well, if not better, you know! You can rest assured, all of you, I have not forgotten you nor will. My mum and dad "send their regards and thoughts to you all". They say it a bit formally I feel, but they mean they have love for the kids and know you are doing your best for them. You have earned their respect and that's what matters.

Now I'll go back to my retreat in my shed for a while, and then meet my friends for a long walk in Nature no doubt, as we often do. They are good friends, some old ones from the

267

Earth, some new ones from here. We all enjoy walking, thinking, talking and asking questions and even arguing - but that's in a nice way! There is always a bit of banter about, that's why it's so enjoyable being here! No more job or pain. So I am happy, free and joyful on that score. Now I have spoken to you, it feels good as it has linked me back to you all and I know I am not completely cut off as I felt at first.

I'll let you go but love you and kiss you and hug you. Do it for me to the kiddoes please. All of you are in my heart. Now I am off for a big walk to clear any sadness and remember the good feeling of having been linked again to you. I'll come back another day and talk again if you are happy with that.

26th December 2008 - *French is spoken. It's Mum.*

The last day of your life will be the most beautiful day of your new life here; you'll see when you arrive and meet us all again, or nearly all. There'll be your parents, your husband but you'll have to bear the grief of being parted from your children for some time. You'll have to get used to it but you will. Please do understand we are not predicting your death in the near future, of course! But this is to reassure you it will not be as horrid as you may imagine.

BR- It does not sound very cheerful news though!

I am only telling you this to reassure you well in advance, as it will definitely not be soon! The result of your life will be a success, you'll see, as you will have managed to publish these books and many others, as we have work planned for you! If you want to know what I have been doing recently, I'll tell you I made more inner trips. I have seen even more people 'unknown' to me yet in fact whom I used to know before! Some were from my own lives, my different facets.

That's why I saw another woman, not the one I've spoken to you about earlier. That was in a really different life!

268

Not in this country or England, but far away in the days of Mesopotamians, or something similar, in the days of ancient Scribes, when the majority of people did not know how to write properly, so someone did it for them. Those were biblical times rather than modern ones.

I was then a knowledgeable woman but I was unable to share my knowledge, because in those days men had more rights than women to make themselves known. I had this intense inner frustration, as I wanted to let people know what I had learnt! I acquired knowledge by listening to wise men of that time in the temples and the arenas where they gave interesting and long speeches on all kinds of topics. Yet women did not really have the right to attend. It was more for the men. But I always wanted to know more, so I used to go discreetly or in disguise not to be recognised!

Therefore, I gained knowledge which no one could take away from me, yet which I could not share easily with anyone without admitting how and where I got it from! This is when the idea came to me to write them down! But for that I had to learn to write. So I had to do that discreetly too! A learned female writer was not 'the done thing'! So I learnt to write, I made some rapid progress in order to apply myself to doing what I wanted to succeed in - knowing the world besides what surrounded me in the little village where I lived. But it was not easy at all. Yes I learnt, I wrote indeed, but I was unable to 'publish' it as we'd say nowadays - because men were in charge of all that! So, I would be revealing my subterfuge!

However, I kept that collection of manuscripts so that the world would find them later, if I died before I was able to make myself known. The world did not know I had done it and they must have been lost since I have never heard about them ever since. But the acquired knowledge I had was not lost because I kept the facts in my Mind and brought them back here.

Then frustrated not to have disseminated them, I decided to return to Earth in a new life as a globetrotter where this time, as a free and liberated woman, I could go round the world and learn what I could and desired to discover! That is the time when I lived without any family in order to be free to do what I wanted when I wanted! I was thus able to learn each time even more, on the spot - without it being men teaching me 'secretly' as they did it before.

However, that life was only useful to me. I did not make any great speeches or write great books. I learnt and discovered for myself, to help me understand the world around me, compared to life in the Great Beyond. I knew who I was. I knew I had lived as a Spirit before coming down to the Earthly world. I wanted to see and 'drink' the difference, enjoy it, appreciate it! That is the reason why I had made the trip from one world to the other. Yet the results were only known to myself, as said before. I did not take the trouble to get them published. It was a personal and private matter.

Unless I can see more, this is all I saw of that particular life, as a frustrated woman because they were impressions, memories and thoughts of those days, rather than visions of clothes and countries and elaborated discussions. I was frustrated and I wanted to learn. I learnt yet I could not make this useful to others. Therefore, I must have died very frustrated and because of that I came back to do as I explained to you. But that **desire to let others know what I had learnt** must have remained within me, because this is what I did during this (recent) life when you knew me as your mum.

So now I don't know where I'll go next, but it will not be for a long time, as I need to concentrate on this new (once more!) life. I have to wait for you all, without my disappearing before you arrive back here, with Dad and I! We have so much to do here that I don't think it will be necessary for me to wander off elsewhere on 'dry ground'! There will be plenty to do in all 'the countries' of the Mind and Spirit. I mean the levels where one can discover fascinating things without having to go anywhere!

So that's it, I wanted to let you know I had made another little inner trip, 'backwards' in a way! But we only see snippets of those lives - just important moments which have left their marks on our Souls and ways of thinking. All we have to do is to look within. It feels as if we dive into it backwards, then we let ourselves go with the flow of our thoughts and we find ourselves back in those times of yesteryear! The aim is to see what there is to learn about oneself and begin to patch the pieces of the tapestry of one's Higher Self. It's what I do when I have fun discovering myself. Me who thought I had only been your mum! How ignorant we can be when on Earth, hey? Yet that's what 'spiritual education' is! One discovers oneself, one understands more and more and one moves forward on the path of eternal progress!

That's it. My big speech is over. I only wanted to share with you the new discovery of one of my facets. Me, the Mesopotamian...or something similar! It was probably some kind of Arabic country but I did not really see myself wearing a veil. It's not what stood out. It was the frustration to be prevented from doing what I wanted when I could have done and discovered so much! Now I'll let you get on with your activities, Darling.

11th January 2009 - *Mum comes on line.*

I'd like to tell you what I've been doing recently. My life has not changed much in a way and yet it has in another. That's because I saw and have done heaps of things new to me, though perhaps not to you. Discovering myself has been fascinating for me lately, as I realise one does not know oneself at all. One needs to do it often to succeed!

Last time I spoke to you, I think it was to tell you about my feats and my 'visit' to a lady from Mesopotamia, which was one of my lives as a frustrated woman as she could not make a name for herself and wanted to learn so much! Yet in those days a woman should not have expected to be able to! So I looked into this more deeply, because I wanted to know what she did and how she coped. I reckon she did have a lot of guts, that 'other me' woman! I had to go much deeper to discover that the more she was learning, the more she sank into a kind of abyss, because the frustration to be unable to express herself and pass it to others hurt her so much that she was making herself ill! She worried because of that frustration. I suppose it was a bit silly, but that's how she felt. She had learnt by reading, listening or hiding to be able to listen. Also by thinking, by linking up with what she thought to be her inner voice, but which must have been her Higher Self or her 'guide', as you call him. Everything made her realise one could study without being endowed with fantastic gifts. All is needed is wanting to learn. That helps to absorb lots of knowledge!

So I saw that my poor lady suffered deeply within because of her hunger for more knowledge and I realise now that I never lost that thirst for knowledge. Yet I was able to quench it, more than once, by making those long trips during a certain period, then in this recent Earthly life, by teaching children to make them learn things they needed to know. However, there still is that thirst within me! Even here I don't stop wanting to discover more! So this is my little journey as a 'researcher'. I went back to very long ago and I can see that through the centuries, I've always had this craving for information and understanding, this enquiring searching Mind! I did not make any grand medical or scientific discoveries, but made some for myself, to satisfy and expand myself. It showed me what the Earthly world had to offer and was hidden from us. Of course, I could only see what I was able to discover, step by step, but it was enough to excite me and amuse and interest me!

So that's where I have got to - the poor frustrated lady has less frustration now that she has reached another of her goals... as the revelation that one does live on after death has been one of my most wonderful discoveries! I know I probably did it more than once, after each 'death' but it does not seem to have had the same impact as this time! Perhaps because I did not remember it as well?

Yet it's worth being noted down: 'Death' is not an end, a blocking wall. 'Death' is only a passage, a tunnel from one place to the other, from one period to another. This should be taught to all the children, so that they grow up in the hope of death and not with the fear of dying!

Dying is not terrible if one does not suffer on that day or that period. I am told that all that is needed is to **want not to suffer,** but one must have learnt to think that way! People need to build within themselves the understanding they can **will** themselves not to be ill or injured when the time comes for their Soul to decide to leave the flesh! Absolutely no need to be in pain. Build up that desire and belief.

Children are never well-informed because adults don't inform them properly! Therefore, adults must be taught in order that they teach children what they need to know. That way they won't be afraid of dying. Of course, one must not let them believe it's not wrong to kill oneself! It's neither the solution nor the kind of teaching that should be offered! It's **the fear of the Hereafter which must be removed,** then the rest can be taught gradually, as you well know.

The next thing I want to tell you is that you have a great need for more calm, Darling. Please don't be annoyed with me for reminding you. I know it is frustration and despair and annoyance, as you are longing for peace and quiet and for things to be done well. Find a solution so that this does not ruin your life and damage your health. There are aspects you may grasp well: All stress is pernicious to the physical body, so you must protect yourself mentally so as not to suffer physically! You'll have a lot to do in the future, a lot of work and you'll need courage to do it. You'll lose courage if you cannot control the frustration, anger, sadness, despair and emotions filling you when things don't go well.

The problems are not always your fault of course, others cause them. So try to escape from them. Cut down on tasks imposed on you, delegate them to others! Avoid chores. If things are not done as well as they should be, is it really that important? After all, for whom are you doing all that unpaid work? *(At the Spiritualist Centre)*. For others who have no idea how much work it involves. Do the minimum and delegate!

About 5 days later, I discovered that Sandra S. had been telling nasty lies about me and making false accusations behind my back for months! She was a woman whom I saw as a good friend and was fond of, whom I helped and encouraged - I looked after her cat and her house many times while she was on holiday - and even gave her the opportunity to get involved with some useful work, to give her confidence and 'importance' (since I could see she had complexes and wanted to feel important!). Yet all her vicious malevolence went on deceitfully, while she kept smiling at me and pretending to be my friend! What a venomous snake!

When I asked my Guide why that happened, to my utter amazement he explained in great detail. The main points being these:

The mystery of whom to trust or not trust is solved. You see, we could not tell you either way until you found out for yourself that you had traitors amongst your so-called friends! So we had to let you suffer a little longer; we had to see whether she'd carry out what she had planned long ago! She had been jealous of you from day one. You had no chance

274

whatsoever! You've been used because she needed a 'friend' to keep her company when she felt like it. But she hated everything you could do or say **because** you could do and say it. She's been feeling like an underdog. And she has always resented you! We could not do much except let you see what was really happening behind closed doors. You have not lost a friend, you have discovered an enemy hiding in the bush! That's safer that way. It could have been worse! *(My Guide followed this with shocking revelations about that attention-seeking, two-faced woman and her spiteful behaviour even towards her own family, including using and smothering her poor husband G. and preventing him from developing his own abilities. I was better off without her indeed!)*

27th January 2009 - *French is spoken.*

Mum here, Darling. I have been waiting for quite a while as we haven't spoken to each other for some time. I see you've been very busy. Preparing this book for publication is a lot of work. I also know you had awful troubles with nasty and dishonest people around you! It's so sad for you. I did always tell you one cannot trust another woman who risks being jealous! It's impossible to avoid. They all are and will be. So you may as well be aware of this fact and get used to it, avoid them, or at least do not tell them anything or confide in them. Treat them as if they are insidious enemies inside the garrison!

I no longer have to cope with this, fortunately. I have friends here whom I can trust totally and my pastimes which are always useful activities helping me 'progress'. I have made a few more inner or 'historical' discoveries regarding my past lives. Apparently I had lots of other lives! It's really intriguing and fun to see ourselves elsewhere as someone else when we assume we 'know' we are who we think we are! Weird but interesting!

I saw a man of long ago, who was 'me'! He still exists and his Spirit is part of my 'Higher Self' as **he is one of my facets.** Yet he has not finished living his life; he continues to do so in thoughts, fancy that! He feels as who he was and has been thinking that way for a long time. He has only begun to realise that he was not just what he knew himself as! *(Note- There may be quite a lot of such slow learners!)*

So I made a little trip in 'time' to see that man. He had a small family and looked after them, but he had greater longings. He felt stuck where he was. He would have liked to travel but could not. There were not many means of transport in those days - it was very long ago. I have the feeling there were only horses, coaches or whatever a horse pulled. But it was expensive to own one or more horses - he could not afford it. Moreover, he had to stay near his family, since he had promised his wife to love her and not abandon her. So he stayed and did his duty. Gradually he 'buried' his longing to travel, since it was no use to him because he could not fulfil it!

After his body died, he carried on wanting to travel so he reincarnated. Apparently he did that several times. It does seem weird indeed that one life was not enough but he had desires, ideas and projects. The more he travelled, the more he discovered reasons to go back to Earth! He enjoyed doing a wide range of activities and saw lots of things all over the world, over several centuries, I reckon! Since then he quenched his thirst but there remained in him, in his Spirit, a constant curiosity for anything new and interesting. The same lies in my own Spirit. We are therefore like twins, but in fact we belong to the same Spirit with a capital S. *(Note- Meaning the multi-faceted Higher Self).*

I experienced this when I 'immersed myself' in periods prior to the ones I had previously seen. 'Previous times' in a way, yet not really - because there is no 'before' or 'after' in reality, since 'Time' does not exist as such! They are impressions of 'before' or 'after' which we give ourselves if we think like we did on Earth. When examining those facets, we feel like the person we see - the 'other me'. We live again those moments as if we were there. So we remember in our very core that indeed that was how we felt 'long ago', in those days! But it does us good because we understand ourselves a bit better: "Ah! That's why I used to have that thirst for... learning/travelling/etc!" It feels good to be able to comprehend those thoughts, those ideas we used to have without knowing why. Now I understand myself better. It makes me feel more 'complete', like a jigsaw puzzle to which one adds missing pieces!

The end of that man's life was apparently sad. He was killed by a runaway, panicky horse who was frightened. As it fled, it knocked down the poor man. The very man who had wanted to spend his life galloping on his own horse, uphill and down dale! It was rather ironic, wasn't it? He remembered it when he showed me his death (or was it someone else showing it to me? I can't recall exactly). He wanted to leave the Earth so the quickest way, in his opinion, was to be knocked down and trampled by a large horse! It did not remove his desire to travel, but it sent him on an even bigger journey - the one towards the Great Beyond!

That's my recent little trip. I thought you might be interested to know your mum had been another man, once more! Also to see that desires one has in one's Soul, one's Spirit, do not die out necessarily with the death of the physical body, but remain within the Self, until one manages to satisfy them thoroughly, to get rid of them... and acquire new and different ones!

BR- Was he the same man you mentioned before, the good chap struggling for his family?

The same curiosity filled him. He had that thirst over several lives, I think. I think this man and the one I saw earlier had a link but he was not necessarily the same man. In fact this is not important, because I realise that what matters is to **become aware of the aspects of the Higher Self.** I must be able to understand them, link them together and comprehend it is in fact the same 'person' who has all those desires, all those 'separate' lives, as it seems. Yet in fact they are only facets of a single and same person.

Therefore, I am beginning to understand myself better. This is what becomes interesting, in fact more and more fascinating! I see how one 'rebuilds' oneself by glancing at the other façades and facets of one's 'Real Me'. This is what I wanted to tell you, Darling. You are enjoying it, aren't you?

BR- Yes indeed! It's captivating.

Yes, I thought it would amuse and intrigue you to see 'your' own mum as someone very different, yet not that different after all! There is so much to see and do, hey! It's certainly wonderful! I also want to tell you that the day I had you, my daughter, did not change my life in a dramatic way, physically. But it did change it emotionally, because I wanted to have you, as you were the girl I had never had before and wished for, since I only had boys before and after you. So you fulfilled very well your role as a daughter to help me have one. But also, of course, you had your own Earthly life to live, that's why you came with me. I am really **glad you chose me**, because I may not have had a daughter otherwise.

As you can see, I am having fun, I occupy myself and you learn some things thanks to it all. I am sure there is plenty more to tackle, but it will be for another and many other times, no doubt! We can't do any better, can we? Wasn't it worth my 'dying and 'disappearing' from home, in order to let you know all this in the end? We shall meet again, so that's what matters.

Now I'll let you get on for the time being. You must have things to see to. All my love to all of you.

(As reincarnation may interest or confuse some readers, I include here a related question I put later on to my Teachers for clarification. I also inserted their answer in their 'Truths, Lies & Distortions').

BR- How is Mum (in Spirit World) helped to see her previous facets? She was also told that they 'still exist'. Could you explain, please?

The notion of 'Time' will confuse your Mind as long as you try to make everything fit in like it would on Earth. We need to take you out of that and into extra dimensions, where there is not such a notion. You need to understand that the equivalent of being 'here now' and 'there now' is possible! That means being ubiquitous, omnipresent, not only in space but in so-called 'Time' to you - but not 'Time' to those who live it, because they would not have the same 'Time' reference as you.

We have to see things differently since we do not have the use of a sun to fix minutes, hours and even years. You need to grasp that the vision of someone in the so-called 'past' does not necessarily mean you need to fleet through 'Time'. It **can be done by going within oneself and FEELING the various personalities, without feeling the notion of Time.** It's more like watching a film of oneself at a younger age when you look at your cameras and recording devices. As you look at things from the Earthly point of view, you'll find it difficult to grasp the whole concept.

Let's look at it differently: The little girl who is now you, say, has been a man 'before' by your time standards. But the Higher Self of that man is the same Higher Self as yours and the same Higher Self as the other personalities that have been and still are forming the whole 'Real You'. So, these

279

personalities have the **common linking point of a joint Higher Self**. And **that** is where the common ground is.

Yet the individual reaction to various 'deaths' is not quite the same thing. It lies within the fact that, say, when one personality 'dies' of a horrific accident, the accident will have reverberated throughout the whole Being of the Higher Self. So they will all feel it and may all remember it. Or may not! According to whatever you've felt coming from 'previous' lives (as you'd say), you will react with various memories at times. So it is not so surprising. But the 'longevity' of each one somehow does not affect the others.

BR- But after a 'death', that life is finished, gone?

The fact that it's been lived, may have an effect if there was something traumatic, say. But if the Soul or personality in question (e.g. male) is 'not gone' as such, it is because the rest of the Higher Self will have absorbed it and it will be part of it. The 'male' influence will fill up the recess of every one of the other personalities which are part of the Higher Self. It will itself be influenced by many other aspects which come from the other 'facets'. So it will live within each one of its facets, whether they are 'gone', 'finished' as an Earth life or not.

Therefore, **they will still 'live' in the rest of the Higher Self.** It is alive because the others are alive anyway as an eternal 'Spirit Being', but also because the influence still permeates every one of them, as said before.

****

CHAPTER 6
My brother's tragedy - Confusion and adjustment - Mum's brave work - Messages transmission - Thoughts sensed as images and feelings - Dave's world tour - Pierre focusing and adapting

28th February 2009 - *During a mediumship 'message giving' practice workshop, I am working in pair with a lady who does not know anything about my family. As part of her message to me that afternoon, she says: "I am also told you have a brother who lives very far away. There is great concern about his health. He is very unwell. Please send him lots of healing thoughts, it's important." This is correct, as one of my three brothers, Pierre, is the one unwell at the moment. He lives in the depths of the rain forest in French Guinea, South America! One could think her sensing he was unwell was good, but saying he needs healing sent could be seen by some as run of the mill comment.*

Unknown to her, he had written to me several few weeks ago to say he thought he may have tetanus as he had problems walking in spite of having been vaccinated. It was still extremely painful for him and very worrying. So I could understand the message and sent him some loving thoughts.

Two days later*: I receive an unexpected telephone call from a stranger asking me whether I am Pierre's sister. I confirm this. The man then goes on to say he is from the French Guinea 'Gendarmerie' (police station). He regrets to have to tell me Pierre was found dead on his bed **on the 28th, two days ago**. He had a plastic bag tied over his head. Some rags soaked with some chemicals covered his face. It appeared he may have committed suicide. He was found by one of his acquaintances living nearby in the little community that Pierre had created for a few people who want to live close to Nature.*

I learnt later he had progressively become more and more paralysed by the creeping disease that struck him. I know that from a young age Pierre had always vouched he would never want to end up as a cripple and would rather take his own life. He was still young and very fit at seventy-nine years old! There is still some controversy as to why the French Guinea hospital (where he had been taken to with great difficulty by one of his friends) disgracefully sent him back home to his forest with no treatment or helpful medication whatsoever! Also, what caused this sudden health deterioration? Was it a cut and dirty soil with resulting tetanus, or was it a particular indigenous insect whose bite causes tetanus-like symptoms? We may never know.

I lost my dear and brave eldest brother because he received no proper help by the hospital and could not stand the agonising pain any longer, as well as the gradual paralysis. He will have been heartbroken to be forced to abandon his dearly beloved cats and the exotic home and peaceful village he created in the wonderful environment he settled in decades ago. Oh! His pain, his tears, his fears.

7th March 2009 - *One week after Pierre's passing, I ask my Guide for some news of Pierre.*

He has 'dreams' of being at home with his younger mother. He has dreams of being loved like a little boy and had love in his heart for her. He has thoughts of being able to escape the pain from the last days by running away from it and he is succeeding.

He had such a shaken, traumatised Mind, which had to be realigned on the right path of thinking. He had lost the sense of where he was exactly because he has never been here *(Spirit World)* as such. But it will be rectified and is being rectified.

282

BR- How are you doing that?

Visions are sent to him of himself being well, healthy, younger and full of strength. He now has that filling his head, to realign the Mind on the healthy feeling track. Then the Mind will be filled with lots of pleasant thoughts about meeting Mother, Father and other people he liked. Then it will be brought to his attention that his 'dreams' are **not dreams,** they are **reality** and it will be proven to him, as we usually do here!

So he will be well looked after, don't worry! It is only a question of gradual adaptation. He is already on the right path; he has seen and sensed his mother many a time. She has been by his side, loving him, sending her tender, healing thoughts to him, so that he feels them and comes back to his own correct reality. All is not lost, just a slight deviation, because of the shock, that's all.

BR- How is Mum feeling about all this?

You have nothing to fear for your mum, she is well looked after. She had been very upset for him when she realised he was so ill. It was just a question of 'time' on Earth for him to come. **It could have been the disease taking him across - or his own Will.** It had to be seen up to the last moment; no one was too sure. But his strength was sapped and that was a sure sign he would give in, so then we knew he'd come across a little sooner - but we were all upset for him to have suffered so much!

It was not 'planned' as may be thought. It happened gradually and the **Will to live gave way** to the total lack of strength and mobility; the paralysis caused by the disease - he could not move! That was the final signal indicating to us he would not last long there and would come across. Mother was upset to see him suffer, she sensed him but it was important she had the courage to send him strength and determination, in addition to as much healing thoughts she could muster, but the

283

healing was more for the Mind than the flesh, as the flesh had been destroyed by the disease of the nerves and muscles.

16th March 2009 - *My Guide explains more.*

The little lady *(Mum)* looking after her poor son who arrived here has been very busy mentally and emotionally. It was a shock for her to receive her own son over here, compared to welcoming new strangers who had nothing to do with her! She had to learn to put her emotions aside to let her love pour out and let him feel it - in order to give him respite, confidence, healing of the Soul and Mind and most of all, Peace of Mind, which he has not had for quite a long time.

It was very painful for her to see the man struggling in his Earth life lately, as he had pains all over his body. The body would not give up because **the Mind was not giving up at first,** until the last days when he could not stand anymore!

He had a shock when he saw her and made himself believe he was dreaming (or suffering from the effect of the chemicals he put on that cloth). He thought it could not be true because he was not used to thinking you would see people as they were. When he saw his own mother, also his own father and grandparents too (in that life), that was a shock! But he could not work out why he should see them so soon when he was 'still in his room', in a way. He thought he was dreaming it all! It was not a bad thing because **it could have gone far worse** if he had kept thinking he was in a dark hole, or in a totally different place where he would not allow anyone in! So then it would have been difficult, or more difficult, to get him out mentally! But he's had his rest; he is feeling so much better now.

BR- Is he still dreaming?

It took some time for him to come to realise there was no dream lasting such a long time. He also thought it was strange the whole thing looked coherent and made sense,

284

nothing is disjointed. Mum was there all the time, not disappearing, not talking of anything else which he did not know. She talked of what he knew from way back in his childhood and even before - as they had planned to be together long ago before he was born, when they were still in Spirit World! His Soul took in all that.

Gradually he started making sense of the fact he had come out of that very painful body and now the fact his own mother was standing all the time in front of him seemed to fit. He had to pinch himself a few times to make sure he was not dreaming, but he had to come to the conclusion there must be some truth in it! So now he is resting mentally from the shock of it all. He has kind of **accepted that he is here**, he needs to gradually assimilate the facts and the circumstances he now lives in.

BR- What are his surroundings?

He'll see himself as he was when he was younger at a certain age he enjoyed. He'd had lots of ups and downs but this age was the best for him. So he is reliving it, then it will help him gradually make sense of it all when he sees his mum has not changed much. He will see her younger too but he knows she was older when she 'died'! So he will understand there is a discrepancy in the ages and he will come to realise what is happening! He will have his own little 'dream like' stories, reliving themselves in his head; he'll have good times reappearing to uplift his Mind and his mood. He'll be happier for a while, so that will set him on the right path for him to be prepared to accept more and be more uplifted all the time.

He had it very rough recently. We have to take it gently, one thing at a time to help him settle, assimilate and accept. It's all within the process of healing. Healing of the Soul, of course, as the Mind is the tool of the Spirit and it has its own way of tackling things!

So your brother is neither completely out of his mental puzzle nor totally settled here. But he is here, he is fine. He is just **resting mentally and adjusting to the great shock** he had to endure and is now recovering from. Mum had a shock too. She has pulled through it as he is here now and she knows he is safer than he has EVER been! She had pains in her 'heart' when she saw him suffer but had not suffered too long as he is back with her and is fine now. No more worries on that score!

11th April 2009 - *My Guide comes to offer some helpful suggestions. Many readers may be glad of the tips.*

You have a very dedicated team here who wants to work with you and you enjoy receiving information from us. You can help your linking up by having more private, quiet time; it will help you get the right balance to reach a passive state.

Another point: There are lots of people in the world who deserve to be told the Knowledge we give you - what you learn from us. Some will waste it, but that's not your problem, it's theirs! It's a total lack of understanding and assimilation of anything which is beyond what they've been told or telling themselves. Reach the ones who can accept, so that they do not get missed out. Just a question of perseverance and not giving up.

Another suggestion: As you progress with our work together, wouldn't it be more beneficial to you to keep a diary of the 'messages' you give to people, so that you can look back and see how much you've progressed with your links? See how images or facts came across possibly as symbols? It is important to know how you are getting information from our world. We would appreciate if you could keep in mind what you had. That way you'll recognise impressions, fleeting words and ways of putting them across as given...

BR- At times it seems hard to get some communicators to give a list of evidential facts or memories to help them be recognised by the recipient wanting a 'message'. Yet at other times others provide the information easily! Why is that?

As the person in our world is more educated in ways of communication and how to send their thoughts better, there will always be a difference. It cannot be expected from everyone talking to you that they'll be able to give long lists of details! **They have to learn** to do it properly! Just see how long it took you to learn to link up with us and how much trouble you can still have at times in quietening your Mind after all those years! It cannot be expected from others who may have much more to cope with! They have the emotions of being parted from the Earth, the emotions of wanting to link up with loved ones, ideas floating all over the place in their Minds, juggling with what they want to talk about... and the first thing they usually say is: "I am here!"

It is understandable you want to know much more about them to give evidence of who the person is but you need to make allowances and be patient with them! Keep up with the practice and **do not get distracted during the link**, so that the person in our world has no worries about 'losing you' on the way, while they also have to concentrate on what to say, how to say it and why they say it, etc.

It is important to think of it as a telephone conversation. If you spoke to two or three people in your room at the same time as you are telephoning someone else, what results do you think will be obtained? Total confusion, upset and lack of clarity. So be firm with yourself and the person whom you speak to on Earth! Because this is where any slacking of the link could come from.

You have nothing to worry about, you are doing fine! But it is worth knowing and remembering that if the medium is distracted, put off or put on the wrong track, their poor Mind could come into it to try and rectify things - or more likely will confuse or misplace information. It is essential to have the link solid, one-tracked and not move from it. Keep talking, keep thinking 'Spirit'! Do not worry whether it is 'taken' or about 'what it looks like' to the Earthly recipient. **Keep up with us** as we are the information givers. The rest is of lesser importance and at times, not needed. After all, the one on Earth is the person most likely not to remember who could be talking, or to confuse the information with someone else's - for example, they think we have a brother communicating whereas it is an uncle!

As we talk to you during the exchange of facts, please make sure you listen to **how we give it** to you and make sure **you repeat it** word for word. It is important - you know it, as you had proof of how essential the reporting of words is! (Of course, avoid shocking swear words, but explain the language used is strong!) It is all the more vital if you have feelings, emotions or memories to pass on. It is not easy to send and even more difficult to receive! You all have to learn to open even more the 'sensitive' part of receiving emotions, as it will be another way of passing over the message which is so much wanted from both sides (sent and received).

There is a big difference between receiving a message saying: "Mother is here. Had a bad leg before dying - wants to say she loves you" and "I have a lady here who did not see you for many years when she was on Earth, but who wishes to say that, though you lived far apart, her love for you never faltered for one moment and never died. She had leg problems before the end. It led her to being a bit bitter as it prevented her from travelling easily and coming to see you. You could not always travel easily yourself, because of your many commitments which she understands very well, as she was very sympathetic and kind." Do you see and feel the difference? That's what we'd like you to be able to pick and pass over. The wordings can be given, but the feelings may be needed too.

BR- You've just given these feelings in words, so why don't you pass them over that way?

It is so important to stay with your link and not falter. That way you'll get words but you'll also receive feelings, which you could interpret in words. That may even be better coming from you, as the feelings will be sent from one person (in our world) **directly** to another person (you). This no doubt will be more personal and better reflected, rather than words passed from one person to me, the intermediary friend, then to you! Do you see what I mean?

The more you practise, the better your link will be if you give it the time. It is essential to have the guidance of your 'guide', to have an understanding of how communication works and how it can be improved, as it helps you direct the flow to your recipient. Or else you could be floundering, couldn't you?

As the link gets stronger when you talk, the person here will have more Energy to send their thoughts along towards you. Therefore, it is up to you to keep the link clear and strong, so that the reception on your side is clear and precise and not wavering towards interferences of your own Mind. It is all to do with being **constantly focused** and not letting little things interfere, overlap or distract you.

You can rest assured we do not get distracted here when we send thoughts! We are very focused and concentrate in an extraordinary way compared to you people on Earth! This last line is important - no way could you Earthly people learn to be as focused as we are here! (Until you came over, of course). So you need to try to match, as much as possible, our focus and concentration. This will help you be more precise and detailed in your receiving and giving information. All of you Humans must try more exercises of concentration!

BR- Can you suggest any good ones?

My own favourites have always been: Listening to your breath and listening to the music of the wind moving the branches in trees. Also, concentrating on the sound of one's breath and then looking at water running down its path. It will be going somewhere but you don't need to know where. Just stare at the water, listen and feel. Pay attention to that and nothing else. Just stand still, motionless mentally. That is the secret! Hold on to what you gaze at and do not let it go. Hang on to the sound of your breath and do not let it go. Hold on to the feeling you get at whatever moment and do not let it go. As you progress, you'll feel more and it will stay longer...

17th April 2009 - *My Guide starts the conversation to give news of Pierre.*

As we are start talking to you, we'll tell you that the dear lady you know here, your mum who loves you so much, has made even more progress lately. She has had to perceive more happenings directly from the Earth as she went to see your brother in his last days. Then she made sure he was going to settle his Mind in the right direction once he was here. That must have been the hardest as she had to control, as best as she could, the way he was going to think. It was important to make sure he saw her, thought of her, loved her and understood he was indeed with her! It had to be done carefully and gently.

She certainly did it very well! She succeeded in bringing him back out of his melancholy and dreams of a kind to realising he was well and truly in this World of Light, where he could now enjoy more peace and quiet than he'd ever had!

He needs some mental rest to have the strength to focus on what is now around him and what he can do with his Mind Power. As he will no doubt understand that quite quickly, there will be no problem, once he gets going full strength. **He needed a lot of love to build his strength up**. On Earth he'd been deprived of real warm love as should be given between Humans. *(Note- He lived abroad alone for a very long time!).* He loved, but it was not as deep as it could have been. His Animals were the ones he really loved more than some Humans. He could not help loving them; those are the ones he lived for. But he could not totally avoid his human companions, because they were there - if and when they were there!

He had to find his feet when he moved to that country over there. Now he is with us, he has to find his 'mental feet'! He is well, no longer ill, as he was told to be careful and not think he still was! He had to be put on the right track. We've all done that. We've looked into his past actions and thoughts that he let us see. We know you were not very pleased with his usual Earthly way of thinking, as you've been told. *(Note- His rigid political views).* All will be done to help him open his Mind, so do not worry. He'll be fine in the end, we know.

You have to get on with the book now. You are progressing well enough, you will succeed. It just has to be given to the right person and get it 'out there', to make it go.

BR- Couldn't you see the book on a shelf and look up the publisher's name?

My dear little one, the book has not really been published yet, so we would have to look at **all** the possibilities and probabilities to see which one made it! It might be possible but is not a fact yet! Instead we'll just say this: You can rest assured you have not done anything wrong to attract all those nasty moments or spiteful people around you, as you've been wondering. *(So-called 'spiritual' people backbiting me for no reason).* We cannot reproach you anything. You've tried to be nice to everybody, so it is their problem at their costs if they choose to be nasty. You will see it later, 'when the sums are made'. You cannot reproach yourself anything if you try your best all the time (as your mother said many a time!). Be of cheer!

You can't be feeling down and depressed every time someone is not nice or even is nasty to you, as you'll have a lot of that to come and you can be sure there will be jealousy and envy when you get those books out! You'll see there will be people trying to criticise you, as well as people wanting to praise you! So enjoy the praises, the love of Spirit for your doing it and let the others 'rot' in their own evil thoughts - until it's time for them to face it and regret it! By then you won't care anymore anyway and it will all be forgotten in your own head! But theirs will be full of their nasty deeds! So why worry? Be of cheer.

We need you to be 'upbeat', to be on the ball and get all that going very soon. We know you are trying and we thank you for it. It's just a question of concentration on this important task, not letting others come first.

30th May 2009 - *My Guide joins me for a chat.*

As you try, so do we, so that we are halfway through to you. We can tell you about your mother if you like. She is quite busy with her new charge, now she's been by his side a lot, to get him to realise where he is and help him let go of his past sadness for leaving the Earth, his cats and other friends. He had to go because the pain was too strong. The need was inevitable and he saw it! We know this is true, but he should have tried to hang on longer if he could have, as it would have eased his actual passing! He would have left the body more easily because the pain and trouble would have severed the link more quickly when he actually did it.

We are aware it is of no help to you and him to say that now! But this is to let you know why we always say: "**Let the body die of its own accord, at its own pace'**. It has to do with the level and intensity of the vibrations, as they have to pass from one level to another. This needs to be done more smoothly than suddenly, as this is often a shock. We are not blaming or condemning him for making the passing happen earlier than it would have done on its own. It is just a question of understanding why **things are easier, quieter and calmer when the body is left to its own device**. This is why, now, he has to readjust gradually to accept and understand where he is.

BR- I think he believed in a God, heaven etc. Didn't that help him?

He believed he had somewhere to go to, but he did not know where, how, what it would look like! In fact he had quite a few erroneous ideas and we have to make him see that. It is not enough to believe you have a 'God' who'll look after you when **you know deep down the 'god' cannot do anything for you** when you are so ill and dying! So his reaction was **anger at having been left to die** slowly and in great pain!

25th June 2009 - *Tomorrow is the 10th anniversary of Mum's departure to a better world. My Guide comes to talk to me.*

Your life has indeed been very hectic lately. That's why it is so hard for you to settle down mentally. Now we can tell you the lady you have in your heart, your mother, is indeed very busy with her new arrival here, her first son. That has taken priority over everything else for her, because it's the first time she has had a loved one following her to this world! It's the first time she is showing others in the family how and what to do here!

He had been very shaken by his experience - you must acknowledge that! He was ever so ill and in such pain! He saw no alternative to speeding up the departure. The only thing his taking his own life suddenly caused is that his arrival here was a little bit confused in his Mind, as he was not too sure whether it was real or he was dreaming it. To him it felt like a kind of dream, mixed with the nightmare of the pain and the fears he had in his heart as they materialised. He saw them as symbolic objects!

BR- Can you explain this please?

He did see **symbolic pictures of his fears,** materialising in kinds of dream-like happenings, because he was surrounded by his fears, his dread of being totally paralysed and the sadness of leaving his beloved forest and his Animals. All that sadness and sorrow became 'real' as dream-like happenings! He had to sort out what was real and not real!

He's been very well looked after, as you can imagine, especially with your mum (who is his too) at hand to try and guide him towards the reality of our own world here. He'd been so shaken it had taken its toll on him. But he now knows where he is and he is more settled mentally and 'physically', so to speak, i.e. he feels whole and normal again, not mangled by the disease eating him up, as he saw it.

BR- I am pleased to hear this. Thank you for the update.

13th August 2009 - *Over the previous weeks, my Guide's conversations referred to getting the books published and advice for our personal lives. Today he 'opens the door' for Mum before she talks to me.*

We'll let your mum come over now, but you must make sure you let her speak and not interrupt her, as she has a lot to say and wants to concentrate too! All that happened with your brother had a great influence on her, we warn you, so be gentle and listen carefully! Don't get distracted or she'll lose her thread too! *(Then French is spoken).*

Mum here, Sweetheart. I have a lot to tell you! I've had heaps to do with Pierre, because he arrived rather confused, muddled up, embarrassed and a little panicky. That's because he did not really know where he was going to 'land'. Although he was interested in what the Jehovah Witnesses teach and they say "God forbids you to kill yourself", he on the other hand did believe it was right to do so! He used to think there was no point in suffering if one is in pain; one should have the right to do away with oneself to stop the torment. But he did it in a very bizarre way! Yet this does not surprise me, as he did everything in a weird way!

When he arrived he looked rather lost, you know. We assured him he was in good hands, but he looked sleepy, as if he thought he was dreaming. He was probably telling himself he was dreaming, because at first, when I saw him, I kissed him and surrounded him with all my love, yet he appeared rather distant, as if he was not really with me! He eventually realised it was me indeed, when I told him I knew he had killed himself, I had been warned he was going to arrive, and we were **not judging or condemning him** for doing so. I pointed out we understood him and were distressed by his suffering on Earth. Yet he did take some time to really grasp it was actually me talking to him and not a voice in his head or his imagination!

We all sent him tons of love and healing and positive thoughts, but I reckon he took some time to 'gather himself'. He had been feeling as if he was made of loose pieces and did not feel 'whole'! But we surrounded him and encouraged him and spoke to him of things we did together long ago, the dogs we had and the children I had (you and the others). I reminded him of Algiers, his military service in the Army with the Engineers, then Colomb Béchar and his life in the Sahara desert and all that. It reminded him of his life with us, then without me and gradually he saw that I knew what I was talking about! So he started to listen with more attention. We were able to make him understand that where he is now is really 'Paradise' and it is not where his forest was! Because for him the Earthly life in his forest was 'his paradise', even though he did have lots of problems with brigands and politicians whom he hated etc!

In a way, it's a good thing he 'relaxed' by strolling mentally in his world of dreams, as he was creating 'dreams' with everything he thought about! Because he had suffered, at times they seem to be awful and painful, then gradually they became calmer. Eventually he understood he no longer needed to be concerned about his Earthly life and his health, as the flesh body had well and truly disappeared - therefore the pain and nightmares had too!

We had great difficulties in making him understand, you know! It was not that easy. But as I was talking to him and showed him in his Mind, activities we did together, he started having some good feelings; he **saw again some good times** when he had fun. This helped calming him and bringing back his Mind towards us, as I think he had forgotten us a bit, you know! His Mind was so focused on his forest, his pain and his anger towards everything that went wrong over there!

So we had to make him comprehend he no longer had any need to be angry with politics as there were now 'impassable kilometres' between that and him! He could forget all about that, as thinking about it did not improve things, in fact it made them worse! Indeed, mulling that over surrounded him with greyness and even more anger, which means the waves of his thoughts were becoming even more turbulent!

We finally brought him back to thinking sensibly and to the fact he was with all of us here. My mum and dad also came to welcome him as he used to know them, yet he was wondering why they were there because he did know they had 'died', but he had forgotten that he used to know death does not really exist and one survives it! However, he did not know for sure what it would be like to find oneself in an unreal world, not 'solid' but spiritual or celestial!

As he was worrying about his house and his family of cats and his forest, that started him thinking about how he got over here. So he knew that he had killed himself, consequently he had gone over to the 'Other Side' of Death! That meant he had chosen to come over and be here, outside Earthly life. Therefore, this is what 'death' was - one saw people one used to know who had 'died' too! We had to make him do such little demonstrations of deductions, so that he managed to come to the conclusion: "Right, I got here because I killed myself. I wanted to die in order to stop the pain, the paralysis and the great weakness. Therefore, I went where I wanted to go! So it must be here. Here it's with Mum, Grandpa and Grandma, yet I feel 'alive'. I do not feel dead and vanished, I feel whole, in spite of the suffering endured on Earth!"

I saw he was beginning to understand when he took me in his arms and kissed me as he used to do a long, long time ago on Earth! I had not seen him for ages since he moved to South America. For me he had 'disappeared' in his forest, as he no longer came over to Nice, so we did not meet and he hardly ever wrote! However, I managed to convince him that I had always loved him and still loved him and he had not lost anything on that score.

Moreover, his grandma and grandpa were present too, with beaming smiles and showing themselves as he had known them when he was a little boy. All this helped him remember who he was, why he must be here, since he could see them and we all spoke of intelligent topics and facts that he knew well, instead of it being like in dreams. In dreams one feels people do not have a continuous conversation and do not mention 'solid' memories of what had happened previously.

All this was rather complicated for me to carry out, you know, because I never had to do it before. It's only because my own mum and dad helped me to remember what I and they had done with him that the series of facts created itself gradually.

Then Pierre was able to realise we spoke seriously and sensibly, without making mistakes which can happen in dreams.

In the end it worked! We conquered, as Julius Caesar would say! We could finally meet again at last, as 'friends and parents', rather than 'enemies trying to convince him', if you see what I mean?

To understand you **must not commit suicide**, one must grasp that **it causes *you* more problems than letting your body die gradually**, in order to give time to your own Spirit, your Soul, to settle down - going from one world to the other without any jerks! One needs to stroll a little from one to the other, pop in on and off, before making the Big Step, in order to have time to become acclimatised. That is why churches usually say not to commit suicide and wait for 'normal' death. From what my friends here tell me, it seems to be true, because I can see that for Pierre. It threw him off the tracks at the beginning.

He is ok now and seems to have finally understood! This is a great relief for me at long last! I was getting worried we were not going to manage to open his 'mental eyes'! I feared he was going to live in a world of 'false dreams' which were no help to him and rather confused him, as he did not know for sure where he was! Now everything is much better. He knows where he is! He has lots to learn - all the things I saw and have studied myself since my arrival! But he will have to find his own system of thoughts and actions. He will need to look at his life again, here and on Earth and to feel all the emotions he ever felt in order to analyse them and comprehend them, therefore to understand himself.

Yet, on top of that, he will also be able to have fun and enjoy this fantastic place he sent himself too rather rapidly, in spite of the efforts we all made here to try to prevent him from killing himself! We tried to inspire him **not to do it,** so that his Mind and Spirit did not have to endure that terrible confusion.

But he did not always listen to his 'conscience' (as he thought it was!) Despite this, we still managed to receive him and we finally succeeded in opening his eyes! We still have a lot of work to do; there is always plenty to achieve here. But I cracked an enormous job - making myself be recognised and accepted by Pierre!

BR- Well done! Am so happy for you and him! When it is possible, could you teach him to speak to me?
We shall no doubt have heaps to do for him to be able to do that, but it will probably be possible, so we'll have to see much later, okay?
(English was then suddenly spoken as my Guide stepped in unexpectedly). All those near you are ok. None are suffering in any way. There will always be regrets not to be with loved ones on Earth, but they are all taught not to cry but send loving, positive thoughts. You'll also be reassured to know your Dave is ok, busying himself with all his occupations. He'll no doubt speak with you before long.

19th August 2009 - *English is spoken as my Guide wishes to speak to me.*
If you wish to talk, we are ready to listen. Make the day useful by achieving some more done for your Mum's book, for example typing, but if you want more information we can tell you the rest of the family is ok, of course! They all have their own activities to see to and we are here to look after you and see to our own activities.

BR- What do you do if you are not dealing with me? What do you enjoy doing?
As we speak, your light expands. As it expands, it shows your thoughts. As **I see your thoughts in pictures and sounds of light**, I learn to understand more and more your way

of thinking and to catch those flying thoughts as they pass by! That in itself is a very big activity which I have to practise constantly, as you provide me with a barrage of fast flying thoughts throughout your day! Do you think this is not enough?!

BR- Poor you! It must be boring to have to do the same thing!

It is certainly not the same thing all the time, as you do not think the same thought all the time, do you? We have lots to do here at leisure. All of it are experiments and discoveries, all the time. We have friends among ourselves who let us see what they think, by sending thoughts and we are all 'at the moment' practising this thought, catching sensations, the sensing of the slightest feeling of whatever! It is important to **diagnose and decipher the feelings brought by the thoughts**, as they are the characteristics of our protégés. So, we learn by practising amongst ourselves and among you, the people we look after. I have you as my main personality to look after, but I do help my friends to assist their own protégés, so that we are helping each other and helping others. We have a ring of people whose job is to lend us a hand to look out for those in need on Earth.

BR- Who exactly?

Those we help, our 'Earth children', in the same way as you see us as your 'Guides' or 'Helpers'. So, we look after those but **we are helped ourselves by our 'superiors'**, as you might say, **who have even greater Knowledge and will guide us even more** when situations are getting tricky and awkward. Some circumstances are even nearly impossible to solve, because the Earth persons have made it so, out of sheer laziness or lack of tuning in to our response to their plea for help, whether consciously or not.

300

They have not 'got the right to demand' help, of course, because all is done out of Free Will on both sides! But they can be assured of our love for them. The help we do our best to give is the help similar to the one given by loving parents towards beloved children, if you see what I mean. All for them, nothing asked in return, so there is no resentment or anger. But there can be sadness on our part if our beloved 'child on Earth' is not responding to what has been provided by us.

The fact of looking after someone on Earth is a learning experience for us too! We constantly polish it and learn to be better and better at it all the time! This gives us lots of satisfaction because that is what we chose to do, you see? We accepted to devote some of our 'time' in this world to the 'years' you will be spending on the Earth, so that you can manage to achieve your 'life plan', as we call it - your purpose for going back there. **We are in charge of making sure you try to link up with us** and not forget your origins and why you've gone back to Earth.

There are indeed lots of hiccups and problems as people are not always responsive. In fact most of the time they ignore us and our inner signals - the ones we give them about the 'right enough' pathway! It is an ongoing activity, a constant reminder both for you and us that there is an extremely big need for Mankind to stay tuned to their Inner Self - and that's where we come in as the 'guidance', hopefully! But not all listen!

BR- Sorry if I've given you 'headaches' over the years then, as my life has not always been all peace and quiet!

31st August 2009 - *My Guide 'opens the door' to more communication.*

If you wish to talk to your Dave, you can, as he is always ready to have some news. He's been very busy 'lately' because he has settled more in his new life. He needs a bit of boosting up now and then, to know he has not completely lost touch with you all. He has no expectation of talking to his sister or brother (*on Earth*), but he hopes you will eventually be able to let her know he is ok and has been communicating for a long time! So we'll let him talk to you now and we trust the connection is good so that you can hear each other. As we link up with him, he has a little trouble making himself heard... so we'll start with him at our side. As you talk, he will listen and hear. Ask him a question, that will get things going!

BR- I hear you have been busy, Darling?

You are right, very busy, even more than usual! We have been travelling, Mum, Dad and me. We've been all over to see various places I have not seen before! You know, that's the best way to travel - no fares, no driving or flying, just going from one place to the other! We've visited countries on Earth I had not been to because we have not travelled that far, you and I. And the job I did took me to some but not everywhere.

We had a good time looking at Australia, here and there. I wondered what the 'bush' was exactly and I saw how dry and inhospitable it can be, so that was not exactly my favourite! I saw mountains in Alaska but that was too white, too cold and snowy or icy! So, I am not enamoured with that either! I went with them to the North Pole in passing, since the North Pole always intrigued me because of its situation. But it has not got much to offer, has it? It's not that easy to define exactly where the 'pole' is... but we had quite a look. I had seen films about it, but I thought I'd have a quick glance close up! More snow, blizzards and ice, so that was not really my cup of tea! I would not have wanted to be an Arctic explorer, believe me!

I still have New Zealand in my heart as it is a beautiful country. The mountains, lakes, sea, rivers are very picturesque. But it cannot beat good old England, you know! We have seen a few more mountains and lakes when we went round Scotland you and I but I encountered bigger ones when I went from here to the famous Himalayas - just for the pleasure of seeing the height of those peaks! Incredible yet rather bare in many areas! So, it's still not the best place to be. Many other countries are to be visited if I wanted to. Africa and the rain forest too, but there are always extremes in regions like that! I prefer the middle of the road, the Continent, where you have a bit of everything without having those extremes of temperature, weather or other conditions.

We do little mental trips like that now and again. It is to show me what I could have missed if I had not been, but actually I did not miss them because they are not the types of places I would want to live in or experience, even just as a holiday! I had the advantage of not feeling the cold or the heat as such, but just looking at it all from my viewpoint and that was enough for me. Mum and Dad enjoyed it too but, like me, prefer old England as a steady base! We've been to see other parts of France too which I had not visited. It was just for a bit of fun, but it's not urgent or essential. Just having a bit of a 'mental roam'!

BR- Where did you go?
I saw bits of the main Dordogne area, as there are lovely sceneries of mountains and rivers. There was also the Massif Central I always wondered about, as you and I never went and it was not so appealing from a map. But as I see it more closely, it's quite nice too. We could have enjoyed that if we had been, you know, plenty to see, lots of walks too.

Anyway, now I have started another section of my 'discoveries'. It is to do with the planting of ideas in people's Minds! Making my thoughts reach them and seeing ideas taking shape and growing in their Minds, like lights and colours!

BR- It sounds intriguing! Can you tell me more about it, please?

The thoughts we send each other are the way we communicate (as you may well know by now!). This is what I need to see happen. As we 'talk', we can **see our own thoughts travel to the other person**. It seems to hover and get into their Mind like a wave of colours, according to what we've thought about! It's rather nice and pretty at times; lots of rainbows produced by my Mind approaching and 'invading' the other person's Mind, which is not visible as an object, of course! Their Mind is part of their own Being, they are like a Mind themselves. **They are a Light which understands** what I am sending them, if you see what I mean?!

As we exchange these 'bombardments' of every possible colour (which is how thoughts come across), as well as images of places or things we think about, the surroundings here are quite colourful, as you can imagine! So we have fun with that.

As I did it gradually, it has taught me to accept one has to be careful how one thinks, otherwise lots of things are sent which one did not really mean to send! It's no good having 'useless' passing thoughts which have nothing to do with the other person and to bombard them with it! It is also unpleasant for them to receive such meaningless messages! It is a bit like having a fly which you don't want in the first place, buzzing round and round your head! So we've been busy altogether!

I have not seen your mum for a while. I think she's been occupied with a brother of yours who has arrived, I was told. It was not one of the ones I knew, I reckon, it's the other one? (*Note- Correct! Come to think of it, Dave had never actually met Pierre! I'd never realised that before!*) He's been ill and very unhappy, I gather. It's always a pity when someone suffers so much that they have to be pushed to actions they would not do otherwise. But he is ok now, I understand. She has been with him most of the time. I had my own 'problem' of adaptation to see to so I have not really tried to approach them, so as not to interfere.

Make my link stronger by telling me about our kids, hey? What's the latest news? I have snippets given to me here, I know that you are all fine, overall. Have you been nearer any of them? I have seen Anne-France working hard at her degree! I could sense the thoughts flying round in her head, the despair now and then, yet the hopes rising again and the determination. She is very determined... like her dad! Many tons of love sent from me to them, tell them please.

Has Jim got any closer to having a famous recording studio? He has been working so hard, hasn't he? He's got determination and courage too, the lad! We've got to say that in his favour. He'll build a mountain and knock it down if he needs to, just with his determination! We love and admire him for it.

BR- (Jokingly) You seem to know all about them! I can't get a word in!.

But I need to know more than what I picked from here, you see. (*So I gave Dave the latest details about the children's lives and my working on my mum's book for publication. The phone rang then but I ignored it. Yet the noise must have disturbed my concentration and my link, as my Guide suddenly joined in to help*). As we link again, we have to remind you that sudden breaks like that don't help at all, but we know they can't always be helped. Dave has been patient and is waiting for you to come back on 'online mentally'. Here he is. You can carry on talking to each other. He's got the news and the details. We have helped with the access to the information which, as you know, has to be **dissected into understandable fragments**. He's understood, so you can carry on with the conversation. He's got something to say now. We've made the link stronger for him to 'ride on'.

(Dave is back) Look, I have grasped what you told me, isn't that good? Thanks a lot. It's great to know things are ok 'over there' (or 'down there'?!). We've been keeping an eye on you from here and sending good thoughts to you all from our hearts and Souls. So it's wonderful to see there are results at the other end! All of us here cannot forget you, understand that! Mum and Dad think of you all too. You may not think so, but they do, in the same way as they think of Marion and my brother Ray and their families! We have a big family over here, with all the parents and grandparents and uncles and aunts etc! But there is a big bunch still on Earth too, so we have a job to think of all of you over there! It's our pleasure, mind you! Our pleasure to think we can help a little by sending good thoughts to help you survive the long haul of Earth life.

I've got something to say to you: There's been a little problem nagging you lately, I am told, to do with the publication of your mum's conversations with you. You know, we can see it all done here! We were shown the cover, the title and the book and the people buying it as a big crowd following you for it... so it looks a really good venture. That's going to be successful, you can rest assured. I wanted to confirm it to you, to help you get on with what you've got to do. I am told to tell you that you have no need to fear anything, it will work out. So you've got to be ready for whatever next steps will come. That's to do with you being constantly 'on the job' and off the mark. You can do it, you can have 'my' determination too, like the kiddoes have, can't you?! We know you have some and have been very brave typing and translating all that. It's been a mammoth task indeed!

All to do with thinking of one single goal, you see. One single goal. Then you know where you are going, what you are aiming at. Like when playing tennis and looking at the other end of the court or the goal at football. All the same. Aim right and keep going without looking at the opposition or the distractions around you. Concentrate and you'll win! We have to encourage you from here, they say, because you could lose heart at times when things don't go well. But it's ok now, you'll see.

BR- Thank you all very much!
It's surprising what Mind Power can do! I know you went on a course about it long ago. *(Note- It's The (Jose) Silva Method of Mind Control).* At the time I was wondering why on Earth you wasted your time and money on that! But now I understand you had not wasted anything; it was very useful to learn all that, as it is what we do here! We have to use our Mind Power to make things happen! So you will be ahead of some other people if you constantly use yours.

(Dave then suddenly switches topic and unexpectedly talks of a young lad I am helping and advising to help rebuild himself from within and heal the emotional wounds. My Guide then joined in again). Make your day useful, my friend. Your Dave kisses you goodbye for now. He says he's lost the mental link but the emotional one is still there. He says: "Kiss my kids too for me. Tell them it's from me as well as from you. Love you all. Take care of yourselves". We love you all from here too, you are not alone at all, any of you. So be brave and carry on with what you have to do.

16th October 2009 - *My Guide starts the proceedings.*
We are not only willing to talk, we crave to talk to you, all of us! We have lots to say if we could get it all in before any disruption occurs! The lady who helps you with the (psychic) drawings wanted to come through too but the line seemed too muddled for drawings to be sent easily. Your family are always thinking of you too. We have your mum here, always keen to chat with you, of course... *(Suddenly French is spoken).* Hello Sweetheart, it feels so good speaking to you!

BR- It's great for me too darling Mum. Please give me news about Pierre?

As I told you before, when I first saw Pierre he was out of sorts mentally. He could not make sense of what he thought were 'dreams'! We had to work hard to make him understand that all that he had to do was 'wake up' and realise he was still there, in a 'dream', which in fact had become reality! Eventually he started doing so and now he is learning to grasp what one must do with one's thoughts. He had created (with his Mind) heaps of things around him and he is gradually extricating himself from them by learning to control his thoughts. He's got his work cut out but he is getting there.

BR- It's important that he learns to talk to me too!

The solution to all this is that he must learn to control his thoughts since this is what governs everything here! We cannot do anything which is not linked to what we are thinking. So, if he started thinking about you, that would bring back lots of thoughts of when you were much younger (this is the period when you mostly saw each other) and that risks linking him back too much to the Earth again for the time being! Not good for him to do this at the moment!

Much better that he concentrates on the 'novelties' here and his mental work. When he is at last much calmer and more solid psychologically and emotionally, I mean when he is properly settled in his new life, he will then have the possibility to 'think back' without endangering the work he has been doing to get used to here and feel at ease mentally.

For the time being I leave him in peace, so that he 'plays' with his ideas and thoughts and can see the results. When he finishes this, he'll have progressed more and we'll guide him towards you.

BR- He does not need to talk to me directly; he could say things to you and you'll let me know.

All right, we'll do it as soon as it's feasible. It's vital to be aware that we have to obey those who know more than us here! They are some kind of psychological counsellors, who understand how the Soul and the Spirit work and what is best to do or not to do. We'll manage it, don't worry.

So, now I'll tell you about my own learning here! My education seems to expand and increase constantly. I watched my journeys of 'dreams in the past', as I call them, though I know it appears to me as if in the 'past', compared to the fact I have just lived a life with you. Actually, on the great scale of the Universe and Eternity, neither past nor present have a place, even less than the 'future', which has a lot of 'scope' when one thinks of all the probabilities! But the 'past' had and has its probabilities too... so this creates **an enormous roundabout of possibilities!**

My lives I saw are the ones **I had activated by living them** and learning something out of those existences . That is how one progresses. I am still fascinated by my 'past lives'. I have been doing more reviews to see what was worth looking at to get to know myself better. I notice that the last life (with you) is the clearest in my Mind, obviously, since it is the most recent. So I see it again and analyse to check where I could have done better and what I learnt out of it. I would have had to sieve it to pick where there were some mistakes, but I think I did not make any dreadful ones. So it's a relief not to have been purposely nasty, as this is what hurts the Mind and the Soul - to have been **wicked on purpose**. Nothing can condone being spiteful towards someone who has not really done you any harm. And if he has done so, then you should have overcome it, so as not to drop to his level of pathetic nastiness. Ah! Isn't it hard to be a saint, hey?

Anyway, at least no one judges you here! No tribunal, no god on a throne. It is **you who examine and pass judgement on your own actions** by comparing with what you know you should have been done. It's not always easy to judge oneself, as it hurts sometimes to be faced with situations where one did not act correctly. But if one now knows it was not right to do so, that means one has understood and that's good. If you wish, you can rectify it 'at a distance in time'! You can say to yourself: "Ok, I shall remove this and live that moment again by doing correctly what I should have done!" Then you can delete the mistake and replace it with the good actions! That's it. So you do not have any remorse for too long if you don't hang on to it mentally.

You may have something to do now, so I'd better let you get on?

BR- Have you got anything else to tell me?
Life here is always beautiful, you know, so one can jog along nicely at one's own pace. I have nothing new or extraordinary to tell you except what I have already mentioned. So we can talk again later.

19th November 2009

Mum here, my darling daughter. I wanted to tell you I did lots of exercises to be able to talk to you via a medium on Earth. I had to practise it, so I hope I'll manage to make myself heard whenever we are at one of the séances you go to. I have to pay great attention to what I think and present it very clearly, in an orderly manner, so that my thoughts don't arrive muddled and entangled! I have to be very careful, but it's worth it when they 'land' properly on the other side!

I knew how to do that well recently, because I did it via another medium and he transmitted what I was saying. He did not say it himself, it's me (and us) who made his mouth say it, but he was not using his brain, not his own thoughts (*Note-This means the man was in trance. Interesting to hear that Mum can practise talking through mediums in séances I do **not** attend. Possibility worth recalling if communicators come through in practice circles as well, when no one can recognise them. They are 'learner drivers'!*)

There is so much to do in such occasions, it's incredible! Yet it looks so easy seen from the Earth! Here I must focus tremendously! I can only think of one thing at a time and not deviate, or else thoughts get entwined and end up in incomprehensible gibberish! So I did my 'homework' painstakingly, like my dad showed me and I practised.

I hope it will work with the medium you'll go to one day! I learnt there is more to do if one wants to achieve more and use that ectoplasmic thingy, but that's much harder to do, I reckon. I will need more practice! I thought of doing it too but I don't know whether I would manage as well. We'll have to see, won't we? I'll do my best anyway, you can be sure of that at least*! (Note- Good to know. But there are not that many séances I can get to nowadays!*)

I have something else to tell you too! I saw again a man whom I had not spoken to (on Earth) for many, many years! I had decided not see him again because it was too painful! Yet I have just met him again 'recently'! We had loved each other. He was such a nice young man, though he was not perfect in a way, as I suspect he was probably using me - but I had loved him deeply! Then we parted, because of personal reasons. And now he suddenly reappeared here! I saw him as he was and I was when we knew each other. In those days he'd been very ill and I looked after him. He has recalled this and it reminded him that I had been very kind towards him. Anyway, he is over here too and we met in passing, as all this is history now! Very old indeed! I had done my utmost to forget him when on Earth, but I always thought that one day I may be able to see him again. Then later, I told myself I looked far too old and horrid to show him all my wrinkles instead of my youth of yesteryear! So I did not try to. Also, he may have got married or divorced or be in some other situation, so it was not worth me bothering! Anyway, he is here, Roger, yes, my 'special friend' - of course, not Roger your godfather!

It's strange that we can meet people again and **we look just as we were at the time we knew each other!** Well, all that is over now. What remains now is the friendship. So this is good. It calms Minds and emotions after all that time!

3rd February 2010 - *I was given a 'message' from a mediumistic person who saw a 'lady in mourning' linked to me. I send a thought to my Guide, asking whether they could tell me who she is.*

My dear friend left behind on Earth, you have just asked me about the lady in black clothing. That was obviously one of the closest people you have near you, a lady always on the lookout for your well-being. She was not close to you physically when she was on Earth, but her heart was, because you have always been linked to her, through the love of your mother. She loves you because you love your mother, who was her own daughter. So you have your grandmother's love around you all the time and she does it silently!

She is not the type to make herself or her presence known noisily, or with attention-seeking gestures! She is quiet and discreet but always by your side, ready to help. She had mourned her husband for a very long time and was known as 'the lady in mourning', or so she tells us. We know she suffered when she passed over here and she was in great need of help herself at one time. Now all is well, she can concentrate on helping those she cares for, whether here in our world or in yours. And you are one of her protégés, because you still are her daughter's little girl in her heart and Soul.

You have the privilege to have her by your side, because she is a very brave Spirit who has endured a lot in her lives, over aeons! She has **great Knowledge**, whether to do with communication between people, or to do with the way we as Humans can feel, whether when we are back here or when we go over there to the Earth. You see, you are definitely not alone and definitely not 'trapped' - unless you choose to be, in which case there is nothing we can do - as you have Free Will to wrap a cord around your neck and strangle yourself, metaphorically speaking of course!

Make sure you are up-to-date with everything to do with that unpaid 'job' you had and pass it on to those who want to have it, then stop caring and worrying about it! *(Note- Referring to my time-consuming and volunteer position as Booking & Admin Secretary of York Spiritualist Centre. I followed their advice and retired at the upcoming AGM).* They'll survive, they'll make mistakes and one day they'll see it's not as easy as it looked! Then they'll possibly mellow down. By then, you will not have anything to do with it, you won't care and you'll be doing your own work for the 'Spirit World'!

All that is needed is to be courageous enough to make the first step, retire, say: "No, now is the end"! So sort out your paperwork or whatever else needs doing to make sure you'll have nothing to put up with afterwards. Get on with it and do what's needed to start the final road to success for both your/our books. Our books are the cream of Knowledge, my dear! You cannot ignore them.

BR- I certainly do not!
Respect them, love them, do them justice and let the world know what you have received! Then you'll be able to smile contentedly and know you have always done your best.

7th February 2010 - *At the end of February it will be one year since Pierre passed over.*

Hello Darling! Mum here. It feels so good to speak to you again after what seems a long time. I spent a lot of time with Pierre here, but it did him and me some good, as we had lots of things to say to each other to catch up and understand one other. I saw what happened because he did not want to suffer anymore and become a miserable wretch, unable to do anything whatsoever! He had organised everything and made his friend promise to carry out what he asked him to do.

BR- Did you get more details?

He told me and showed that what happened was for the best for him at the time, because Pierre could not stand the thought of being weak, immobile and paralysed. His condition was continuously worsening and 'the end' was very near anyway. The sight of his beloved cats comforted him, yet at the same time saddened him as he knew he would no longer see them and they'd miss him. But he knew they would not be abandoned and would be looked after by his friends.

BR- Why didn't he use a gun to end it all, instead of using 'chloroform' or whatever chemical he used?

The sight of blood would have horrified his friend and the others nearby and would have made a mess! It would have been awful to see, on top of the fact it could have looked like a murder! So it was not worth making those people suffer. A bag was more discreet for them; they would no longer see the face of their dead friend! It's far worse seeing the mangled face of someone one loves, or even just with dead eyes. Pierre reckons it was much better to hide it! Personally I would have chosen to blow myself up but he preferred to use the other way. I don't quite fully understand, but it was his own idea. Perhaps he assumed he would fall asleep gently and painlessly?

He says it all happened fairly easily. He knew he was 'falling asleep' and was surprised to see me and thought he was dreaming and I was in his dream! This is what delayed things here, as he kept assuming the reason for his 'dreaming' was the chemical he breathed in to put himself to sleep for good! He only came round to grasping the truth when I was finally able to make him understand that he had not dreamt all those conversations we had been having, but we did truly have them here, in this new world!

BR- How is he feeling now? What does he do?

He has nicely 'put on weight', mentally! Apparently he had been ever so ill on Earth, that he was terribly thin! So he started eating (here), mentally of course - since any food here is always 'mental' because imagined and he told himself that he was gaining weight and recovering his strength. He must have rebuilt himself as he used to do 'over there', by eating good fresh fruit and vegetables he loved. Then he went for walks in his 'mental forest'; he imagined himself back there, but fit and in good health.

He needed to say farewell to it, but also to see himself one last time where he loved to be, but in better conditions, that is he saw himself when all was well, without any hassle. He wanted to live again his forest life without the problems he had known! In my opinion, it was a bit weird not to try to escape from it, but he preferred to do this in order to make himself grasp that he had quenched and satisfied his desire to be there. Once this was done, he could allow himself to be elsewhere. Rather strange, I reckon, but we cannot interfere with what someone wants to with his Mind!

BR- Does Pierre know where the friend buried his body?

The flesh body was not something he wanted to see again, you understand? He made that mental trip to see himself again when he was happy there, not when he was miserable, ill then dead! He made that journey in his Mind by rebuilding what he knew to be the most beautiful and pleasant over there. He then lived again all those good times of lovely strolls and satisfying work. It was not to witness dreadful times but to live again what he would have loved to always have, yet which was gradually spoilt by other humans, illness etc.

The most amazing was that he kept marvelling at the inner peace he had when he was there: "My peace, my forest, my quiet life, my peace of Mind", that's all he kept sighing and mentioning! So strange! One would have thought he probably had lots to think and worry about! Yet his best memory of the place was that! Well, he probably needed it, it did him good and he also cured himself of the desire to be there, by immersing himself into it one last time. He emerged from it refreshed and invigorated - after all his recent traumas!

He had to be explained many a thing here relating to the influence of one's thoughts on one's surroundings. He had to learn gradually, like I did too, that what we think becomes reality in front of our eyes! But it took him some time to control his Mind, which is understandable. It's always rather mind-boggling to have to do that, to see things happen without realising we have produced them ourselves in the first place! He is feeling better now.

We need to teach him NOT to think of the 'past', for a while at least, so that he does not go backwards and end up having to start all over again! If he saw himself at the time of his illness and his death it would make him live again all the terror and horrors of those dreadful months - and we have just managed to make him get out of them! Not very good psychology, is it?

Now he has his own mental 'cosy corner' where he has fun with his own thoughts and his own books, just like I had mine! He has always loved reading so this helps him. He has

316

learnt that now the essential for him is to settle down, to really establish himself mentally and 'physically' here. Well, not really physically, of course, but to feel he belongs here and is part of his own environment, so that he has his feet well implanted on this 'new ground', if you see what I mean. That's what he has to do and he seems to be happy about it; he looks reassured and peaceful.

Yet it had taken quite some time to get him out of those 'dreams' he thought he was having! It was rather like talking to a zombie or a sleepy child dreaming with his eyes wide open! He was frightened to go out, scared to hurt himself and he believed he was going to be told off if he did 'something wrong' and all kinds of silly little nonsense! But we succeeded gradually. My mum and dad and I spoke to him, pouring love on to him with all our hearts. We finally won and that's all that matters!

Pierre needs to be given a lot of love to reassure him that he is loved. He has started being less shy or 'bearlike' than he used to be. He has recently begun speaking more and sharing what he feels, how he sees himself and what he is learning! So, things are much better. Yet there will probably be some times when he'll think again about his Earthly life, then we'll have to see what happens! It could make him have some regrets therefore it will depress him, or it could make him angry and therefore destroy his inner peace! This is why we are guiding him towards far more important topics, that is his settling down here. This is what matters now, do you understand? **His Mind must be completely focused on this world** here and feel relaxed and at ease with it. If he did not feel properly established here, he would have 'nightmares' mentally and would find himself living them! Blast! That would upset all he and we had managed to do so far!

So this is has been my main occupation for quite some 'time' now. But I did not lose sight of my own development. I, therefore, learnt heaps of things by doing that work for my own sonny! You see, after all, he is still my own little boy in my heart, my little 'Zaton'! *(His childhood nickname)*. I also prefer to do it for someone I know and love than for somebody I had never met before, hey! It is understandable, isn't it? So that's me and my activities!

My own dad and mum were here too, as they both loved him a lot and he loved them too. We've got used to having him here and going and seeing him in his 'mental den'! Not that we could see where he imagined he was! But he said he was in a peaceful little forest, sitting at the foot of a tree, either reading or gazing at the river etc. So he must have created for himself such a little haven and he pictures himself in it. This is good, it calms the Mind and the Soul, doesn't it?

BR- Many thanks for all these details, darling Mum. You did a really good job!

I'll now go and see what your dad is up to. He told me he had been doing some experiments, so I'll try and see whether I can understand what he was trying to explain to me. I don't know whether I'll manage it but I must always try, otherwise I'll never know!

BR- Have you explored other past lives?

There are people who appeared in my Mind from time to time. It feels as if I remember an old dream. I seem to understand they are people whom I had been a very long time ago, who are coming back to the surface of my Mind. I am coming to this conclusion because I have not seen them here before, then they suddenly appear like in small 'cameos' and I am certain, deep within myself, that I recognise and know them - without really recognising them! As this kind of situation happened before (not identifying them, then learning they were 'me before'), I am now getting used to it!

It's quite fun to see oneself in little snippets, rather like trailers of films - you know, no story, just a few shots to give an idea of the tale. Well, that's how I perceive them, now and then - they just appear when I am not thinking about it. It has perhaps something to do with what I am thinking or doing at that moment, which may have some connection with that particular personality? I have no idea, but it could have! Anyway, that's me and my life recently.

You see, we never waste our time here, if we don't want to waste our eternity. I have had my work cut out ever since I arrived here, haven't I? I beg you to do your best so that our book gets published and sold to people. I know you have had some terrible setbacks, but in our Minds here we can still see the vision of that book on shelves in bookstores. Therefore, it will be there! Do everything you can so that it happen please!

BR- Yes, I assure you I am trying hard! Do you know I went to visit Mich' last month? (My brother Michel, in New Caledonia, Pacific Ocean).

I was told about your trip. I am very pleased for you. I would have loved to be able to do that too, but I would probably have been too exhausted by this very lengthy journey to the other side of the world.

BR- Have you managed to see his home from where you are now?

My inner life showed me places like that. Yes, I went to see him by thinking of him and going round his buildings and **sensing how he feels** when living there. I saw that what matters to him is to have some comfort and the freedom to do what he wants. Also space, he loves to have space around him. He hated Nice and the furniture there and all the books. He seems to have reached a level of inner contentment, which is essential for him, isn't it? He also has his Animals whom he adores, so that's what matters. I am told he was extremely happy you went to visit him. It was important for both of you that you saw each other again. You see, it was worth it and everything went well without danger or unpleasant incident! A big trip into the unknown is always rather frightening, isn't it? You've done it, that's good. I do wish I had been able to do the same! I just did not dare. Perhaps I should have? But you know, one gets used to being at home, without getting the hassle of trips and possible problems outside one's comfort zone! It's rather lazy in a way. Moreover one needs money and good health to go wandering like that, doesn't one? *(Suddenly, English is spoken! My Guide pops in).*

Look after yourself now. Do your tasks and chores to get rid of them as soon as possible, then you'll feel the freedom you've been longing for. It is imperative for the work you have ahead. You have a burden that you absolutely need to shed now or over the next few days or weeks of your time.

BR - You mean the Spiritualist Centre?

Yes, that place and the unpaid work you do there. Just slip out, let them sort themselves out. Why restrict yourself to fastidious, mundane tasks a monkey could do, when you have the ability to teach the world the beauty of Spirit life and the truth that no one dies? You need to expand your wings, yet you have been forcing yourself into a hole! You need to fly instead of staying on the ground! The hassle it gives you is not needed by, or of no interest to, the rest of the world which you need to teach, or rather we need to teach via you. Make it happen. Follow your own path. You have taught only a handful of people compared to those you can teach! Make the leap! There are millions looking for the Truth, Light and Knowledge. Dedicate yourself to them. That's all we wanted to remind you!

****

CHAPTER 7
Healing Process - Shamanism - Mum's message at séance - Mum's past lives - Pierre's introspection - Mind's layers of perception

18th February 2010 - *As my Guide started the conversation, I asked him to send lots of healing to my brother 'Touky', who is currently suffering terribly from a slipped disk.*

You have made your plea very clear. We'll do our best our end. Keep the thoughts, intention and your love going towards him, so that the stream of your loving Energy can be built on with our own stream to aid rectify this unhappy situation. You have to assist us as **this guides us to help us focus on to the personality** you know as your 'brother' in this life, yet who has been someone else at some other 'times' of the periods of your Earth!

You can always rely on us doing our best to help someone in distress or pain, but you can be of assistance too by sending the right loving, concerned and caring Energy, so that the two blend (ours and yours). **We can work better on the confluence point, the junction**. This is where it is meant to go. We know where you are, you know where he is, so we concentrate on to **where you focus.** We send the necessary powerful Energy to heal what can be healed, repair what can be repaired, or send strength to put up with what cannot be repaired easily.

BR- Are you telling me some of it cannot be repaired?

We are saying what cannot be repaired is always helped on an emotional and spiritual level, to give strength to the personality to put up with the physical trauma. This is done in general. We have not said this in the case of your brother, though there will no doubt be bits which are worn out and can't be repaired. But we can assure you that we are doing and will do our very best to relieve what pain and trouble he has. You will have to think of him to help us focus in his direction better, if you don't mind. The matter of Spirit over Matter is of great interest, if you want to learn and discuss it? You need to know more about this until it really becomes second nature to you, because this is what healing and recovery is all about!

If people do not **use their Mind to get healing power to their injured bodily parts, or Mind parts**, they will not have any good results! The injured party should use **their** Mind Power over their flesh body, because they are the ones involved in it. They are better placed than anyone else in either world to make their own body feel or get better!

But we know and understand Mankind is not so receptive to this Knowledge and Understanding. So we can only do our best from this side, to help them power their Mind and their flesh body with the relevant Energy. Their flesh body indeed, as that is where the problem occurred in the end, but there will always be some 'reason' or other for the flesh to be damaged!

Apart from obvious physical accidents, there could also be some **underlying, subconscious cause** as to why the personality would wish to be free from their daily chores or duties or life encumbrances! This is always at the back of anyone's Mind - to be freed from burdens which have possibly accumulated over a long time and make you feel down and fed up and wishing for freedom of Mind and movement.

We are not talking of physical movement - but movement in the sense of the Spirit of the person wanting to be free to achieve some things which, perhaps, their lifestyle or circumstances or other people have been preventing and hindering. We know it is not easy to always live happily and do what we want on Earth, as we have lived there too, at some point or other!

322

So we'll come back to the point of rising above the flesh matter and giving the Mind free rein to visualise and 'make visual happenings', i.e. to see things as they should be, **SEE the body healed!** Because that will lead to a gradual transference into the flesh. All that the Mind thinks and feels, does and will become reflected in the flesh body, as this is indeed a reflection of what the 'Spirit person', as you call it, the Inner and Higher Self, wishes to achieve.

BR- Thanks. Any news about Dave?

All is well with your Dave, don't worry. He has not been able to talk to you much lately, not only because you have been very busy, but because he has been too! He has been immersed in the depths of his own Soul. He has been discovering some of the other aspects he is made of and that has given him a lot to think about. He is happier now, much more settled and full of his newly discovered information. As that is new to him, you can guess he has a lot on his Mind and is pleased about it too!

5th April 2010 - *I want to ask my Teachers a question.*

BR- I know 'Animals' are Spirit Beings. Please tell me what happens to them when they pass over.

As a so-called Animal's Spirit leaves its body because it has had enough of being on Earth, it will automatically come to a world of beauty, peace and tranquillity. It will enjoy peace of Mind and body but there will be no real, 'solid' body. It will know it is no longer in pain, say, if it had some before. It will **enjoy the peace of Mind which all 'Animals' constantly seek**. That is why being threatened or in danger makes them so aggressive. It is the same with Humans, isn't it? So the 'Animal' comes over and bathes in peaceful surroundings suitable for its type, for the time being.

As it progresses towards more shedding of that last 'personality' it had, it will mentally rise above that way of thinking and feel at one with peace within in general. This is what all Beings aim for - peace within as an overall feeling of contentment and stability without any tendency towards any particular feeling. All stable within. No unrest towards joy or sadness, as this is a tilt one way or the other. The all pervading feeling is what all who have understood it call 'nirvana', as I understand your words. But it has to be attained by shedding all thoughts of knowledge-seeking or emotion felt. It has to be Pure Peace within brought by peace within itself! Not by doing something to reach it. It has to just 'be there'.

This is what 'Animals' can do much better than Humans, because they can be content with their lot on Earth, if no one hurts or upsets them. They can enjoy being comfortable and love the moment, instead of hoping to get something else or planning something! You have to understand that **'Animals' come on Earth for a different reason from Humans' goals**. They want to know what it is like to have a physical body to be manipulated by a Mind, a Spirit, but they don't come to experience a wide range of activities.

Usually, contentment in that body is all they seek, if possible, once their body's needs have been seen to. So, whether a hen pecking around or a cat sunbathing, they are all there to be happy with their surroundings and their lot. Wild 'Animals' are the same. As long as they have what they need for the present moment, they are fine. It is Humans who bring trouble and pain, most of the time.

BR- Yet they are in danger from predators, while they are looking for their own food?

The predator would not attack and kill them if they knew the mouse (or other 'prey') is not ready to leave its body!

BR- Did I hear that correctly?!

You can rest assured you have grasped my meaning: **No one dies whose Spirit/Higher Self has not expressed the strong wish (deep within) to leave that flesh body.**

Therefore, the wild 'Animal' eating another will not use one who wants to stay longer, but one who has sent (invisible to you!) **signals it's had enough** and wants to get out of that flesh body! It may be a younger or older 'Animal'. That makes no difference. Age has only to do with the flesh capacity to survive longer. There is no age in our world; all are 'young' and fit. So the 'Animal' being eaten has already 'gone out' in a way, because its wishes have been heard. That's why it does not mind its body being useful to the hungry hunter. Now, this is the law when Animals are left alone in Nature, without the interference of Mankind and its greed and nastiness.

If you have an 'Animal' in a laboratory, being tortured by men to make experiments which have nothing to do with helping Humans (yet people imagine it has!) then the situation will be different in a way. This is because the 'Animal' there may **not** want to die but will be forced to if the torture is unbearable or the poison injected is not survivable! It has been interfered with; its life plan may not have been to be hurt! But the cat stolen from its home to be experimented upon did not choose that as a contented life!

On the other hand, you could have some very advanced Souls who have chosen to **sacrifice** themselves and their poor bodies to **prove to Mankind that all experiments on 'Animals' are useless**, because no survival of the flesh will be achieved by drugs or treatments provided from cruel experiments! **Survival** of Humans (and even 'Animals') **will only come if that patient,** that sick Human, **has chosen to stay longer in his body** and not leave it yet, i.e. not 'die'!

The abhorrent use and **torture of any living creature**, whether Human or 'Animal', for any other purpose than loving

325

them is not and **will never be part of the Universal Law!** No law will ever, ever accept you should or could hurt others in **any** way! It has never been and will never be accepted. *(For more understanding of Spirit World's Knowledge and detailed explanations on that topic, read their book 'Truths, Lies & Distortions').*

Be of cheer *(addressing me, BR)* as you have well understood this point long ago. You have been brought up to know this and you even went beyond what you were taught as a child - you do not eat, hurt or kill them. You have grasped the Law from within and have succeeded there, well done. But do not let others deter you and fight you. Just let them be and they will suffer their own fate when they are shown, once back here, what they did wrong!

On the other hand, remember that to be physically healthy, people need a healthy Mind. If they don't think healthily, they'll end up with an unhealthy body. That is the other rule to always remember. The peace you gain and live by within, is paramount and essential to a healthy, balanced body. You'll have to **shed all unnecessary stress**, so that you can reach a peaceful balance within with no regrets, no anger, no desires for other things than achieving your life plan and its lessons. If you have achieved your 'Life Plan', you will not need or want to stay on Earth. If you have not achieved it, you will need to stay on Earth, so as not to regret not to have completed it.

So make sure your Mind is calm and balanced, so that the body is calm and balanced, therefore healthy, that way it can last longer in this physical world until you have achieved the technical and physical things you came to do.

As you *(me BR)* personally have to be quite fit to be able to finish off what you came for, you do have to pay attention to these words and apply them. Do not let lack of sleep, hurried eating and stress from others sap your inner strength - because if your inner strength is depleted, you will not have a strong resilient body! And where will you be without a flesh body which can carry you around? You will have to be back here and have a baggage of unfinished business and regrets and remorse to have failed yourself! So that would really be shame, wouldn't it?

BR- What about Animals' bond of love and affection for Humans or other 'Animals'? Mum saw her pets. Also, I was told (in a 'message') that I have a donkey in Spirit close to me, though I have not owned one.

What Humans call an 'Animal' is a Spirit Force, a Being made of 'Spirit' who **chose to wear the garment of flesh as an 'Animal'** of some kind.

If you have had pets who have been loved and well looked after, they will always remember that love and that bond and will not let it die. It will always be part of their own Being, so they will sense when you come back here and it will attract them back to you on the vibration of love or friendship. You have been told of a donkey because you have sent love to many a donkey in your life and one in particular. A little donkey you saw in a field who had been hurt and your inside cried for him. He felt it. That's why he comes close to you at times, to say thank you and give you his affection.

But there are Animals who have not been loved as pets, so they have no need to be near Humans when people pass on, as they have no links with them. They will go straight to a 'peaceful pasture', a resting place and will feel good and free.

Those who wish to pop back to be near Humans they've known, or even do not know but they wish to feel or keep feeling the love from another person, will chose to stay near. That's why your mother sees lots of cats etc. But they are only there because they choose this type of association and it makes them feel good, contented and at peace.

BR- Where does the belief in 'Power Animals' fit in, like in shamanic healing?

Those Animals are **symbols of qualities** needed for that particular time or situation. Bears or lions are for strength and courage. A mouse can be for someone who needs to hide more and be quieter. All sorts are shown for the Human Mind to comprehend the qualities needed to strengthen or back up their personality on Earth.

You have to understand those were ways of expressing concepts which are hard to put as a picture. What is the picture or imagery of strength, courage, kindness, wisdom? You need to have a symbolic object or 'Animal' to express and explain it to Humans who can only understand what they can see, touch, smell or taste. This is why those 'protective Animals' have been and are projected in the Mind of the teacher and even the student.

BR- So it is only a symbol? There is no real bear or owl coming close to inspire the Human?

The imagery is most important because how else could a Human tell another less knowledgeable person what he wishes to impart to him? It is indeed just an image, a symbol. Just a picture as an explanation in drawings, if you like.

But the fundamental point, the thing to explain, is the quality and that is what is to be valued, sought after and aimed at. **A quality is something to cherish and treasure**. Find it, get it, keep it and appreciate it more than a precious stone or money! It is impossible to put some value to it.

As you strive towards it and get it gradually, you'll find that the idea or thought or picture of a strong bear, or a gentle cat, or little owl, will be pleasant, soothing, reassuring, all the more if you love 'Animals'. The shaman healer himself may find this imagery helpful, because it is a way of sending and giving healing to the person suffering or in need of help. This is why Shamanism has been in existence for a long time because the Knowledge could easily be passed on, since a picture is worth a thousand words, as you say. You can describe an image. People can make statues or symbols of such 'Animals'. Ideas and concepts are practically impossible to draw, paint or model out of clay! **As people think, they create things and situations** - anything in front of and around them! So people can create such pictures from their own imagination and visualisation! If they do, these creations do not really have a life of their own; they'll stop existing when the person stops thinking about them. This is the same for everything and anything thought about! People need images to understand and that's what Shamanism provides - an image of protection, help and guidance.

BR- While on the subject: I met some shaman ladies doing some very good healing work, but their intriguing method could come across as particularly unusual to anyone only used to Spiritual Healing and laying on hands. Could you please explain the Shamanism belief of 'Soul retrieval'?

(NOTE – Wikipedia definition: Shamanism encompasses the premise that shamans are intermediaries or messengers between the human world and the Spirit worlds. Shamans are said to treat ailments/illness by mending the Soul. Alleviating traumas affecting the Soul/Spirit restores the physical body of the individual to balance and wholeness. Shamans may visit other worlds/dimensions to bring guidance to misguided souls and to ameliorate illnesses of the human Soul caused by foreign elements.

The shaman also enters supernatural realms *or* dimensions *to obtain solutions to problems afflicting the community. The shaman operates primarily within the spiritual world, which in turn affects the human world. The restoration of balance results in the elimination of the ailment. Shamanic beliefs and practices have attracted the interest of scholars from a wide variety of disciplines, including anthropologists, archaeologists, historians, religious studies scholars and psychologists).*

What we see as 'Soul retrieval' may be labelled differently among other cultures or beliefs. What you are dealing with there is the understanding and comprehension that any hurt endured by a Being will register in the 'cloth' of its inmost Self. This is what the 'Soul retriever', the shaman, heals and does his work on. You have to see every Being as a multifaceted Being made of many millions of pieces. A puzzle-like Being, but it's also 'Beings' in a way, as there are many lives superimposed which create the 'final' Being (so to speak)!

Each Soul has its own propensities and characteristics. This is true for each time a person goes back to Earth, so the Soul of **that** particular life will no doubt have to endure (say) many knocks and hurts, but it will not always heal well. As this Soul is left rather damaged, when the Being goes back to another Earthly life, the 'new Soul' of the 'new person' still has the 'canvas' of the 'previous' one floating over its own present Soul's canvas... if you understand what we mean with this allegory? It is important to see how **all the bits of various lives** interfere and impose themselves or, rather, **have an effect on each other** over centuries of your Earthly time.

Since we talk of so-called 'Soul retrieval', I'll explain to you what happens when such actions are taken. If you have someone with lots of traumas in their present life, that person will feel unsettled, confused and unbalanced in many areas of their thinking and emotions. This is because the effect of the traumas and the pain will still linger.

So the shaman goes into a trance link to pick up those feelings and emotions. He goes and absorbs and understands how that person felt at the time and he 're-lives' it for the patient. He then talks to the patient's Mind and Spirit or, more exactly, to the Soul of that particular life and person, saying: "You are suffering, we can help you heal now from those bad days".

The impacted part of that Soul will react to the healing thoughts and Energy. That damaged, traumatised part of the current personality will pick those healing, supportive Energies and will either resist being helped, if it is still too traumatised and scarred - or will accept. Healing will occur when those damaged parts accept to pick themselves up, to shake off the hurt or memories of the hurt.

What a shaman sees as a 'piece' of Soul 'floating away' towards the 'land of the Dead' is not exactly as it is supposed to happen. The 'piece' does not actually float away as the Soul is not a physical object. It is its **Energy** which 'flies away', in as much as this Energy is getting lighter, finer and 'getting away' from the heavier environment of the Earthly vibrations and ways of thinking! It is a bit like a fine mist floating away from a heavier cloud, which may be close to the Earth due to atmospheric conditions. It has the desire to be free again, like when it was in our (Spirit) world.

That is what the shaman senses - the **Soul's desire to be free** from traumas and Earthly conditions, to get away from those happenings. The longing to be free is always linked to the original condition of being a free Spirit Being of Light and Love, as in our world. So the yearning to escape is reflected in the part of the Soul which has suffered the problem(s).

That is what the **shaman sees and senses as a picture.** It is to explain those complex concepts in a more understandable way. Therefore, for example, if you wish to go and have that kind of healing to help sort out your emotions and sore parts of your Soul, you are more than welcome to do so, as it will guide your Self back to being and feeling whole and balanced again.

BR- Would 'normal' hands-on healing achieve the same result as quickly?

As you ask, we'll answer. What you call 'normal' healing is healing! It is transference to the patient of superior, calm, energising Energies coming from the Superior Realms of vibrations. What you can have as 'healing' is the same as you can have in shaman practice. The Energies are rebalanced and reunited, smoothed out, as you blend together all the 'constituents' and 'layers' of what constitutes a spiritual Being, which you and we all are. So you could very well get the same effect with 'normal' hands-on healing. But **it depends on how strongly the Energies are channelled through!**

The best healer on Earth will have a tremendously wide 'opening' for the Energies to get through. He will have a wonderfully receptive access to our world and will blend extremely well with what he is receiving. Therefore, he will be able to let it pass through, unblocked and with ease.

But not all healers are that open and clutter-free! All and most human Beings have clutter on their channel line! So it will be less free flowing and less powerful, in a way; less all-embracing and invasive. Healing will only be as much as that channel allows and can cope with, as the Energy flow needs to be uncluttered, unfettered, not distracted or diverted from what it is doing. Do you see what I mean?

BR- Yes. Perhaps one day I'll go and receive some shaman's healing to experience it?

The lady you know is well known to us (the one with 'Animals' in her heart). You will do well with her as you have some affinities and you'll get on with her all right. You can try. It will not be harmful, of course and you will be able to get some rebalancing done 'underground' on your basic Self. This should help you feel more stable and calmer emotionally, we hope.

BR- Could she do it knowing nothing of my life's events? Or does it help to tell her at least the basic upheavals?

What is needed is a focus on the person, to help sort out the bad bits from the good bits. The lady will need some idea of where to go but it is not absolutely necessary. You could try without telling her anything, though refusing to do so will look rather rude and possibly hurtful or unhelpful - thus creating 'bad', or rather 'not so nice', vibrations between the two of you!

You'd better give her a little but not too much. Enough to make her feel she is tuning into your life and Soul, but not too much, if you feel it's invading your privacy and 'feeding' her too much. You can rely on **this** lady, she is honest. We have the probabilities and possibilities in front of us as we speak to you. We see you going there one day, for yourself, not to help your friends. This is what we pick - you getting on well with her and being helped more than you are expecting. That's all we can say.

17th June 2010 - *I took my friend Christine Shepherd to attend for the first time a private séance (about a dozen people present) with the famous and genuine British physical medium Stewart Alexander. The evening, as always, was fascinating and uplifting, with great displays of the astounding skills of the Spirit scientists. My friend , whom* **nobody else knew**, *was treated to the amazing and mind-boggling personal experience of witnessing at close range 'the passage of matter through matter', carried out by Spirit scientists, a demonstration I experienced personally some years ago at a similar séance.*

This is when Walter, the Spirit communicator in charge of this well-tested 'feat' of superior physics, actually dematerialised a looped cable tie securing the medium's wrist to his armchair, and released the medium's arm, this while

Christine was holding it firmly under her own hand! Then he rematerialised it! Walter then gave her the cable tie still looped to keep as a souvenir. Anyone familiar with cable ties will know it is impossible to open them up. After every séance the only way to release the medium from his chair is to cut off those secure ties from round his wrists and legs.

Christine was thrilled to receive that extraordinary memento, just like I was when I got mine, which is amongst my most precious possessions. Later on that evening, she was also one of the attendees who had the joy to receive some evidential direct communication from both her own parents, speaking to her via the medium's trance. Several other attendees also conversed with Freda, the lady communicator whose task is to facilitate conversations between loved ones in the Afterlife and the recipients in the séance room. Then Freda suddenly said:"Oh, I have someone in my world who is calling out somebody's name. It sounds like Rick to me. Rick, Rick? Can any of you understand this? Sounds like Rick I think" No attendee could. So I only said: "I would understand Rix."

Freda continued: " Oh, that must be it because the lady here is now nodding vigorously and smiling! She was calling 'Rix'. I feel it's your mother, my dear. Would that be correct?" I agreed.

Freda carried on: "Your mother mentions her bracelet. Does it make sense to you?" I replied: "Absolutely!" Freda added: "She says you have her bracelet, it's her bracelet!"- I exclaimed: "That's spot on. Marvellous." Freda said "She is pleased about this. She also brings a memory of baking apples, she enjoyed cooking baked apples. Strange thing to talk about, but that's what she shows me!" I laughed: "Oh! That's true! I had completely forgotten that she used to often do this as she loved them... whereas I really disliked them when I was a child and I moaned when she cooked them! She is now teasing me!"

Just then Mum tried to speak herself, using the

334

entranced medium's vocal chords! She actually uttered a few faint words! Unfortunately I was not close enough to catch what she was saying.

Freda came back: "Sorry my dear, she could not manage it clearly. She was so keen to speak today that she pushed herself forward! She also says she is very close to you, especially at bed time and when you go to sleep."

*All this is correct! Of course my surname is Rix and it was easier for Mum to convey that short name. Regarding the bracelet, Mum bought me my gold bracelet (a replica of the one she wore) for my engagement several decades ago and used to be very upset if I did not wear it. That evening I had it with me, hidden under my sleeves, but **no one** knew as they could not see it! Mum also seems to sense when I stay up too late and tells me off often for going to bed late - and I know we often meet while my body is asleep, which she mentioned as well! Finally, I was also unexpectedly told by Walter the Spirit communicator: "You have a man in our world with the letter **P.** I am told that we must tell you he is perfectly all right now, he can walk. It's important to tell you he CAN walk now!" As **no one knew** about my paralysed brother Pierre, this was great unexpected confirmation that he was fine now!*

19th June 2010 - *My Guide starts the conversation.*

My dear lady should be pleased enough with the result, considering her mum nearly did not 'get in' the loop of conversations! It was due to her cheek and determination that she made herself heard and spoke loud and clear for Freda, the lady in charge, to hear her and pass it on.

That lady in charge has her attention turned to the Earth link and listens with great concentration on both wavelengths, so to speak. She has her awareness turned to Earth people, but at the same time to our side! That's because those here who want to speak send their thoughts intensely towards her, to let her know what they wish to say. It's not as easy as it sounds and takes a lot of determination and attentiveness, like your poor mum had to have. She also tried to speak through the medium but that was not as successful as could have been, because there was a loss of power of thought halfway through. But it was a good try though!

BR- Indeed! Amazing! Poor Mum, she must have been disappointed! Don't worry Mum!

Your mother is no longer distressed about it, because she knows you were and are very pleased to have heard her say those words via the medium and the lady in our world. So there was some communication between you two and you know it was your mum!

We shall now proceed with the rest of our talk, but you'll have to talk to your mother first, as she has been waiting patiently to have her say. You'll find it easier nowadays, you'll see. You'll understand her even better because there has been some adjustment of vibrations. We've got your mother here now, make your link. (*Suddenly French is spoken*). Mum here, Darling! Can you hear me?

BR- Very well!

You see, I did try to let you know I was there and you understood perfectly, didn't you?

BR- Yes indeed. I was so thrilled!

Me too. **I was so happy to be able to actually hear you**! It was a pity I could not make myself understood clearly when I tried to speak through the medium but it is extremely difficult, you know! There are heaps of things to do and think for it to be a success, so it's, as always, a question of practice! But I was delighted you grasped the 'Rix'. I kept telling her to make her say it!

336

There is something I must make you understand now! It seems to me that I have been here for such a long time now *(Note- Eleven years by then)*. I realise there are Earthly things I am beginning to forget! I have to make an effort of memory in order to remember, would you believe? I feel my life here is now the clearest and sharpest! I see the others, including this last one with you in a kind of fog and I must make a great effort of concentration to think of things to say as 'evidence' and memories! This is crazy, isn't it? One would think one would always remember everything, forever. Well, it is not so, sorry!

I am not forgetting you or the boys, of course, but I realise **little details of my** (Earth) **life are becoming more and more blurred.** I worry somewhat about this when I want to speak to you! So that's it! Don't bear me a grudge if I look daft by not recalling things you would perhaps have thought of! It's essential to know this, you see? One forgets gradually many small details which are not important. *(NOTE- Interesting point! Mum is progressing, which means her Mind is shedding off unnecessary Earthly labels and information. That's good).*

BR- Fine. On another occasion you may have more time and be able to recall more. It does not matter. (Short silence... then my Guide steps in to rescue the link).

There is a need for consistency for the flow to be more even and coherent. You'll have to do your bit your end too. It's just a question of getting the vibrations into gear, so to speak, so that they match and blend. You'll hear your mum again now, concentrate please.

(French is spoken again). We are online again Sweetheart. You see, there are often little problems but in the end it still works! Do you want to know what I have been doing lately? Well, I have visited many a place in a rather bizarre way since I don't need to move physically. I was able to

project myself there mentally by just telling myself this is where I wanted to go. I saw other countries I did not know and had not seen before.

The theme of my travels at the moment is the fact I have at last properly understood my life plan for that last life (the 'recent' one with you). I see it again with the emotions and the constraints I have experienced, to see how I overcame and faced all that! But the places and countries I visited are in a way the equivalent of a 'gold star' or lollipops as a reward! So, say, I perhaps examine sad moments, but straight after I pop across to Paris or India or Japan or Australia, just to have some fun and show me something pleasant and different! This is so that the unhappiness of the inspection and introspection is not unpleasant or too permanent in my Mind - otherwise I would or could be surrounding myself with gloominess, which would spoil my joy, my 'eternal life'! It's good, isn't it? A spoonful of sugar makes the horrid medicine go down!

If it interests you, I'll tell you that Pierre's grandmother, my first mother-in-law - the nasty bitch who gave me a hell of a time and had set Pierre against me - must have finally had a guilty conscience and faced it! *(Note- This news is absolutely unexpected and unrequested! It had never crossed my Mind. I am delighted for poor Mum!)* She came to **ask me to forgive her** for doing me so much harm! She knows it was so wrong to have done that without ever trying to rectify things when Pierre, herself and me were still alive on Earth.

At least she actually turned up and spoke of it of her own accord! She also went to see Pierre and explained to him the lies and calumny she told in the past and apologised... and asked for forgiveness for doing us both so much harm! Because of her, practically all his life poor Pierre thought that I did not want him and did not love him, which is not at all true, as you are well aware since you know the truth! I do remember all that, as it broke my heart and I cried for years and years!

Anyway, we talked and finally decided it was over and done with. The best was not to talk of it anymore. Pierre has properly understood now because we all showed him the truth by projecting images in our and his Minds. So, at long last, he and I understand each other!

He has also had his own memories to sort out and analyse. It took him some time but he got there! You see, we do have some work to do, haven't we? But there are also good times of pleasure of all kinds, as you know. Pleasures of the Mind are the best as they last much longer!

Well, Darling, that's the main bulk of my activities because all those little inner and outer trips took me some time. But I also wanted to practise as much as possible means of communicating with you via the medium etc. I did what I had to do to think and concentrate properly. Perhaps it was not the best result, but you understood, so it was worth it!

BR- It was great. Well done and thank you!

29th June 2010 - *A medium friend was due to give a 'reading'/sitting to a stranger, a lady neither of us knew. But before he arrived to do so, I offered to give her a (free) quick sitting while she waited, as I enjoy the practice. I was pleased to be able to link her with three people in Spirit World who chose to come through and whom she recognised. Each had some advice to pass on to her. One of them I recall was a grandfather. But then my medium friend arrived, so I stopped tuning in and he did his sitting. Fairly soon after he started, it seems the client's departed mother came through and also there was mention of a lost child, close to the sitter's heart. I was surprised and disappointed those had not come to me too, as it would have been double proof for the lady. Later on I decided to ask my Guide why this occurred.*

You can rest assured we did not let you down with that lady's sitting! Those communicators in our world, who come to a medium, choose the medium (in this case you) because they feel at ease with your Energies. **You** cannot choose as such who will come and communicate via you, because they have got to be able to link up with your Mind and vibrations. But it was still useful to this sitter.

BR- Yeah, but why didn't I get the mother and the baby, whom she was glad to hear from?

The mother was due to come to you too, but she was **gradually** building up her Energies so it took her a little longer! She would have spoken to you, but then your friend arrived and tuned in, so she went to him. You cannot feel bad about it; you did well and gave what you got. We cannot be responsible for who chooses to go where! It is the choice of the communicators!

BR- Well, I am a bit disappointed all the same.

Many mediums feel the same so no need to beat yourself up! It comes as it comes, that's the result of the experiment. All sittings are an experiment in communications between the two worlds!

12th July 2010 - *Having attended many a physical séance over the years, I recalled times I sat during the wonderful and famous 'Scole experiment' in Norfolk. Among numerous astounding happenings, some cats and dogs had materialised too. I decided to ask my Spirit Teachers about it.*

As we understand it, the process of materialisation is a process of Energies being blended in a certain way, so that Humans can feel, sense and hear the bodies this produced. Apparently it is not too difficult a process if one knows how to do it. But the puzzle in your Mind is how an 'Animal' can have the right understanding of the procedure, to be able to apply it to itself, is that so?

BR- Yes, correct.

Well, we are told it is a question of mental Energies being channelled in the right direction. If you know you are going to be made into what looks like 'solid' to Humans, you learn how to channel your Energies the right way and follow the advice and guidance of our expert scientists.

Some people may say: "Why or how can an 'Animal' be able to juggle all that understanding? It's 'only an 'Animal'! ". We'll answer: There is no such thing as 'only' an 'Animal'! It is a Spirit Being, like all Beings in our world are! And though there is a slight difference in ways of thinking and perception among such Beings - who, for example, have been an 'Animal' at some point - it is imperative to understand the main core of the Being is an Intelligence built in the Being. A Being of Intelligence with a Mind that can achieve feats because it is a Creative Power!

So the main answer about the séance is: The Being you think of as an 'Animal' **has not always been an 'Animal'.** Its feeling for the Earthly world may have been so strong (for example, especially towards its masters or companions) that it may wish to sample their presence again by coming close to them, as a body of flesh or 'fake flesh', if we can use this term for materialisation. Therefore, as it has feelings and emotions, which will lead to creative formations, it will help the construction of a solid (to your eyes and senses) body of some sorts.

It is essential to comprehend that the body always reflects the Mind and the Spirit's emotions and wishes. "Even in an 'Animal'?" some may ask. Of course, why not? An 'Animal' is a spiritual Being, a Being from our world, so it will do so automatically!

BR- Will it be aware/conscious of the fact it is in a séance, an experimental environment, i.e. not a home life set up for example? Or will it imagine it is one?

The Being choosing to come back temporarily as an 'Animal' Being (e.g. dog or cat) to please the feeling and emotions of a person, will do so because it had some attachment, some links, with that world, either directly with one of the participants, or with them because they love cats or dogs. But it could very well be that it chooses to come and try this just for the joy of feeling itself as a solid 'flesh' body again! To feel linked to the Earthly world, but without any worries as to how to live there with concerns about food and pain etc. It just enjoys being in a 'solid' body again for a while, just for the pleasure of it, that's all.

It's well known that most Beings love trying new experiences, new things, just for fun. This is therefore what could be done from our end - appearing solid to those who cannot see us otherwise. The puzzle in your Mind is the fact that a dog would choose, or learn and comprehend the concept of submitting itself to a process to be made more 'solid' (as it seems to you). But you need to remember once more what we said before: **ANY physical body is the solidification of the thoughts, ideas and emotions of any Being, any Mind in the sense of 'Spirit Being'.** This means ANY creative creature!

All 'creatures' are creative anyway, because they have that Inner Urge and inner power to produce more of themselves; to extend themselves; to progress in the sense of expanding their Selves towards more accomplishments! So this is no surprise that a 'one-time dog' would wish to make himself be aware of and experience the delights of a new experiment with links to its old feelings for the Earthly world.

BR- Sorry for the very stupid question, but for the sake of argument would, say, a fish, be able to appear/materialise in a room but without being in water?

As we told you before, it would be for the pleasure of coming back to Earth to re-experience briefly what they had enjoyed before. So it would be very doubtful that a fish (even if 'he' wished to do that!) would be able to cope with not being in water if he rematerialised as a fish! This is because that is how a fish lives - breathing in water, not air. So you'd not be able to have him 'alive' in a hot séance room with no water but just air!

BR- True! Many thanks for your explanations.

27th September 2010 - *My Guide comes forward, using English as usual.*

We are near you all the time. Your mother is here as usual, always very glad to talk with you. Are you ready to receive her discourse? We are nearby if there is any problem with the communication. So we'll leave you with her now. Be of cheer, your mum is very happy! *(Brief silence then French is spoken).* My little Darling, it seems to me we have not spoken for a long time! I wanted to tell you again that I love you and everything is fine here as always! Would you like me to tell you what I have been doing recently?

The main thing is to always learn something and do useful things which teach others or ourselves. So, lately, as I mentioned before, I have been the teacher for people who have just arrived and are not sure where they are. This is exactly what happened to me when I came over! And here I am, now doing and saying what was said to me! I have to encourage them not to cry and not to dread the future for their family on Earth, as that would have a negative effect, not only around themselves here but also around the loved ones left behind! So, they are taught to think in a more positive way.

This is my 'big' job at the moment, as there are lots of people arriving here with this problem. Some of them know a little about the Afterlife, so it's a little easier. But some are completely lost and don't know what they are doing or where they are going. They mentally 'run' left, right and centre searching for I don't know what! It's probably somehow similar to the 'dreams' Pierre had when he came over and believed he was still in his forest, so he felt confused at first.

Having some visions of both worlds at the same time is most bewildering. It is far better to see oneself in only one place in order to cope better. That is what my job to 'rescue refugees' entails. I have to show them what we can do here, how pleasant it is and definitely worth living in this world! This has an 'educational' side to it for me, as I learn to teach others what is to be done. It makes me practise even more, as I must demonstrate examples of 'manufacturing' just using Thought Power! It is fun for me and amazes them, therefore it's good for everybody!

On top of that, I still look after Pierre, though less than before of course, as he needs to be left in peace so that he can adapt more and more and find his feet. He is evidently calmer and happier than he was when he first arrived, but those unsettled moments are 'past' now! He has managed to overcome them and we are all very pleased! He still has a lot to do to totally master his thoughts but he's getting there progressively.

He had a look round his 'estate' here. He feels safer in a kind of forest that he built with his imagination, so we let him be there! He constructed again a kind of dwelling like he had 'over there' (on Earth) and that helps him get his bearings better. He feels more at home. That's all he needs - his own den, like I had too, so that he can 'escape from the crowds', as he says! Though there isn't really any crowd here - except people who want to see him again and welcome him.

Now we have all understood he still prefers solitude to people's company. Therefore, we leave him in peace with his own thoughts, his little occupations and habits! He still has routines which he had over there, I reckon! He still deals with the same things he used to do. So I think the best is to let him do what he wants. He will teach himself, at his own pace, what he really requires and how many things he has in fact no need for! He is at peace and it seems to me his Energy Field and his Soul are much calmer, so that's a good sign!

As far as I am concerned, I have no longer any need for a den, a 'home', as I am far too busy between sharing myself between my friends, my own travellers arriving here and my other occupations. It's incredible how much there is to do, yet all that is fun and interesting. All tastes are catered for! So, we don't get bored here, do we? Certainly not me! Nor Dad, who is still busy with his scientific activities and who certainly has not finished doing that! It's your dad I am talking about. As for mine and my mum, they have evidently far more experience after all those years here, but we all do useful and pleasant 'work' here. I have told you the main points so I'll leave you with all my love, my darling daughter. I have three sons but only one daughter! I send you all lots of kisses.

(Whenever I tuned in over the following weeks, my Teachers dictated even more information for their book 'T, L & D').

17th November 2010 - *My Guide starts the conversation.*
We have your grandmother here. She is delighted to come near you and would love to talk with you if you want. Enjoy the experience of having her close to you once more and being aware of it for a change. You do not always know she is there, yet she is and has always been next to you to guide, influence and encourage you. *(Swift change of communicator).*

My little granddaughter, you have made the leap between you and me. I can now feel your thoughts and sense you can receive mine. I just want to say I love you very much and am indeed very near you in your dealings with your world and the teachings you have received.

BR- Thank you, I love you too Grandma. Please tell me about yourself.

Well, life here is always happy, my dear, you know that. Though you won't realise how wonderful the place is until you come here again one day - but not for now, as you have far too much to achieve first!

BR- Have you seen Pierre?

We have all been to see and look after your brother, who has come over at last. He'd been so ill, the poor man. We were very concerned for him - his state of Mind as well as his physical state. But all that is over now and he has settled down, his own way, like we all do, no one can do it for us.

He had been such a lonely, private person all his life that he has still got that side of the personality he has just been. That's why, for now, he has his imaginary wood where he 'lives' here, so that his surroundings are not too different from what he had known. But this time without the worries, the fears and the disease! He has his Animals around him; he feels their love and the peace he needed so much during the last part of his Earthly life. He did not have enough peace of Mind and had too much anger, resentment and fury at what was going on in the Earthly world!

He has now understood that it is not necessary to think about all that; he need not fret about it, he has left it and understands that is 'their' problems to cope with, not his to 'solve'! He can now enjoy relaxing in that Nature he loved so much and this is what we are pleased about - to have got him

346

out of his mental nightmare or wild dreams. He had to settle mentally first. Then everything calmed down around him and he felt and now feels much happier within. We are happy to keep an eye on him at a distance, so as not to interfere with his private thoughts. But he is all right, don't worry about him.

Another thing to tell you is I have not been as happy in my life as I am now. You are all around me, all those I love, both you and your family on Earth and your mum here, as I can feel you all. So you are all part of me in a way, whether there or here. I care so much about you all I have no regrets about being here of course, but I also want to let you know that you and your brothers and your children are **my** family too! You may not have realised that **I have watched over you for all that time.**

(Note- Grandma cares a lot even though we have never known her on Earth, as she passed over when we were babies or not born).

I cannot prevent things from happening, but I can do my very best to try and soften blows and encourage you all when you are feeling down. And I try to inspire you to do the right or better thing. This is all I wanted to say - to let you know that you have someone supporting you with so much love from here. I am not the only one of course! As you know, your mum and your dad are there too! But we, Léon and I *(Note- Léon is my Grandpa, her husband)* do not usually make ourselves known as much as the rest of the family. So I'll say it once and for all: All of you have all my and Léon's love to help and guide you through your life. We have been here a long time now, so we have learnt a lot and are glad to pass on what we can, when we inspire you to do the best you can.

BR- Thank you ever so much Grandma Léonie, I love you both and am very grateful for all your help.

20th November 2010 - *After my Guide gave me a lot of advice and discussed my life, he then announced that my mum had been waiting to talk with me. She swiftly came 'online':*

My darling daughter, you are here, so am I! Thanks for waiting for me. I wanted to talk to you too.

BR- Hello Mum. It's great to hear you. I love you!

I do love you too. I have heaps to tell you about because I have made more 'historical planned trips'! Yes, I had to plan them, organise them in my Mind so that nothing gets muddled. There was so much to see and do!

BR- Were they your own lives or History?

MY lives of course! That is what is the most important and interesting now, as I must observe properly what 'shapes' me, what I am composed of! I had previously realised and seen that I was not 'just' your mum but had been other people too. And that is screamingly funny, I assure you! I saw myself as an old man, another old woman and also a young lady from elsewhere. It feels so weird!

I recently saw a rather more particular facet. It was a life such a long time ago that I am not quite sure when in Earthly terms. It was in the days when there were Roman soldiers in most countries. In the days of invasions but also Roman civilisation which did quite a lot of good!

I could see all those soldiers around me and I was actually one of them - how about that, hey? Me! A Roman soldier! How could I have ever imagined this? But that's what I saw and felt. As this is the essential part - to sense how one felt in those days and why. Then one can compare it with 'later', throughout other lives, in order to see whether one has learnt anything, or one has somehow improved, one way or the other.

Well, I saw that fortunately I was not nasty and not a

malevolent soldier! I did not harm people! Phew! I was worried in case I was to discover I had tortured some or thrown them to the lions - but I did not! The span of life I examined showed me that, in that life, this man had been who he was just because he wanted to see what good one can do when one conquers a country and civilises the inhabitants. He did not want to murder them. He aimed at being able to show them how to live better and be less like 'savages'. I noticed he was kind-hearted and tended to look after people as individuals. He dealt with them as if he was acquainted with each one, rather than treating them like vanquished losers. They had not really been vanquished but there were Romans there. So, over years or centuries, it allowed them to have better ways of living and more comfort. Roads were built and made more comfortable and useful than the stones they dumped here and there on muddy paths!

Therefore, he was a good man and that life of mine was not shameful. I felt I wore a Roman uniform. The horse I had was my friend throughout that life as far as I could gather. I also observed that I was aware you must not harm people you do not know, simply out of ego or for the fun of it! After all, they are like you. They are no less human than you - you are equals. All that is needed is to reduce the differences if you have more knowledge than them, by showing them how to live better, learn more and understand more.

As for me, I was delighted to realise that, in the end, I did more good than harm there. One always talks of 'conquests' and 'victors' and 'defeated parties' but I did not want to have those sad aspects in my own life. When I went to Earth to live it, I chose to be a soldier to make a favourable difference to some and not to let myself be influenced by others who could be more violent and full of pride. That's why I was able to give myself a 'good mark' for that particular life and have a little smile full of relief!

Then I had to leap across the world, would you believe? The lives I examined did not necessarily take place one after the other. In fact I am not too sure, as I think there is no such thing as 'Time', which means we **observe the choices of lives as forming a kind of circle** without any beginning or end! Therefore, it is not too clear to me whether one life is 'before' another or not.

So when I leapt across the world, I was taken to Siberia. Yes, SIBERIA! Can you imagine? You must be wondering why there? I too wondered... because I could not grasp why anybody would want to shove themselves in a large freezing cold hole like Siberia! That's what surprised me. And you'll see why. I had only mused over the possible reasons for some people to live over there when, suddenly, I saw myself in that region! Not only did I see it as if I was visiting it via a film, but actually saw myself as living there! No, I am not dreaming, neither are you!

I saw it as me, a Siberian woman! I was in fact a woman from a rather undefined era, but I had very long and warm clothing. Several layers. It was a kind of thick, coarse cloth with lots of bits of skin over the lot. There was a succession of thicknesses so it was heavy to wear, as I recall! Not comfortable at all and rather ugly! But I reckon I was not concerned about the ugliness and the 'look' of the times! I had to live, to stay alive. That is all we had in Mind. Have enough to eat, to drink and be warm enough when asleep, so as not to be so cold that we would die! It was a constant worry: not to be too cold and to be able to move and eat enough to survive!

I saw some reindeer and some other kind of Animals with horns like that. I noticed a furry Animal, I think some kind of bear but I was afraid of them, therefore it was not a tamed creature. I was always scared of everything - of the cold, of the lack of sun, lack of light and lack of food! We had some sort of hut and we were all frozen if we did not move about.

There was a fire but it too had to be kept alive! It constantly needed wood and other plants which we put in to burn in order to keep the fire going. It was not a good life; unpleasant, poor and not happy at all either. One could be poor but happy, but there - no way! Not enjoyable at all! I wondered why I had wanted to go and live in such a country! It looked to me as an utter waste of time. Why not treat oneself to something agreeable?

Well, it was demonstrated to me **that life over there was a comparison** between being poor, starving, being very cold and frightened - and having a much more pleasant life like I'd had 'before'. That was my life as an elegant Roman lady - well fed, well dressed, living in the sunshine and much happier! So, that was definitely very different indeed! Luckily I did not want to go back to that Siberia! What a miserable life! What a terrible thing that your dad's poor father was forced to go there!

(Note- My own father and his family were Russian-born and lived in Russia before the Tsar was overthrown. My Russian grandpa Mikhail was an honest Forestry Commission Supervisor. At one point he refused any involvement into the shady dealings of a nobleman. The latter took revenge by pulling strings and having Grandpa Mikhail 'relegated' and exiled to Siberia!

Eventually one of his sons, my own dad Nicolas, became a trainee Officer in the Tsar's Russian Navy. As a young adult in 1920, sadly he suddenly had to go where the Navy went because of the political events which overthrew the Tsar. That meant finally ending up in Tunisia (French land in those days) where France had allocated a naval base to the Tsar's Navy. The young officers training carried on for a while but when the fleet was disbanded, my dad Nicolas was awarded one of the grants offered by France to some young Russian officers. My dad eventually moved to France where he

went to University. Later on, he took on the French nationality.
Sadly, he was never able to see his close family again).

I hope and assume your Russian grandfather Mikhail may have had a slightly better life in his days than my Siberian past life - but in my opinion, it still was not a good place to live in. So you see my adventures never end.

We have fun doing this because we know that in the end we did not stay in whichever place forever. We know we did wake up from that particular 'dream' (if you see each life like a dream) and we have lived many others! And that for the time being anyway, we've got to the present point, which is 'now', that is to say that 'Other Side' where I am and where I talk to you from, at last!

If you want me to carry on talking, I can tell you that I have also seen Pierre again from time to time, to make sure he still knows where he is and to check that he is feeling all right. He likes and prefers to be on his own for now. We are just 'allowed' a short visit in passing, to give him a kiss and assure him of our love for him. Otherwise we can see he is well (of course, since he is here!) but he could have made himself feel unwell, you know! So it's good to notice that he feels much happier now that he is well settled and he simply does just what he wants.

BR- Does he know how to control the power of his thoughts?

He has loads to do as he is constantly building himself some new things - a boat, a house, even an aeroplane to fly over his 'forest'! He keeps himself busy! He has understood that we can use the power of our thoughts, so that's how he practises, because he wants to use it doing and making things that he fancies doing, not what somebody else would like him to do! Well, that's fine; we leave him in peace enjoying himself and learning more and more. So, that's all regarding your brother and me. But I have also seen your Dave in passing. I popped over by casting 'a glance with my thoughts', so I can tell you he is doing all right and has fun with his activities. He appears cheerful and contented, not saddened, as he seems to be deep into things which interest him. I could not quite see what he had in Mind but it looked as if he was absorbed in them and they gave him pleasure.

That's just what is needed here - to be able to delve into various interesting activities to enjoy ourselves and learn more. That way we do not let ourselves slip into depression by ruminating on the fact that our loved ones are not with us for the time being. "For the time being" - those are the magic words which allow us to carry on living happily here! Otherwise there would be no joy if we thought we would never see again those we love and have left behind on the Earth! So there it is. Everything is fine here, as usual.

(Note - Lovely for me to have Mum giving me updated news of my departed family, just like she did on Earth, she was the hub in Nice, keeping her four (adult)children scattered across the world informed by passing their news around the family).

As for you, I know you will 'soon' have our book as a real book - no longer as just sheets of paper or on the computer. A solid book in your hands! I can't wait to see it and to hear you when you talk about it in public, because **I shall come close to you when you discuss it and make speeches**, don't worry! We shall both be there, hey! No question you should be alone since we wrote it together. Then you'll also have the follow up *(this)*, volume 2 to publish. So, you'll have your work cut out and lots of great results! Your brothers will find it more difficult not to believe it is true once the public accepts it.

BR- Mich' says emphatically that he does really believe! Touky probably does too; but he constantly wants even more 'solid' evidence. He does not always properly grasp how things work from 'the Other Side'. Did you understand what I've just said? (My Guide steps in, taking over in English).

Make yourself comfortable for a while. Have a rest. Your mum has understood what you told her, we helped her. So all is well this end. Have a little break, you deserve it. *(I have been conversing/listening/writing with them for two hours!).* We all love you for your efforts and your loving attitude to all those who matter.

16th January 2011 - *My Guide first commented on recent happenings. Then he adds this:*

Focus your attention on what you hear and is said. That's the only way we can keep up the flow, which has to be smooth and uninterrupted for the thought to come over clearly and correctly. That's all you have to concentrate upon. We'll do the rest. We'll take this opportunity to ask you to do something now. *(Note- I have no idea what he'll say next!)*

You have not done any (psychic) drawing for a long while and we are all disappointed at the missed opportunities! So we'd be grateful if you got going again with the pencil.

If you want to get the drawing right, you'll have to do it the way she teaches you. *('She' is the Spirit Art teacher who took over my tuition after the previous (male) tutor seemingly gave up on my lack of 'regular dedication'. He had been a great artist when on Earth centuries ago).*

BR- I am sorry! I had so much to do. But it's also partly because she does not do portraits like he did! She's gone back to doing boring exercises of squiggles and shapes. I guess it is to ensure she and not my Mind has control of the pencil? But it's frustrating for me!

It may be very frustrating and even boring, but she knows how to put it across for the best. So it is in your interest

354

to do as you are asked. Then you'll see it will have been worth it! We'd also like to add this, so please listen carefully: there is no need for you to worry about the past. You have all done this and it's no good. You now need to focus on your future and its apotheosis for it to be worth having lived it and come back here eventually full of relief and joy for having achieved it as you wanted to do it. If you fail it's not because of not wanting it. It will be because of lack of focus and determination. But you have both or nearly both, so you need not worry. Focus on both books and what you can do with each. That way the 'lesson' will have been put across to the public awaiting for enlightening.

BR- Which lesson?

What you'll want to **'teach' them about what you have discovered**. All will be fine. Not everyone will listen, not all will believe, but you'll be pleased to have the majority on your side and that's all that matters at that point. The essential is to have made some people open their Minds and let the light shine in.

Now we'll tell you that your dear mum has been very busy as usual. She has been focussing on the degrees of concentration one can achieve and what it entails and brings about as a result. She'll have been concentrating on various aspects of her life here and on what is beyond the 'life' she imagines she is having here, compared to the states of Mind she is encountering as she delves into various ways of thinking!

There are **ways of projecting one's thoughts and Mind**. That is what she is working on at the moment - the variety of possibilities which the Mind can offer and trigger if focused in the right direction. The Mind has no limit whatsoever! A Mind is not an individual package, isolated from others who think too. All thinking is done at a superior level in our World, superior to what you do on Earth! On Earth you do think, but you focus on your world of Matter. So your thinking is related to that world most of the time whereas if you could focus on what we feel and sense here, you'd see that the consequences of our 'thinking' are not always the same as you would have experienced on Earth! As we feel the need to experience more within ourselves, say, we are able to plunge into our own layers of perception - and that is without physical senses, remember! So be sure to comprehend the difference.

OUR thoughts are triggered not by physical sensations or happenings, but **by internal feelings and emotions or urges.** We look out for various feelings leading to diverse and possibly unexpected outcomes. Those could be from another 'aspect of oneself' as had been known on Earth, or from another 'aspect of oneself' that had **not** been known on Earth but perhaps elsewhere!

Leads will help the Mind find its ways around the conundrum of situations that had not been remembered, or were even never lived as such! The point being: experiencing new experiences, discovering new levels of sensations and vibrations with their own repercussions! Avenues opening to even more discoveries of a kind no Human would understand, as it is **not within the range of human experience.**

So this is what your mum and dad are going through and playing with. Just the game and joy of experiencing and discovering more! What else to do? Why stay on the same level of sameness? Why not look further outside one's present state? And that's what it is all about.

As you are not talking to your mum at the moment, we wanted to let you know why. It's because she's been **focusing her Mind Power on other directions**, directions which are not directions towards you and your love or her love for you (which will never go, never be lost!) but towards other things, as said before. That is why.

If you wonder what your present husband has been

doing so far, he too has had to 'tackle' various jobs, in the sense that he's had to learn a lot of new things - new to him from his point of view as an Earth person fairly recently arrived here. But he is doing well and experiencing what he needs to do. He has to find out what range of thoughts his Mind can gather, acquire and create in order to make sense of the Whole he is, in comparison with the one and only 'aspect' he had known (as 'Dave') when on Earth with you at that particular period of both your experiences.

It is always exciting to know more about oneself. There is nothing more intriguing than discovering one is not just one personality but many! And then gradually knowing what each one has learnt so far to ensure that the accumulation of Knowledge from all has been, or is being, of some use to the 'you' now - if you see what we mean?

BR - Yes perfectly. Many thanks for this update. I am very proud of their progress!

16th April 2011 - *I am sitting quietly by the river in Newby Hall Park (Yorkshire). My Guide comes first.*

There is a little lady who would dearly love to talk to you now. She's been waiting for a long time to be able to do so because you have been so busy and so has she. So we'll let her in. Make sure you know it's your mum - don't doubt or argue. Be relaxed and let her in, whatever language your brain takes it. It does not matter if you receive it in French or in English. It is converted! The Mind of the recipient can adapt to any language because it is really thoughts that are sent. **Thoughts are not always in a specific language or words**! What is sent is usually made of **feelings, impressions and images** - which are meaningful to both parties- which get translated into words by the Mind who has words for it. The brain then helps convey them to the pen. So let your mum speak now.

(Swift change of communicator). My darling, we've made it! It's so good to talk to you again after all this time. I've been ever so busy, you could not believe it! We've done so much, my friends and I! They've shown me so many different ways of going deeply within and **exploring one's Mind**. It's a marvellous tool when you come to think of it. I am still amazed to have been able to do it.

BR- Please explain more?

We've been to a quiet place as often as possible. I've made some trips within myself to see what I could discover about myself that I did not know! We went together in the sense that I was doing the work myself but they were guiding me 'from the outside', so to speak. It was a question of suffocating the thinking part which wants to analyse everything and letting the feeling part surface and show you things that have been buried there for a long time.

So we went deeper and deeper within, because I had to understand what the 'rock foundation' of my own Real Being was - not just the mum you know I was for you. I still feel that for you, don't worry! But I discovered I have been so many other Beings on Earth and also, at times, just here, without 'going' anywhere else! I have to think of words to tell you this and it's not easy as **all I have here are impressions**! It was like going to a carnival and seeing all those disguised people and knowing that all of them had been or were me in one way or the other! It's fascinating because you can't believe what you see at first. It's like seeing a big fat man and telling yourself: "No way could have I been him!" Yet you know you have been, because you can sense the way he feels and thinks! You know what he will be doing and saying, because you have been in his 'head' or, more exactly, your Mind is his Mind too! Just that little bit extra added by the focus on that particular life or personality. It's not easy to put into words or for your Mind to pick up what my impressions have been.

One of my favourite 'aspects' is the one when I was alone, travelling all over the place, discovering things! When I was involved with people, whether family or work colleagues, I always felt a bit trapped by the necessity to do right by them all the time. But when I was free to roam and learn and discover whatever I was encountering, it was real happiness as I could do what I wanted, like here. Pure freedom on Earth is rare so that's what I truly enjoyed - the beauty of Nature and the freedom to find out about things, about the material world which has always fascinated me.

That is what is at the bottom of 'Me. I long for the freedom and love to read or learn and encounter new experiences, new facets, which I had no idea about. That's what 'progressing' is and I love it, you see! You, Dad and all of us, I think, have always been like that, haven't we, in this recent life of mine? Well, I have 'had a ball' recently, making all those extra discoveries.

I have felt the pain of losing loved ones, whether people or Animals, but I have felt the joy of having Knowledge poured into me whenever I looked for it! Nothing is held back from you. It's always there to be drunk at, like a fountain of pure water. But you need to be up to it and wanting to reach it. So this is what I have busied myself with - making trips into the 'Me' of yesteryear and accumulating Knowledge from all quarters, if I can say that.

BR- Can you give me some examples please?

The list is very long! It's hard to recall because they are all instant flashes of recognition of many things at the same time! It's like seeing a kaleidoscope of oneself in one go, one glance! It's taking in the sight of all those squares and shapes and colours and **not** analysing them individually for a long time but **understanding them at once**. Yet now you want me to tell you about one or two 'shapes'? That will be hard, you see! All those exercises are done to teach me to know myself better and more deeply. But I have also done other things. My little Sweetheart, I have other things to tell you too.

I actually saw Pierre. He has changed a lot since I last told you about him! He has now completely accepted that he has no need to 'lock himself' in his favourite forest. Of course, he can go to it, but this is not essential for him to feel at peace, as he can get that everywhere here! All is needed is to focus on what he enjoys and not bother with anything else. He's accepted he has left the Earth and in a way rejoices now, as he hated politics affecting adversely what he believed in. He wanted to rectify everything and could not. He had in Mind the idea of a perfect country, yet that utopia is impossible!

So now he is beginning to concentrate a little more on what he can see here and what can happen if one utilises the power of one's thoughts well. He's made a few trips within to get used to doing it. They don't seem to have been big trips but he's started to grasp why he felt as he did.

He had numerous fears when he was young - fear of the kids mocking him, fear of displeasing his father or me, fear of people whom he could not trust. When living in the Sahara he was dreading scorpions and other such dangers! He was very frightened but never admitted it to anyone, which means all **this was bottled up inside him as a big block and disease of fear!** On top of that he had always been terrified of ever becoming or being paralysed - or of becoming retarded mentally!

Well, he did not turn into an 'imbecile' but the disease paralysed him and led him to make the fatal gesture of committing suicide, because he could no longer bear the idea of getting completely nailed down and immobile for the rest of his life. He knew he would die of it anyway, so he acted to speed it up. This is why, once here, he needed to cleanse himself of all those dreads accumulating in his Mind, in his whole Being in fact!

360

He is much more at ease with himself now and is less of a 'grumpy bear with a sore head' too! Since he came here, he has been smiling many a time! He feels free from all those dangers and fears which he was constantly burdened with, included the frights and dangers in his South American forest as there were plenty too! Yes, he is well, he looks much happier and is interested in what he can do with his Mind and new life here. I reckon he has not had time yet to look into his 'past' lives, but that will come, there is no rush! We are free here and not bound to minutes and hours!

(Suddenly my Guide steps in unexpectedly to say):

You wanted some news of your Dave. He is fine, of course. He has been very busy too and will no doubt ask to talk with you, as it has been some time since he last did it. We wish to help you. We'll be able to combine both your Minds so that you can speak to each other more easily. We want to say he has been a 'good lad' and done his homework thoroughly to be able to progress here. We know he always was a good worker and student, but this has topped the lot! All of you have done well. We are waiting for the link to get stronger. *(I wait for a few brief moments as I remain relaxed, sitting quietly by the river. Then I hear Dave).*

This is the life, isn't it, darling! The life we both love - in Nature at the edge of water. You like it, so do I and did I. You have to be here to see even much better mindscapes and waterscapes! We have such wonderful scenery here, it's indescribable!

Do you want to know what I have been doing for all this time? Well, we are always busy here. It's not a holiday camp in a way as there is something to do all the time, but since it's not compulsory then it's fun! We (My mum, dad and I) have been looking at our lives!

My life on Earth has been busy. I can see all that learning was not always easy and caused lots of stress. It pushed me onwards and I achieved; am pleased and proud of it. But it's nothing compared to having tried to be a good father and even husband, though I don't know whether I always did well there! Maybe not all the time, we know about this.

So, I have been looking, thinking and wondering what I learnt out of that particular (recent) life. That was to teach me certain things. I learnt to communicate with people at a higher level than I had done before apparently. I am told I have lived before and this is a lesson to complement what was lacking before, or so they say.

I still have to complete this 'inspection' to compare that with previous experiences in other lives, but it's interesting and even intriguing. You had spoken to me about reincarnation and I always thought you were potty or mad, as I could not see how one could reincarnate! That was more like a Buddhist or Hindu way of thinking to me and religions appeared like brain-washing in my opinion! But now I am being convinced that it is not the case and one can indeed 'go back' if one wants to, as long as it is **for a purpose.** I think I understand better now what it's all about.

You had said that one day I'll understand - well, you were right! It's beginning to dawn on me that we can live different lives as different persons, because it's all in the learning. What one has not learnt 'before', one can learn 'after'. Simple, isn't it? And yet it is **not even compulsory** - one can choose! I think **I'll WAIT till you are all back here** before I even contemplate such a trip possibility! It is too much fun here to have the mad idea to give it up to go and trail all over the Earth life. I feel happy enough here, I don't need that... not yet anyway!

BR- Have you seen bits of your previous personalities?
If one wants to, one can have a look. I have not really tried as such, as it means having to focus in a different way to

look for other aspects of oneself somewhere in the 'past' (which is not really a past as one has no real Time here!). So, I am waiting to finish what I have been doing and inspecting that recent life. I feel it's too soon to examine other lives yet. I am curious indeed, but I have not been able to concentrate my Mind enough to see in that direction. You'll be told as soon as I get some information, because it will be fun to see myself as someone else totally different, won't it and think "that was me" and I did not even know I had other 'me'!

We are constantly learning here, it's amazing. But it's also very useful, as you can guess and no doubt know. How else would one know one had been on Earth before and been so many different people and probably will be some more in the so-called future! It's incredible - until I came here and realised it **is** credible and even more, it does make sense! So that's where I am at the moment. Happy to potter round with all this.

BR- Have you met some old friends? And have you had to quench some unfulfilled desires?

When the time comes for you to be here, you'll see many of your old friends in the same way as I did. There were not that many, because I was not that old when I passed, but there were a few people I knew who had gone before me. It was good to see them again.

As to your second question, whether I had to fulfil wishes, you can be sure nothing is left to chance here! It's important to feel whole and with no gaps in your learning or your heart. No longings. So this is why I first had to look at what I liked to do on Earth, which was all sorts of sports like tennis, badminton, squash, football. Then I realised that was to give me strength and stamina. As a child, I had felt I was not strong, not a 'big boy'. So, I took up those sports first, because at school and Uni we played them, but also because I wanted to build up my muscles, my body, my strength - and perhaps also

363

my ego, my importance as a lad! So we did see this - but since that, I realised there were a few other things I liked doing, like painting- and I did that quite well indeed by the look of it! So we have a few gaps filled like that.

Piano playing was my sister's forte, she was good at it. I would have liked to play like her, but now I am here it has become a lesser interest. I am not too bothered actually as I feel that longing has gone, because I could and can now listen to some far better music than I would have been able to play anyway! A piano is nothing compared to a whole orchestra or big band, so why bother? I have not tried to be a pianist here. It's not so important.

Much more valuable to me is to discover what I can do with my Mind and invent new ways of creating all sorts and seeing what can be seen in this world! A world which I thought did **not** exist, as the Church was saying things but I always thought it was rather rubbishy! I could not see how you would have a 'god' sitting and watching over you all over the world and 'knowing everything' etc! I could not quite comprehend that!

I knew one had to be as kind as possible, because that's how I had been brought up; I would not want people not to be kind to me. So it made sense. The rest did not seem sensible. So you see, I was not 'religious'. You did well not to call upon a vicar for my funeral! I would have turned around in my lovely coffin! This is to say you did well to understand I was not interested in religion!

So to come back to your question. I was not in need of fulfilling any unfulfilled desires as I am fine now. My desire had been to walk, walk and clear off a long way from that hospital where I was tortured and trapped! After that, I felt much better, though I missed you all a lot, especially the kiddoes. Now I am free and I am not unhappy, you must understand that, so **do not fret for me**!

BR- We love you and think of you.

You can be sure I am ok and know what goes on with you on Earth. I've asked and I am shown when new things happen. Anne-France is having a new job soon. It will be new learning in a way but she'll cope. Jim is not so settled but he'll never sink. He is made of tough stuff and we cannot let him go under. All our thoughts are with him and her, of course. We cannot ignore you and we won't. You can rest assured we are all with you and thinking of you, so be happy in your lives, as much as you can. We'll do the rest this end.

You *(me, BR)* have a lot of work ahead of you, I am told. You have the book you wanted to publish round the corner. *(Volume 1 of 'I'm Not Dead')*.That will take you a lot of time but you will be very successful with it, because you are telling the truth about our world here. ("Our world", hey! I am here too now!) You can rest assured you'll be looked after well too, so do not worry or fret. All will be well. You can go now. Love you all. All my love to you too my little wife, forever.

****

CHAPTER 8

**Volume 1 published - Mind Energy: basis of everything -
Oversoul's facets - 'Purple Dot' - Suicide bombers -
Transplants - Ray's passing - Parents' past lives - Science
cannot create Life**

12th July 2011 - *Morning. The first batch of forty of
volume 1 of 'Mum's books': 'I'm NOT DEAD: I'm ALIVE
without a Body!' arrives from the publisher! I open it on the
dining room table with Mum's photo standing in the middle.
Talking to her aloud, with tears of emotion in my eyes, I tell her
I hope she is able to witness this very Special Moment! And I
thank her for having managed those fascinating and
enlightening conversations. As I was pre-booked for speaking
and doing a mediumship demonstration tomorrow, at a
Spiritualist service in Bridlington, I wanted to use the
opportunity to promote 'our' book. So I needed to have some
copies now to sign and sell. The printer kindly sent that batch
ahead of the rest.*

16th July 2011 - *My Guide opens the way by saying a
few words.*
We need to tell you that your mum has been waiting for
you to ask you to speak with her, as she wants to congratulate
you from the bottom of her heart! Make sure you can feel her
come close, so she can blend her thoughts without having to
fumble for words. She'll send her thoughts and you'll receive
them in words through your own Mind and brain. It is a
delicate **system of transmutation**, but it does work much
better from our end, I can assure you! We'll let her speak now.
(Mum starts speaking, introducing herself humorously).
**This is the lady who wrote a book from the Other Side of
Death!** That should be something extraordinary, shouldn't it?!
We can't do any better than this, hey? Seeing our own book in

print in a world of flesh and blood, yet we are here in a body of no flesh or blood! We have so much joy in our hearts, all of us, for what you have achieved. You've done so well in the end! It was such a pleasure to see you open those packets of books. **We were helped to see you do it** as you had asked your Friend here to escort us, so we could see you perform the ceremonial Grand Opening! We are so proud of you for your superb achievements - translating all those pages and being able to produce in the end something incredibly impressive and of great value to the Souls who will read it! We are absolutely and eternally grateful and proud of you... (I am editing her flow to shorten the text, but Mum went on with even more praises and thanks as she was so happy!)

You made it look appetising and informative and absolutely professionally presented, including our own photos too! Who would have thought when I had my photos taken in those days gone by (Note- One of her at 12 yrs old, another one in her twenties, one with me as a toddler etc.) that I would be on the 'Other Side,' watching them being produced in a book - which I had in a way dictated from beyond my grave! It's absolutely mind-boggling to think that is possible! And yet I know it is, because I have just witnessed it with my very eyes...of 'non-flesh'!!

BR - Thanks Mum. I am happy for you too. Have you discovered more about your Self?

(My Guide steps in). Your mum has been extremely busy lately, as she's been into deeper states of Mind to show her things she had no idea about before. It is rather difficult to explain to you as words are not always conducive to descriptions of inner states, of course! But we could try to explain a few things. This is first to do with the influence that one's Mind has on absolutely everything one ends up being surrounded with.

367

If the Law of the Universe was not based on Mind Power, there would have been different results. But **everything and all are made of Mind Power,** Mind Energy and Creativity built in everything that exists, therefore it reproduces and has repercussions on everything else! That's why the Law has no other outlet than Mind repercussions. We repeat: Whatever one does has to do with Mind Energy, i.e. the Creativity built in everyone and everything that exists!

That in itself has not only amazing consequences, but also astounding outlets, results and upshots, as well as unexpected and often unplanned possibilities. It is a never ending game of Mind fragments bouncing off other Mind fragments - if we can use the word 'fragments' to try and make you understand that as a Mind thinks, the myriads of results are of astronomical dimensions and repercussions, as said before. So your mum is beginning to delve more and more into that side of things and will no doubt have difficulty at times telling you about it. But we could always be there to try and help her put it across, if we can manage it ourselves!

You have parents with great intelligence and interest in what can be learnt and discovered. So you are 'lucky to have inherited' from them that thirst for Knowledge. Except that to be honest you had it yourself in the first place too! You wanted to have them as parents, so that they could urge you through your life to be on the lookout for Knowledge and try to absorb as much as possible! *(Note- Mum always prodded us when children: "Don't waste your time. Do something intelligent and/or read!"*

Make the last leap to get things going with your book promotion now! Make sure everybody knows it exists! What people do with it is their problem. There could be a lot of touring. Will you be prepared to be on the road all the time? Will you have your life and your cat organised for that kind of life? We suggest you plan carefully your outings and itineraries so that you don't suffer from extra stress. It is exciting and exhilarating at first. Then it becomes a chore and is exhausting! So you'll need not to overdo it and do your best to spread the days instead of piling them on top of each other. You may benefit from the rest in between far more than you realise!

BR- Thanks for the advice. It's very kind of you. (Thursday 28 July 2011 - Evening - Found my little Holly dead in her little 'Holly-Wood Manor', the wooden den I bought for her and which she loved. She was the very underweight baby hedgehog I rescued last Winter and nursed throughout the whole freezing Winter and early Spring [in my airing cupboard for constant warmth!] before releasing her in the garden again. She trotted happily in the garden for months afterwards in Spring and early Summer. So it was a shock to find her body had died!

30 July 2011 - *I want to ask my Guide a question.*

BR- Could you tell me about my little Holly? Why did she die? Can you see her?
We have someone near us, a person who looks after those who come over to make sure they feel all right and get settled in happily. We have your grandmother here, who has welcomed your baby hedgehog. The little Animal is fine now, don't worry. It had been quite ill during its last days or period of time when it could not move much. It felt very ill and its inside was sick. We sense an inner body illness, something that 'ate it up' from inside. It could not move, felt terrible and died eventually. We know you will feel quite guilty about it, but you could not have known because your little Animal was not outside during the day. It was to happen anyway - because it looks as if it only wanted to stay on Earth a short time and not go through another of your Earthly Winters. It could have decided not to.

BR- How do you know?

The Soul of this Being is very easily read, you know. We can sense its thoughts and its aims. It wanted to try life on Earth. It did. That was enough for it, as it had experienced the freedom of running around and the affection you had towards it. Its Soul knew of the caring attitude you had towards it. It sensed it. So all was not lost. You gave it love and help, food and freedom. You could not have done more. Do not feel bad about its demise. It had to be one way or the other. And that's the way it went. Make sure you don't suffer from its absence. It would be a pity to spoil your life while it is happy here. You have nothing to reproach yourself for.

BR- Thanks. I am quite upset but I'll try. Could I have some news of my family? Dad, Pierre or Dave?

There is a gentleman here you could speak to, if you want. He is very busy with his own life, but he will no doubt be pleased to share some of it with you - the man who shared your life at one time. "This is Dave!" he says. We'll let him come over and talk to you himself as he has now learnt to do it properly on his own. You can listen and let him talk, ok? *(Sudden change of communicator).*

Bienvenue! Welcome to my world, my little W—- *(his pet name for me).*We have not chatted for a while, have we? Well, I must say, I am very impressed with the big book you've created out of the conversations with us all here! It is quite amazing you could do such a thing in the end! Well done and bravo! You have conquered the silence between the two worlds, as they say. We have been looking at your book as you opened it. We wanted to know what you'd get when it was finished. Your mum is full of joy and laughter at the thought of being the instrument who made that happen! We must say - it is a great feat! We can talk of more publishing if you like.

370

BR- What have you got in mind?

I am told that you'll be publishing more from now on. You'll be as pleased with it as you are with this one. So get cracking! And let's see the results once more! You've done very well indeed. I am once more abashed and ashamed to have doubted you and mocked you when you were trying to tell me about all this stuff on the Afterlife. You could not have been more correct!

Now I'll quickly tell you what I've been doing, so that you don't get too tired writing it all down. This is Paradise indeed. I have not stopped enjoying what I am doing. Please tell our kids that this is the right place for me now, except you could not be here yet, all of you. Not yet. Not for a very long time, unfortunately for me!

We (my parents and I) have been looking at ways to analyse one's recent life and why it has been of good use or not. It is important to do things like that, obviously, because we need to observe what we feel and are able to achieve with our thoughts. But also why we did certain things and what happened as a consequence. It is vital to the process of understanding oneself, as none of us is 'just one person', as I have been told many times now! We are not one individual. We all have various personalities within ourselves, forming our Overall Outer personality. A kind of Big Giant made of lots of little persons who have learnt many different things (over numerous lives) and bring home the knowledge for the Big Giant to be aware of. It is a bit daft to say that, but you know what I mean. I know you'll think I may not be talking like I was when you knew me! But I am trying to explain things which have got no solidity. So I am looking for words to express that in a kind of symbol or picture.

BR- Have you seen any of your other personalities?

Not quite yet. As you ask this, I saw a picture I recall

encountering. I was looking at something and realised it was a familiar scene. But I could not place it at once. That was not to do with what you and I knew when we were together. It was not even to do with when I was on Earth this time! I had the feeling of a 'déjà vu' scene! That must be from some 'other time' which I have not quite recalled properly yet. I'll have to get deeper into it, because it sounds intriguing. I mean, I had never, ever, thought that one could possibly live or have lived several lives! So, that's why it seemed so preposterous!

But now I am here, I am beginning to see there might be some sense into doing so. That way you can learn and discover much more for much longer periods! You don't have to live for a thousand years - as you could not anyway! You just pop in, live it once and pop out. Then you may come back, young again (as a different personality) to live elsewhere and learn other things during that span of lifetime! We know we could be doing that for long stretches at a time, but this is going beyond what I know for now. I'll tell you more when I have experienced anything new and interesting enough to share with you.

Have you got other news for me? How are our kiddoes? I know they are ok, as I have been able to keep track of their happenings over all. We have helpers here who are a bit like newspapers or TV! They tell us the main points about our families' lives on Earth! This is why I can share most of what you know. I only hope Franssou *(his pet name for our daughter Anne- France)* can stay strong with the hassle she has encountered at work! I was told it was not the ideal place she had hoped for. Jim is still trying hard with his own recording studio. It has been a big chunk out of his 'capital'. We can only send them both all our love and positivity, hoping to attract good results all the time.

I have to tell you that your mum came to see me to share the joy of your (and her!) book being done in 'real form', as she said! A solid book to sell, not a lot of pages on a computer! We've had a laugh and a joke about all the photos and we are pleased you chose some good ones. Neither she nor I would have liked to look old or ill! We must let you go now as I am told you have someone else who wants to step close to you and do something with you. So we'll all say we love you all, my little darling and both kiddoes too.

BR- Do you know your brother Ray has been very ill with his kidneys? We thought we may lose him. (I was losing the link... so my Guide stepped in).

Let it be known that there is no danger of this man *(Ray)* to come over just yet. He has not quite finished his chosen path and plan. He'll want to stay a little longer for the sake of his children. We know life can be changed at any time by the body's 'owner', but we feel at the moment that's what the outcome is. You'll have him for a bit longer, whatever length 'a bit' may means as it is up to him as a Soul to decide when he wants to 'come home'.

But we know your **Dave has met him many times during his brother's sleep**. It cannot be discussed in detail unfortunately, because it is a Mind to Mind meeting each time, so it will be their Minds knowing the outcome. But you can rest assured he will be all right for a while anyway. We hope for his sake that he does not suffer, nor does his family. We'll have to let you go now, as your Artist Lady is waiting and has been doing so for quite a while now. So please let her do her practice work as it is much needed for us all to achieve the plans we worked out. All ok now. Bye.

*(This Spirit lady Artist is practising doing psychic portraits via me by using my pencil in 'Automatic Drawing'. It is an amazing communication. Personally I cannot draw portraits and don't particularly like doing so anyway! But I learnt to **let her** manipulate the pencil the way she wants by*

influencing my hand. So if she can control my pencil to her liking, she'll be able to draw portraits of people who show themselves to her in Spirit World, to give evidence of their survival).

1st August 2011 - *During my weekly home group for trance circle practice. Amongst us tonight is a heavily pregnant lady, Beverley. It is her first time as a group member. Matthew, a younger Spirit communicator talking through Ellie, one of the trance mediums, comes regularly and chats with us about his world and ours. He is aware of us as our main Energy colours rather than our flesh bodies.*

I ask him: "Can you tell us what colour our new friend Beverley's Energy is?". *Straight away without a moment hesitation he replies:* "She is a lovely Blue - With a **Purple Dot** in the middle!" *(pointing directly at her 'tummy bump')*

We exclaim: "Oh! You see the colour of her baby? You see it Purple? That's a very spiritual colour! 'Purple Dot'! How about that as a name for him Bev, you were wondering about choosing names?!"

Matthew replies: "Michael".

We ask: "Oh, is that what he wants to be called: Michael?"

Matthew: "No, he is fed up with that name. It's up to his mum to choose a new name. He was called 'Michael' before he chose to come to her! *(He is speaking as if he is looking at snippets of a film).* I can see he used to live in a hot country. Am not sure of the name, it's sunny, it's very warm... His skin was dark, but not very dark, kind of lighter brown... I think he wore some white clothing... He loved playing in the sea. Loved swimming... Swimming like a fish!.. He was fishing too... His house was white and brown, with an orangey round roof. It's made of some solid stuff like... er... bricks made of mud... He rode a rusty old bike... He really loved playing in the water...

We ask: "So he chose Bev as his new mum?

Matthew: "Yes. He is coming to do a job that needs doing. Job on Earth."

I ask: "Is he with you in your world then for now?"

Matthew: "NO! He is in there, with his mum. (*Pointing to her tummy*)

That absolutely unexpected and unrequested, yet so natural, conversation thrilled us all, especially Bev and her mum Betty. The trance medium had not met Beverley before. None of us had discussed the baby, all the more since the birth was not due for another couple of months. So we were delighted to get the surprise revelations and fragments of an obviously 'past life' and the feel of the other personality which 'our Purple Dot' had been - at least as a youngster elsewhere abroad!

24th - 25th September 2011 - *My first 'Author's Table' at Harrogate MBS Festival, promoting and selling my book ND:AWB Volume 1 and my first public talk on authentic insights into the Afterlife - with questions and answers - was very well received by a large audiences - about a hundred people!*

27 September 2011 - *One of my readers asked me a question. So I want to pass it on to my Teachers.*

BR- Since we usually see in Spirit World what we believe in strongly, would a suicide bomber, once he's killed himself in order to kill others, find himself where he believed he'd go - a happy place full of fun and plenty of pretty girls to pamper him etc? (Their answer below is now also included in their 'Truths, Lies & Distortions' to reach even more people).

You are right to think he will imagine he'll go to a lovely place filled with lovely girls and other pleasures. Unfortunately for him, it will **not happen** that way, because he has acted against the wishes of his Higher Self, the 'Real Him'!

If he had acted according to his Higher Soul's wishes, he could have had those pleasures for a while...but he would soon realise they are temporary and 'self induced'! He would not even be able to react to them as he would on Earth, because the **senses of the flesh would NOT be there**...so he would not feel or taste what he would feel or taste in the flesh!

As we said, the Higher Self/the Total Being Self would not be happy and would not agree with what he has done, since he has taken a Life! So the result is likely to be very foggy instead of pure and clear.

BR- But the Mind creates and is the tool of the current Soul (who is a bomber for now!) So why couldn't he see all this 'fun' at least for a little while?

As the Mind creates, that (man's) Mind is still linked to the Superior Part of his Whole Being (a **facet** of which is the **criminal** you speak of). So the Higher Mind will impinge and intrude on the results of the criminal's Mind.

Minds are not just 'tools' to pick up and use and drop. Minds of individuals are part of their Whole, Higher Beings. They are not little utensils in a corner, detached from the reality that they are a Whole, after all. It is the very essence of their Being which has that faculty to make things happen to them.

If criminals make things happen in their imagination which are not suited to their evil actions, i.e. which basically they do not deserve - they will have problems! Because their actions went against their Higher Soul and against the basic and fundamental Law of the Universe: **"You will not harm or kill any other Being - and you will help any you can** during your travels to that (Earthly) sphere!" So they cannot create anything 'good' for them! They produced 'bad', unkind acts against the only Law there is, so they cannot reap 'rewards' from it. This is the basic, fundamental and direct result from their own way of thinking - you think nastily, you receive the boomerang effect of it! You cannot produce light and joy out of hatred and crime.

Taking any life is against the fundamental aim of the Creation of this world. Anybody who has injured, hurt, killed wilfully, cannot possibly 'reap rewards'! This is simply because his own Higher Self, his own Real Self, will be revolted by the acts that the Lower Soul has committed! Committed against his conscience which **will** have tried to dissuade him from doing wrong, doing harm!

The harm done will always reflect itself in the thinking of the perpetrator. That means any **harm done on purpose,** with strong intentions, will be mirrored in whatever thoughts he sends. He will be sending dark, hateful, gloomy projections around himself. So he cannot expect to see sunshine, beauty, joy... and pretty girls! No 'pretty girls' would want to approach such a darkened Soul, whether on Earth or in this World!

We have tried to explain as best as we could. Do you think you have understood the dilemma he has put himself in? He is a 'lost' soul, as long as he does not realise what horrendous harm he has caused. When he does, he will be so full of remorse and regrets (eventually, we hope!) that he will not think of pretty girls and wonderful happenings to please him and his non-existent physical senses! He will be filled with burning regrets and remorse at the sight of what havoc he has caused.

He may even somehow meet those he murdered at the same time as himself! That will not be cause for joy and enjoyment! That will be the beginning of his **own inner hell, within his own Mind!** He will not need to be 'sent' anywhere. He will have built his own blazing hell and hole in his own Mind and Soul. It will take him 'time', more than likely, to try and surface from that - only no doubt to want to make amends somehow to those whose lives he's destroyed and shattered.

We cannot think of any worse fate than feeling guilty and eaten up by remorse. Each personality judges himself individually - not someone on a jury bench, or a big judge in a wig, or one on a throne or any other kind of deity! There is only ONE judge - YOU! So the criminal will be the most severe judge one could imagine - himself! And THAT is sheer Hell in itself!

10th October 2011 - *"Purple Dot" is born safely - at 16.06 hrs - as **Alex** (Brown). He is another Spirit Being coming to Earth to help improve life on it. Watch this space!*

23rd November 2011- *I had been discussing transplants with friends, so I decided to ask for clarification from my dear Teachers.*

BR- Could you give me some information on what you think of organ transplants? Some people think transplants have an influence on the body of the recipient. Could you please clarify? (Their answer is included in their 'T, L & D' book, since it is part of their teachings).

As we see things we'll say this: The transplant of things of the flesh has no influence on the recipient on a 'spiritual' level. The Energies of the flesh do not clash with the Energies of the spiritual which have emotions linked to them. Remember the fact a body of flesh exists is because the 'Spirit' person chose to have that particular body as a vehicle. If the vehicle is deemed not acceptable or not needed any longer, the personality will leave it for a trip back to realms of Energies where physicality does not come into it.

The realm we exist in has nothing to do with the type of Matter you are used to. So, when a body of flesh is no longer any good to you, you can leave it behind and not focus on it anymore. **Focus is what helps keep it alive**; the focus of the **Will** to live in it is what will keep the personality attached to its flesh body. When he/it loses that interest and attachment, the link will break for good.

As you'll see with many transplants, some are accepted and some are not. The reason for this is that the Lifeline/Energy-giving channels have not linked up properly, i.e. the donor's organ has not adjusted itself to the Life Energy of the body it goes into (the recipient). **It needs to be on the same frequencies**. If there is anything out of tune or out of line, it will not work and there will be no blending. It is an essential part of the receiving or losing out.

If the donor is of a different blood type, the body rejects it outright. So, in the same way, if the donated organ does not resonate accordingly with the personality receiving it, the personality as a 'Spirit Being' will not be able to 'manipulate' a link up with that new organ!

BR- So, will there be a need to 'analyse' and match donated organs with the recipient's vibrations - such as 'pitch seeking'? And what about the rumour that the donor's aptitudes, actions in this life and 'past lives' memories' could affect the recipient?

If the donor had 'bad attitudes' or criminal ways of thinking, all this will create negative activities and Energies emanating from his organs and all cells! By their very nature, they would create a wall of 'negativity', not acceptability, i.e. the recipient's body and Soul would not accept it! Because you cannot pass on 'nasty' attitudes or thoughts since the recipient's Soul and Spirit would not accept them. Hence, rejection of the organ!

This does NOT necessarily mean that an organ which is rejected signifies that the donor had 'bad' vibrations or attitudes! NO, it would only mean the vibrations' frequencies did not match, for many reasons. But when you ask: Would an organ affect the person receiving it? Yes, it could, in very small ways, possibly... but certainly not in negative ways, **only positive** ones. As we said before, the receptivity of a body to a donated organ needs to lie in the way the Spirit Being of the recipient's body accepts and can match the vibrations of the organ- and vice versa.

If the Spirit Being cannot find ways of manipulating and handling what has been added to its flesh vehicle, it cannot help it survive. The organ needs to be on the very same wavelength (and other aspects about vibrations we cannot go into now! It is too intricate!) But basically that is why and how the organ can or cannot be accepted. No one has found ways yet to match them for that. If someone can learn to match spiritual vibrations with what is already there, then the acceptance of a life-giving organ will be much easier.

As with everything else, there are always possibilities! But if someone is absolutely intent on leaving his flesh body for good, then he will **not** get better and will not be saved by an organ! He will 'die' anyway and this will be blamed on 'organ rejection' by doctors. Yet it would not exactly be 'organ rejection' in this case but the Spirit Being not wanting to stay on Earth! Not the fault of the organ!

On the other hand, it may well be that a new lease of happier life could be offered to the patient, as he has a new, fresher organ which will help him live better. So, that may trigger his own Higher Self into changing its plan for a while and staying in the body for the time being, for 'a little longer' - as there is no time limit to be charted in Eternity, no need to clock up time! If there was no urgency for the personality to leave the flesh and come back, then it might well stay a bit longer - and thus give people encouragement to share their body parts to help others.

BR- Can I ask another question: What is the Spirit World view on organ transplants?

As Beings of Mind and Light, we have no specific 'views' on transplants, as it does not affect us here. If you mean: Are there reasons why it is 'wrong' or 'right' to carry them out? Well, we'll say 'why not'? If you do some good to another Being, why couldn't you help them even after you have left your own flesh body, since you, as a Spirit Being, decided to discard it?!

There are no rigid rules against it or even for it, except that it may be seen as following the Law of the Universe: 'Do not harm any Being and help them if you can'. If you can help them, then there is nothing wrong with that. Nothing.

So, there is no worry about doing transplants or receiving them. You will NOT be turned into a monster or criminal if you had their organ! And you will not become, say, the best artist in the world either. Because after all, **all** your Being's own vibrations have to fit well with the new ones! So the new 'part' could possibly bring a lighter, or more cheerful, or a touch more artistic angle to your personality... but it does not mean you'll become the best player or artist in the world. It may **enhance your own** innate abilities if you have any in that direction already and possibly 'encourage' them. But remember it is only ONE organ or piece of flesh, not a whole vehicle of flesh! So the influence would be fairly minimal, if there was one!

Conclusion? It is not to be worried or concerned about, as the overall Being has the upper hand on what it does with its vehicle - and the added 'spare part' has only a small 'role'; it is only a small part of it, it is **not** the whole vehicle nor is it the whole Being. Is that a bit clearer now?

BR- What about some allegedly 'studied' cases when a recipient supposedly showed similar tastes to a donor's?

The question about people receiving an organ and feeling or thinking like the donor is not too big a 'problem', as far as we can see from the information we received. If, say, a donor was a 'bad' person (with nasty habits) it would make no difference to the recipient. It would not carry over from one body to the other the nasty attitude, because they were not attitudes of the Higher Self.

BR- But the body is a reflection of the Soul, so organs may reflect it?

The basic personality is a 'Higher Self' who has an aspect of itself projected as a Soul who is **intrinsically good, as it is part of a 'Spirit Being'**, which means Kindness and Compassion. So the reflection of the nasty attitude (if ever there was such a reflection!) will not be in the organ. It cannot be, simply because the Energy of the Higher Being within that Soul would wash off/overcome the 'passing' nasty attitude, as it goes against what all Beings are basically composed of.

Little habits may have influenced a little if it is already part of the personality of the donor AND the recipient. If the recipient was ready to change his habits on that not so important level, this could perhaps be a trigger for his own 'possibility', his possible taste or skill, to tilt that new way. But it is not to be worried about as far as getting 'bad influences'!

BR- Would transplanting a mathematical genius' brain (or other part), mean that the recipient could become a genius in Maths?

The transplant of a piece of flesh can carry only so much of the Energy of the personality. And the brain is not the Mind!

BR- But isn't it said that every cell or so is like the acorn containing the whole oak tree? A kind of hologram?

The meaning of our message is we cannot see why someone would **become a totally different person unless he wishes to do so** and change. If he wishes to change that much, from being useless at maths to becoming a genius, he must have already had some 'seeds' of it within himself; he must already have that great possibility in his Mind and way of thinking and in the **abilities he chose to have** before coming to Earth. Maybe he was a genius' before' coming to this life, in which case such a transplant (assuming there was some of that Energy in it!) would only awaken an old latent gift and reawaken his 'previous' abilities - IF that's what the recipient would want for himself! No way could a recipient become 'possessed' by another person's empathies or abilities or worse, hatred, as this is not the kind of thing the higher Self would accept to have - as it goes against the grain and the Law of the Universe!

BR- Has the flesh heart got special Energies (as some people say), since it is near the emotion centre/chakra/vortex?

It you think a heart of flesh (whether of a chicken or a man) would make a difference to the way a man becomes kinder or not, you are **wrong**! If he is kind in his behaviour towards others, it is simply because he has let his own Real Self come through, as all Beings should do! If he is nasty, it has nothing to do with the heart of flesh! It's to do with his Mind, his way of thinking, his attitude to life and others, his ways of reacting to what he may have suffered. So there is no way a heart of flesh could influence people to that kind of degree!

They will not become a 'Mother Theresa' if they have a heart transplant! They may no doubt get a new lease of life, from having been unwell to being well now and **that** may give them relief and gratitude for still being alive - so they'll be grateful to the donor. Their attitude to life around them may change for the better, but that has **nothing to do** with the Energies and vibrations of the piece of flesh that moved from one body of flesh to another - his.

Since the flesh is the reflection of the person who chose to have this body, when he built his vehicle for the Earth trip, then he will have designed it in accordance with the Law of Compassion and Kindness to all. Therefore, Kindness is part of it and could 'influence' anyone - if you so believed - because it outmatches what the other person is composed of. Nothing to do with the flesh heart.

If you want to talk of little habits, hobbies or new activities similar to the previous owner of the body parts, then it is a 'coincidence', which in fact is only a **merging of Minds at a higher level**. The recipient may well link to the Mind of the previous owner, who has made the gift of his organ, therefore he may be on the same wavelength, which could create coinciding tastes and interests.

That is more likely where the link would be, rather than the actual flesh piece! Their link would be via the flesh organ, yet not actually transmitting the habit or interest via the Energy of the flesh but via the link of Mind to Mind - they connect to the other's way of thinking. Since all Beings are linked anyway and have been over aeons and distances that would not be any surprise.

This is what we'd say to those who enquire: Look for the link of Minds and Souls at the higher level, at the level of those Minds' and Souls' wavelengths - **not through the piece of flesh** which may break out and die, yet the interest in the hobby, say, would still be there afterwards! It would not necessarily 'die', would it? This is because the Mind of the donor and the recipient's Mind had a link beyond the Earthly, physical aspect of the body of flesh.

BR- I am concerned that though organ transplants are acceptable as such by your World, we must remember they have become possible originally because of numerous trials on poor vivisected animals. They suffered and died for Mankind to practise those first transplants.

We'll say this: If you think we should condemn organ transplants because of their original 'invention' being made possible by Animals actually being used and tortured for it, yes, you are right - we would not accept them as something to praise. The idea of replacing a heart etc. is very clever and laudable, but it has unfortunately been made possible by some Animals sacrificing themselves to make it feasible.

We have that dilemma too - but if you started all points of view from 'You should not kill anything and anybody', then you would look for different ways to help Mankind! Transplants were unfortunately made available because **Mankind decided to torture Animals to do that kind of work.** The sad thing is that Mankind has never put Animals first; it's always been themselves first, which is very deplorable.

We'll have to point out that Man would not be on Earth if he had not chosen and designed his body to be on Earth for that particular length of time. As we've told you before, if someone chooses to live a long or short life, it's only due to the person's Soul wanting to stay or leave when they decide! So if the heart or liver is not working, it could be a signal that the person's Soul is not willing to stay any longer and wishes to leave. He will leave anyway, even if he has a new transplanted liver or heart!

So why is he here after the transplant? As we explained earlier, he may have decided to stay a bit longer as that transplant gave him a boost, a more comfortable life and he may have changed his mind as to the length of his Earthly stay. But it won't be forever!

So, if he had realised what harm had been done to all those Animals used as 'guinea pigs' whose hearts etc. were taken out to practise, then he as a Spirit Being may not have wanted it to happen. After all, many transplants do not work because of the vibrations not matching, or because the patient did not want to stay anyway, so that was a wasted organ transplant!

But we can see the human dilemma - now that organ transplants are feasible, it seems unfair not to offer or ask for them. That is entirely up to human Beings to decide. If and when their conscience and their Spiritual wisdom make them realise (once they are back here anyway) that it all stemmed from Animals' suffering, then they may change or would have changed their views and probably would have left their bodies earlier, so as not to drag on the scenario and lead it to an 'imposed' or 'more likely' transplant.

It shows that Mankind's responsibility spreads a long way over generations! Many people will never even think of what happened when the first transplants were successfully created! There will have been numerous attempts before, leading to the deaths of numerous Animals tortured and killed for nothing. But that's what Mankind does and their lack of knowledge of what should be is tremendously wide! So...make sure you tell them!

22nd December 2011 - *Dave's brother Raymond passed over Sunday morning 4th Dec. His funeral was yesterday, Monday. I waited until then to try and ask Dave what he knew of Ray's arrival and whether his brother is aware of where he is. I don't know anything about Ray's own belief or lack of. His sister and brother-in-law are limited by the traditional church indoctrination. Ray may not have seen Dave yet, if Ray's Mind was too closed! Unexpectedly my Guide steps in first!*

When they wrote the various bibles throughout centuries, they always meant 'to tell the truth' and help people they were in charge of, or whom they thought needed teaching and enlightening. It is still the same nowadays. They think they are doing the right thing for the right reasons. Unfortunately, the crowds they speak to these days are far more advanced education-wise and far more refined than those of centuries ago, which means a lot of the religious 'teachings' are obsolete or downright grotesque, when you think of some of the advice given by those who fancied themselves as teachers or 'shepherds of the masses'!

The old teachings became less mysterious to the masses when they understood that the resurrection they spoke of was not so much physical (as a new flesh body) than spiritual - the Mind is still alive, as the Spirit lives on - so the personality has not died and still exists. It took some time for people to sieve (out of what was imposed on them) what was proper spiritual guidance and what was exaggeration, fear of the State, fear of the Church, the political angle and the religious aspect! All those were too often intermingled or had a profound influence on the books to come and the religious teachings implanted in the Minds of men and women.

When those in your present world come to realise that some of the old fashioned indoctrinations do not apply to the lives you all lead nowadays, or the old books do not fit in with the new book and teachings of the man Jesus, then there will be a far greater understanding.

As the bird flies away from his nest, he can gain more altitude to see better from above and afar, so should your Mind be able to do the same. As you feel lighter and less focused on your world and more turned towards our voices and thoughts, then you should feel lighter and more enlightened. We want to bring this to get you going on our pathway and listen to what we have to say.

You have here two men from our world who have recently met each other again, as the reunion was most unexpected for the new arrival *(Ray)*! He had never imagined he would be able to see his mother and father accompanied by his own younger brother *(Dave)...* and yet feel as good as he did when he was younger and healthier!

This man has just passed over recently to our world and needs to say to you that you were right! He thought you talked rubbish when you said *(at Dave's funeral)* that you "knew one never died as such and you knew the other world existed and one could communicate!" He had a snort at your words then - but he is nearly remorseful now!

He has seen his own brother, mother, father, uncle and many others who have been waiting for his arrival for some 'time' now, as we could see from here that his Soul was fading; it was losing strength and hold of the flesh body. When the parting of the two occurred, **the Soul felt refreshed the moment it left the ailing body** of flesh. That 'gave it wings', so to speak! The moment the body was left behind, with all its pain and weakness, the Soul and Spirit of the man felt great.

It's in that state of Mind that he 'arrived' here. 'Arrived' in the sense that his focus was no longer on the flesh and physical world, but on what he was looking at in wonder! Having his own mum and dad with the brother he lost not so long ago and found again now was such a sight for him that he was practically speechless! He felt in awe yet full of joy. He could not comprehend at first how he could still see them since they were 'dead'! But the two parents stepped forward and embraced him joyfully to make him feel again how he used to feel when he was in their presence. He loved being home with them when he was younger and healthier. He loved going home and sharing tea and jokes with his father. He loved his mum's cooking and baking, he had a 'home life attitude' and never lost it, he says. So now, seeing them back with him after all those years was an astounding shock that took him by surprise and that left him 'blank' for a moment! But they made sure he understood he was ok, still alive and so were they!

Dave, his brother, had his say too, to welcome him: "You are all right for good now lad! No more pain and trouble ever again! How about that? I am used to it now but I know how you feel because I had the same shock when seeing Mum and Dad. We are all ok here and so are you! No need to fret or worry - you are all right for good! *(Note- Long standing family joke: For decades, all that Ray would say over the phone was: "I'm all right". We could not get much out of him past that!)* No more illness, it's all gone so no need to think about it. You'll be fine here, we are with you and we'll show you round. You'll enjoy it like we do, so don't panic!"

They took him round to his 'place'. They had built a nice house like the one he had on Earth, so that his 'landscape' was not too different to start with. They knew he would have need of a 'home' as that man was a 'home bird', as his mum called him. That little house was just right for him. But the thought of his family left behind started sinking in, as there were none of his loved ones from the Earth in that new house. However, his brother and parents made sure he understood what could be done and how to cope with the loss and parting.

It's never been easy and never is for anyone to find themselves here and know their loved ones are still on Earth pining for them! So they got talking to each other and settled him down with calming thoughts and jokes too, as they never stopped laughing with joy and happiness in their hearts. The atmosphere was constantly lifted to make him feel light, good and healthy in order to help dissipate his gloom whenever he thought of his wife and family left behind. We have ways here to help those who've arrived and have to settle after an arduous journey. So we can assure you he is looked after.

BR- I knew he would be, somehow!

There is a man who wants to speak to you directly now. *(BR's note- I guessed it would be Dave)*. We have got him now, love, he is fine! We've told him all about here - well, not all, but lots to help him understand he has nothing to fear. We've had a great time laughing at all the goings on in both worlds past and present. We tend to reminisce. It's more fun to reminisce from here, believe me, darling! It's so different and so strange to say: "When I was on Earth etc." It feels so weird even when you've been here for quite a while, compared to him who's just arrived very recently.

We've been shown his funeral! My dad asked that someone (from our world) did what they did when it was mine. *(Note- See Vol.1 ND: AWB - Spirit 'video' of the event!)*

They showed him what the place in the church looked like, with the coffin in the middle and people all around - but they avoided showing him the crying crowd as that would have upset him too much! They moved him to seeing the funeral drinks and 'munch', as he called it. We did not look at the coffin closely as it can be a shock to a newcomer. So he was shown it briefly in the church, but they did not dwell on the fact that the body was in it as the thought was still too raw and the family is still too close.

(My Guide steps in with more details). We saw them in the room for the reception, as then they were a little more relaxed. That black dress suited his wife, he said. He liked her in black as she was fair when she was young and he liked it and the contrast. We had to see a few 'speeches' or 'toasts', but the overall effect was to show him that people loved him and cared and came to the final farewell. But none seemed to know **he was not really in the box,** but happier in a way, by their side, so to speak - though not quite, as we could not let him come too close mentally and emotionally; he was still too shaken by the thought of his grieving loved ones. We are used

to showing people what they can cope with when they want to see what their 'send-off' was like! They usually enjoy knowing who'd been there and who said what. So the speeches and drinks etc. are more what helps the one who has gone, than seeing his body being put in a hole or burnt, which can be rather unnerving, or triggering previous unhappy memories of funerals!

As you have plenty of time ahead to make those who don't know the truth think, we'll say this for now: That little man who's just arrived amongst us *(Ray)* is most happy for himself to have found his family again, those he had lost. He had been very, very hurt and grieving when they'd all gone, one by one. He was indeed very upset. His Soul suffered the blows each time and that was no good for him. He suffered emotionally but would not talk about it. He could not discuss it because he felt and thought he'd put a burden on those who had also lost the same loved ones. **So he kept his feelings and his pain to himself** and thought the years going by would help heal the rift inside him; one great big rift, a canyon! He had lost his mum and dad way back in your time, but the loss was in his heart all along, all the time! He missed them very badly because he lived where he'd always been - in the same town as them. So that constantly brought back memories for him. He could not talk about it but he did feel it.

Now he has found them again, including his younger brother, he is over the moon at the ease with which they can not only communicate again like normal talks, but also the fact they've picked up conversations which they had 'way back'. As he says: "It's like not having been parted! We carried on with 'local chitchat'. That was not my style, but mum liked to talk of what people around had said or been up to. And I was glad to share news with them". *(After this exciting and reassuring report, my Guide then discusses private topics).*

25th December 2011 - *I send a question, mentally, to my Guide.*

BR- Any news from my dad or mum or even Pierre? But please do not disturb them if they are busy!
My idea of fun has never been spending hours in front of a 'telly', believe me!

BR- This is a funny thing to start with! Who is speaking? Is that you Mum?
It's Mum here indeed. How are you my darling daughter? We are on the same wavelength and it feels very smooth and easy to send my thoughts into your Mind now. We'll tell you what the three of us have been doing recently - your dad, mine and me.

We've been trying new experiments. It's new to me anyway, even if the dads have done it before. So we'll say it was more trips into our Minds. This time it was to see **where the three of us had met before**, if ever. It was to find out who each one of us was when we were someone different 'before' and why we came back as we did 'this last time'. So, I saw 'me' as a soldier in a foreign country! A very old soldier when I saw him. He was poor, as most soldiers were. It felt rather Napoleonic Wars time. *(Note-Early 1800s)*. It was not enjoyable indeed! My dad and yours were there too. The three of us were there! As different soldiers, not related. There was a need for soldiers to protect the country.

BR- Which side were you on?
I am pretty sure I was one of Napoleon's soldiers as I saw the tunic, the uniform, like I remember them. And my dad and yours were too. All together as keen to get out of the army if possible, but it was not feasible - we were stuck with it, as it happens! So, we saw our link was pure camaraderie and

392

friendship. We were all subjected to poverty and hardship, yet ready and willing to help each other for survival.

That was interesting indeed, because I did not know until then that I'd been in Napoleon's armies. It was not fun! Lots of injuries and deaths. But during our flashback, we did not see or dwell on that obvious side. We were looking for our mutual connections. That's how I recognised your dad, by his bravery and ideas too, to help us concoct ways of being more comfortable; he was very resourceful! As to my own father, he was too - always the kind man he still is, helping all those who had fallen, injured or dying, not letting anyone suffer on his own.

My friends of 'then' became my husband and my own dad *(in her recent life)*! Funny to think of it that way, but it had to be examined to see where we came together and why. We had always been helping each other and had a link of admiration as well as friendship.

As for my mother, it was different. She was not in that war anyway. She was not a man when I met her. She was a woman again - a very devoted religious nun, a 'sister'. She had a strict upbringing and strict rules in her convent. We met as I was a pupil of hers in one of my lives. Just a young pupil who grew up of course and learnt more and more afterwards. My Mind was a boy's Mind, I was a little lad! That was in my younger days but it was useful. Everything she taught me made me want to learn more and more as I became older and started my travels.

Like my present dad said: This time round *(in the recent life)* we chose different roles to be able to maintain the friendship and the warm links, but the Knowledge had to come from different directions and from different roles. We had to change parts for our own purposes in this recent life where we knew each other as a family. But we still had the fondness for one another and all continually loved to learn and pass it on. So that has survived until now too!

You see, we do have a great time here! This is the kind of 'exercise' I am doing at the moment, as I want and need to build up a longer and larger picture of who I really am on the larger scale. That is a kind of 'family tree of myself', with my various aspects and personalities being the members of the 'Me' as a whole family of One Being... if you see what I mean!

I'll tell you more about other lives later, when you can take it in. We can see you look a bit tired and I am told you've been writing for a long time today so your Mind and concentration are fading a little. Therefore, we'll leave that for next time, if you like.

BR- Yes please, don't forget! I am tired as I took down eleven large pages of dictation from your world! And I also spent a long time earlier with my Spirit Artist, who practised doing some psychic drawing through me.

We won't forget! We also know your Dave has been meeting up with his brother and that has been a momentous reunion, as the two men used not to believe in 'all this nonsense', as they said! They never thought, when on Earth, that they would be meeting each other again one day! Well, it's happened! So that's good. For it could have gone wrong if, say, the second arrival had not opened his Mind enough to see his family here. If he had been ensconced in some rigid beliefs, he **may have not seen them** waiting for him. So it's good indeed. He is here and they are having a good time together making up for all the years missed! Now we'll let you get some rest and hope you'll come back and want to talk to me and us again. We love you for all your efforts. Try to sleep more and you'll feel better for it! We'll meet more often that way too.

7th January 2012 - *A friend forwarded, via internet, a video which came across as quite 'powerful'. I want to know my Teachers' views on it.*

BR- I have just watched a video of Princess Kaoru Nakamaru from Japan. She sounded sincere and spiritual. Since lots of people seem to panic about December 2012, as if it was a doomsday time, she made many very bold predictions, such as there will be "three nights and three days of total darkness due to come to the Earth ("No stars, no lights" etc) and "Some governments are aware of it but keeping it secret (Ten thousand élite people 'saving' themselves underground - but they won't be saved!" she said). She also mentions she opened her third eye in 1976 and since then has been 'communicating with UFO people'. She claims: "Inside the Earth there are very high civilisations"- She "relived thousands of past lives etc..." What can you tell me about all this, please?

The lady was not wrong when she also said you all have to purify your way of thinking on the Earth, because the way it is at the moment is not to be proud of overall! Of course, we are talking of those who cause great harm to Humanity and the Animal kingdom, as well as to the Earth itself which is indeed suffering a lot within its inner structure.

The inner suffering within the Earth's emotional Energies does and will reflect itself on to its outer reflection, i.e. the outer surface. So, there are bound to be lots of upheavals which cannot always be recognised by Mankind as such, since they will simply think it's the Earth core of magma surfacing, because of ground cracks etc. We know there is more to it than this and you do know it too, as we have told you many a time.

The simplest solution to any outer upheavals is to solve the inner upheaval! That will be most difficult in the case of the Earth and its core, because so much damage has already been done which cannot be repaired. That's very obvious, as **the inner structure is made of pure Energy which has been manufactured by us,** in our world and transported and transmuted into physical forms! Which means all that is left for Mankind to do is to destroy the harm they've done, in order to rebalance the damage! But to destroy the harm they've done, they would need to reshape and reconstruct the inner Earth altogether!

That's what is needed - to reshape the inner Energies of the Earth by sending it constantly unlimited and huge amounts of loving balance and calming influence! But the result cannot be seen or felt overnight or even over a century, as you know it took far longer for the Earth to be created and have achieved the progression it is at, now as 'now' is the point where you see it all. We see beyond and we see 'backwards', as far as your point of view is concerned.

As it was asked: "What are those days and night of gloom and darkness?", we'll say: It is not evident to you but it is evident to us those are **not physical days** of darkness, i.e. so many hours of no sunshine - but phases of inner 'blank'. That means the world you know will have to be very still and silent within itself. The tumult it knows now will have to calm down and come to an inner standstill.

It is not really physically possible, but people will have to teach each other gradually and spread the word all over that there is a **need for inner stillness**. That means the hour they spend doing it could become eventually a whole day of your time. We know that probably sounds like 'utter rubbish' to you or anyone else reading or hearing this! The lady got some information from her own tutors, but the information was transformed and translated into '**misunderstood** words of Mankind' - not words of the Minds of those in our world!

If you had three days and nights of nothing but sheer darkness all over your world of material life, you'd end up with utter chaos, deaths and destruction - because the civilisations you have built (relying on machines and electric power etc.) will have no way of coping if all this was cut off.

If she means there will be "no sunlight, moon and

396

stars", because the sky will be blocked out by thick smoke of volcanoes or similar origins, you will still have terrible destruction and deaths and chaos. And this is not, definitely **not,** going to happen all over the world as you are looking ahead of your current year! You will have destructions, as has happened before, caused by the Earth still moving, the planet shaking, so the seas moving too. But you will not have this imaginary total blanket of no light or sound and visibility! You cannot have that.

BR- Could it be created by Mankind and secret weapons such as HAARP etc?

The automatic response to this is NO. You will not have Mankind literally destroying the Earth with their secret engineering of weapons or other such inventions. You'll have to trust us on that, of course. We cannot prove it to you until you see that none of this has happened as the years go by! Don't forget that there were such awful predictions when the years changed from hundreds to the 'famous' 1000. With that, it was 'forecast' by many that the world would end and no more life would subsist! Ha! Did that happen? No! So there you are.

We are telling you there will not be such horrid, unbelievable upset. But that does not mean the world does not badly need to be healed. Of course it does! All that is needed is for Mankind to start (one at a time and all together if you could do that) to transform your inner attitude to yourself and to those around you; to change your views on what really matters; to see that your body of flesh is only a reflection of your inner thinking and goal to be on Earth for that particular experiment - and that the Earth and its occupants are definitely NOT the centre of any universe or 'Big Plan for Eternity'! The Earth Life is only a very small part of what can be done when one is a 'Spirit' Being, as you know it - and only for those who chose to be alive in flesh Matter for that particular Experiment!

If it had been the centre and pivot of some grander 'Plan', there would not have been as much Freedom of Will exercised - as it would have been far more restricted and 'directed' not by those living there, but by those detached from it, somehow 'governing it from a distance', if you see what we mean? So forget that idea - as we think most or a lot of people have understood nowadays that the Earth is only a speck in the Universe that you are partly aware of!

We'll now come back to what we were saying about the **need for purification and purity of thinking,** as much as Man has not quite grasped yet that you are all totally equal! No reservation. No condition. If that had been completely understood, it would have solved a lot of problems. But the need for it will never end as Mankind has waged wars over centuries, wanting to subdue their neighbours or even distant ones, to try and obtain supremacy over them.

We also know that within the hearts of many, there is still very much scorn or hatred of anyone who is not like the one who is resenting them or giving his opinion. Racism and utter lack of 'brotherhood' has always been the main pitfall starting so much harm and hatred. So we'll say, yes, get people to purify and improve their way of thinking.

As to the idea of people living forever underground, this has been a fable which has been perpetuated for quite a long time! We heard it when we were on Earth ourselves. There have been people indeed who did live and some still do in small 'packs and tribes'. We know there are some smaller areas where there has been intense activity underground, in the sense that some communities have created their own little 'haven' of peace and quiet. But if there were 'large civilisations' underground forever, practically, don't you think they would have been 'spotted' by now?

The Source of information we have is of the highest kind, so you need not worry as to whether we only have 'partial' information, as you say. (*He'd picked a passing thought I had!*)

BR- Sorry I didn't mean to offend you, I just want to give the public 'the highest and the best'.

It is of no importance whether you 'offend' us of not. We know you are not intending to be rude. We have no objection to people disagreeing with us or wondering, because we are here to teach what can be taught. The only limitation is the Mind of Mankind and the amount it can absorb!

BR- You mean mine, or everybody's?

No, we do NOT mean you are limiting what can be explained, but we are limited by how much Mankind in general can absorb.

Regarding those underground supposed civilisations, as we said, there are a few groups of people who can live in such subterranean dwellings. But as to calling those "highly civilised people", we would not go so far. Mankind would imagine there is an equivalent version underground of what is above ground! On the other hand, some of those underground dwellers have not got the materialistic and self-centred views and attitude that some of your so-called civilised countries have! So we'll reassure you - no huge civilisations are hiding underground.

That lady (*Japanese Princess*) may have read books or else she may have been mistakenly led to believe that the Beings she can reach with her inner abilities, which are good indeed, have nothing to do with a Spiritual World, but are more of some Earthly origins. Or she think she talks to outer space civilisations!

Make sure you have not wasted your time talking to us by confirming again that all of you have nothing to fear, no fear of such cataclysms. There is **no** wiping out of light or daylight or nightlight. There are clouds and smoke and pollution, yes, but that's happening anyway. But we mean there won't be any big upheaval of no light etc.

Secondly, you have nothing to fear or worry about anybody you know nothing of suddenly surfacing from the inner bowels of the Earth, as that would not happen in such a way! Only 'minor tribes' but not 'huge' civilisations!

If any of you worry about this nice lady's words, you will get nowhere! You only need to take her words regarding the fact she is highly sensitive and has lived before and has come to say so, as she recalls those times. But she is not quite correct regarding some of her other comments, except she is definitely right where health is concerned, both of the Mind and the Spirit, as well as health of the flesh body, which is far too polluted by too many with wrong ingestion of wrong food!

We have covered the main points of what needs to be said. You have work to do on other projects, so please do not delay yourself more. Thanks for asking. We hope we have given you satisfactory answers.

(Stop Press Note- I want to point out that my Teachers' explanations, above, were dictated in January 2012 , twelve months BEFORE the end of 2012 when supposedly "the world was going to end", or at least be hit by gigantic catastrophes! Looking back, they were correct - we are still here!)

Over the following months I was reminded sternly by my Advanced Teachers that the publication of their dictated book 'T, L & D' had been delayed far too much and this interfered with their overall teaching plan. I had to give it absolute priority and get it out to the world somehow! I felt guilty as the Knowledge it provides is indeed of great interest, even though at times it will look 'controversial' - or more exactly, 'stepping on the toes' of rigid or narrow-minded established views! So I worked full guns for months receiving more dictations from them and polishing its presentation in a reader-friendly way. This is why there have been practically no conversations with my family for weeks on end! (Stop Press Note- After a few technical hiccups it was at last published at the end of October 2012).

10th June 2012 - *6.15am, for a change! Mum comes for a chat.*

Oh la la! Yes indeed ! I did ever so many things! I went into my Mind at levels I had not been before - adventures of inner journeys. There is such a wide range of activities we can carry out here, it's unbelievable! There are explorations at every step of my Mind. I visited people I did not know before, who showed me how I can concentrate on myself and 'dive' into my Inner Self in order to uncover more about my identity. Those trips inwards help me get acquainted with the 'Whole Real Me'. That way not only can one see lives 'before' or 'after', even if you want to just focus on one, but it reveals aspects which were unknown to you.

That's how I was able to **discover my Self as a kind of sparkling light** and **perceive my Spirit as a multi-coloured radiance** flickering and illuminating all around me! I realised I could sense the fundamental 'Whole Me' and that is an extraordinary achievement! Because my 'Higher Self and Real Me' is not just the aspect you are aware of as your 'mum', but also the total sum of all the other 'me' that I know of or don't know yet - at least that I am not aware of consciously! I understand that they exist but one must learn how to contact them and grasp they exist.

It's extremely fascinating to do, because once you've seen your Real You, it's so refreshing, so exciting and superb! Absolutely invigorating! There is nothing better, for the time being anyway! The funny thing is that we do this for pleasure, it's not a job, a chore or punishment. The way it happens is a bit like dreaming; one relaxes and sees what goes on by diving into it with the intention of doing it: "I want to see the Real Me, what I am made of." And that's it!

It all starts gradually; one feels lighter as one sees moments of thoughts, remarks made, fears, memories, incidents which marked you. Those are happenings that took place 'before' (or perhaps even 'after' I assume) but they are things which are linked with experiences I have lived and felt. There are also my hopes, my wishes to succeed and improve.

Now there is something else I want to talk to you about. It's important that you listen carefully... (*Then Mum discussed some private matters in my life, of no interest to the reader*).

14 August 2012 - *Relaxing in a park. So I decide to 'tune in', hoping to get some news from the Other Side. My Guide starts the conversation.*

This is an unusual time for us, to find you more relaxed than is customary for you! We are joking. Just to let you know we like to feel you calmer and at peace. We'll bring you news you wish to hear about your family. There is a queue of people here who'll be delighted to talk with you. We could let them do it themselves; it might be even fresher coming from their Minds. We have your mum here, she is always first in the line up! You can talk to her now. (*Change of communicator*).

My darling, there is not much time. We've got to see the second volume of my book out! (*Note- This is the one you are reading now!*) It's important everybody knows what we get up to in this world! I've been doing so many different things! We've been out and about, your dad, me and others too, to see what there is beyond what we normally experience here. There are many 'levels' of ways of thinking. We can think 'tightly', like about everyday things and actions, which brings about the creation of objects or scenery according to what we think. But if we think more deeply, we discover there are 'corners' in the **recess of our Minds which have not been tapped into** yet. Those are the ones which have a lot of interest in store because we have reached levels which we have not been to. If it is very personal we do it on our own, individually. If it is not, then we can go as a group or in a pair.

BR- In a group or in your Mind?

We can look at something together. For instance, if I project out a picture from my Mind, then we can all observe and analyse it- for example, if it is a case of past lives. A past life is personal in a way- but not so 'private', because you don't get as embarrassed about it as for a 'recent' event. So the group also enjoys the inspection and observation of what one person has to look at. It is not done as a judgement or a punishment or a debatable topic. It is just to see what was offered by that life and how it was successfully followed, or not. If there was anything really and truly private in it, we would not look at the details, so as not to upset the person in charge of his or her own experiment.

This is how I have looked at many aspects of my own lives and own Higher Self. It is so essential to discover what we have built for ourselves over centuries and centuries, if we can look at all that! There are plenty of opportunities to develop our own Self and extend our Knowledge to become even kinder and more refined spiritually, i.e. if we were not very kind before at some point(s), we could try to improve that more and more over times ahead.

We see those various lives as presented in a kind of circle, or **as if each life is a spoke in a bicycle wheel,** as I told you before. So we find it **hard to say this life was 'before' that one**. Yet we 'know' somehow which one may have preceded it simply from the happenings.

In one of my lives I looked at, I had a nasty time when I was extremely poor and 'felt lost' as a child. I had no family, so to speak. No parents around. I must have been an orphan, as I could not see why there were no parents there. They had either disappeared at my birth, or else left and died later. I was unable to get the reasons, because what mattered in the introspection was to see how I, as a 'lost child', coped with the lack of family's love, affection and guidance.

There was that nasty old lady who seemed to have some power over me - as if it was some sort of institution or place where I was and she was running it. That would have been fine but she was actually rather harsh, cruel and impatient. Not kind at all. That's why we were shocked to see that I had to survive that environment and yet I managed not to become bitter and nasty as I grew up a bit older! There were not many other kids around me. I may have been on my own or with with any companions - because what was shown to me and stood out was the loneliness and the sadness in my heart. I was most unhappy and lost within myself.

That's why over the years 'after' (and centuries no doubt, as I could not quite place 'when' that life was) there were always people around me who loved me and whom I loved. I had a great attachment to other people close to me. I felt a family was important; it had to be respected and appreciated.

BR- Do you know more about that life? Where? Who you were?

This is where I need to think hard because my Mind was only focusing on what I was looking at, on the point of view of the learnt experience. It was not an examination of dates or 'facts to report', just experiences to feel. I noticed I did not have many clothes; they were more rag-like - so poor, not looking terribly clean either! All dull and drab and pitiable.

I was a young boy, I think; it felt like a lost little boy who could not fit in anywhere with anyone, as no one really cared who or what he was. He felt so abandoned and lonely, with no view on the future at all! He was in his 'mental hole for now' at any moment - that's what was so sad. No hope, no joy, nothing to look forward to, you see what I mean?

We stayed only long enough to see what the pattern of that life was and what the outcome and the 'lesson' were. When we came out of looking at it with impartiality (as there was no judgement in all this, just observation) we realised that I managed, over time and lives, to overcome that feeling. I did not let it drag me down, but over centuries I looked to fill up the gap and the hole created by the sadness of that life experience. I replaced it with lots of love from and for my families of the times I lived. Many times, many lives! That's where you, my kids, came into at one point. You had to be my family and me your mum! I had wanted to give you all my love and feel yours - in the same way as in other lives I was not able to have children for whatever reason - so I needed to have that lack fulfilled too.

It's all very strange to see those needs exacerbated to the point of becoming a terrible **urge** for one situation or the other. This is why we need to analyse our lives as we go along to take stock of what we feel and how we have - or not - fulfilled the needs we want to work on.

(I am more and more disturbed by a dozen brats in the park constantly screaming for no reason, howling and incessantly calling for 'help' for nothing! It broke my link with Mum).

7th November 2012 - *Months flew by as I have been busy fulfilling some public speaking engagements to promote Volume 1 of this present series and at last the long awaited 'Truths, Lies & Distortions' - as well as polishing the presentation* *for publication of the book you are now reading: Volume 2 of ND-AWB. Today I tune in, in case someone may wish to speak with me. No doubt at least my Guide will be close by.*

BR- How is Mum doing? Is she busy?

We can tell you she is deeply into **examining** all sorts of levels of thinking, from anger to joy to resentment to hope - the **whole range of human emotions** - to see how they react with or against each other. It is a fascinating subject because it shows how one needs to control that power of rage and anger, if one does not want to affect one's life's Energies- both in the physical body and the environment one creates around oneself. Your parents are very good at doing this kind of inspection and investigation. They love learning and discovering, so it makes them very happy. We can't barge into their exercises and mental trips as it would be unfair to interrupt them.

However, if you want to know more about what they are doing, we can tell you it is a type of introspection. But the aim is simply to compare emotions as they have so much influence on the flesh body when you are on Earth**,** since **the body is a reflection** of what is felt!

As we feel here, we tend to only want to sense Kindness, Compassion and Joy. We want to avoid anger because it leads to nothing- except unsettling our peace of Mind and our surrounding Energies too, as well as our inner Energies. It is important for all of us to keep a balanced inner state in order to be more receptive to what is going on both in our Mind and our world - as well as in yours, because we have to look after our protégés! Therefore, we need to be aware of your own ups and downs and traumas and joys. So we need and train to always stay calm and try not to get troubled about all the things that churn you!

406

BR- You must get upset seeing what goes on in the world!

Yes, of course it is distressing! But the solution is not getting upset. The solution is to feel the reasons and causes and to send the right kind of loving Energy to help rebalance the situation. We've had lots of practice as we've all been here for quite a 'long time'!

BR- What is your explanation of the 'Aura', so that people new to this topic can understand?

The 'Aura' you see is **not** the whole body of Energy you are made of. The Aura is (only) the part which some of you are able to perceive with your inner vision, as it seems to 'escape' from your flesh body or surround it. The truth is that your whole Real body - your Energy Field body - is made of all those colours and vibrations. It is **not just outside** the flesh as said before. So the number of vibrations you get as it spreads out create the frequencies that people can pick. When those colours (i.e. vibrations) stretch and intermingle with the outside world's vibrations, it creates a wall of interference in a way, or else it blends. So the vision of it that you get is the **mixture** of your outside world and this emanation. The emanation itself is composed of the Energy you are producing at your inner level, at your thinking and feeling level. Your thoughts have got an unstoppable output of moods and ideas!

The **thoughts and emotions and Energy produced have their own rhythm and frequencies** that they pour out. But you need to understand that the colours you see are vibrations of the **intensity** of the thoughts and ideas produced by your own thinking mechanism (i.e. your Mind) - but it is also your whole Being discharging some of itself in it. 'It' being this **layer of vibrations which need to keep the flesh body going.** It is an intricate mixture!

407

You need to grasp that you see a layer or so of a many-layered 'body' or field. And the field is produced by the very fact that you will constantly think and will constantly exist, whether the flesh body is there or not. So the 'Spirit Body' or Energy Body that you are will always emit such light and colours, i.e. vibrations. They can always be sensed and received by those who are able to perceive them.

Therefore, to sum up:

* The body of flesh is the 'visible cover' and tool of the Real You for this particular Earthly life.

* The Energy which governs, drives and keeps alive the flesh vehicle, comes from the Inner Being, the Real Being who will survive, i.e. your 'Spirit Being.'

* This Energy field is multi-layered and is composed of all the emotions, thoughts, ideas and wishes you constantly have - but also traumas and happenings which will leave their mark since they are part of that particular life.

There is no mystery about the 'aura'. It is absolutely normal to have that field, since all Beings are Beings of Light and those on Earth are no different - whether People or Animals!

What is interesting is that when you discard the flesh vehicle, you still have your Energy field as part of you and you can be seen in our world as such as a Being of lights, of vibrations, which reflect your own Self, your way of thinking and feeling. So you are in no way invisible! On the contrary, **your actual thoughts are far more visible** in our world than they are in yours. We see what you think and feel - and you see what we think and feel. That's about it.

BR- Have the colours any meaning?

In our world, we do not need a book of interpretation for the meaning of the various colours' vibrations! We just 'know' what is meant by any vibration emanated, because we see and sense the Whole Being and its thoughts! It is not quite the same in your world. So you need to acquire your own awareness and information as to what each colour you sense **means to you** - because your Inner Self will know the significance of any individual hue **you** can pick. It is not up to us to give words of definition. We do not use words and labels here! We have instant knowledge and recognition of what is what.

8th November 2012 - *Today is the 30th anniversary of my dad's passing. Already! I also want to ask a question to my Teachers: What is your view on these claims I've read on the Internet? The media claims a US scientist had 'created life' by synthetically 'creating' some kind of minute cell that 'multiplied'. He boasts he 'created a new cell'. His team sequenced the code of a tiny bacteria - using a computer code to artificially reproduce the DNA in a laboratory - synthetic chromosome made with chemicals - and developed a technique of stripping another type of bacteria cell of all original DNA and substituting it with that artificial code. Then the synthetic cell was' rebooted' and is said to have 'replicated'- To those scientists, to replicate means 'being alive'! A lot of other scientists do not agree it is 'new life' as the media claim; he just mimicked it.*

We can answer this as we have the facts and Knowledge in front of us - they have not. We can tell you this: If you think a couple of cells made of synthetically reproduced chemicals, or even just chemicals, are going to create whole Beings with a Mind and thoughts and emotions and a Creative Power, you are all wrong! The truth is no Life exists in anything unless the activation comes from the 'superior Being' who will want to use those cells. If it was not so, then you'd have a constant proliferation of myriads of cells all over, non-stop, without any meaning and goals!

All it takes for those Humans who work on such experiments to believe they've succeeded in 'creating life' is a sign of 'movement' or multiplication, as you said. Yet it is not true! Life is **not** simply multiplication if it is done 'automatically' like a robot. A robot can multiply things yet it is not a living Being!

So we'll say you need to see into the Energies behind each cell and the channels within, which may have given it impetus to reproduce or multiply but it is not 'being alive'! You'll have to have many components - and we mean MANY - to create what would compose a body!

Therefore, the odd cell creating itself at random, like in this so-called experiment, is not going to reach very far. Even if it got a few cells multiplying, it would only be a **replica of the same original one**, but with **no intelligence** and aim behind it! No Knowledge of anything and it certainly would not be able to reflect the moods, thoughts and goals of a Being which it would supposedly be part of! This is not science. This is not life creation. This is **robotic** manipulation!

Sorry to disappoint the pundits who imagine they can 'beat' all teachings from Our Side. They will NEVER be able to replace Life. Real Life, Life giving Life, Life that is a Force beyond human manipulation of pieces of cells that will disintegrate after a while anyway! If those things were really genuinely alive, they would live properly and create other things, create other Beings - not 'objects 'made of chemicals! Thinking loving Beings? That is not the case.

25th November 2012 - *I wonder whether I could have a conversation with my Grandpa Léon as I have not heard from him directly, though I know he is always helping behind the scenes. My Guide 'opens the door'.*

If you wish to talk to your grandpa he'll be very pleased to acknowledge your request. He has not been at the forefront so far, because he sees no need for it, since your grandma has been doing all the talking and explaining! He concentrates on sending you his love and caring attitude towards you. But if you think it would be nice to have him 'finishing off' your present book, he says he'll be more than honoured to draw near and talk to you. He's been coming close for years but you've not realised it was him. So here we are now, for that "special event", as he says jokingly!

(Sudden change of communicator - Grandpa is online!) If we have not spoken as such before it's because I've never had the opportunity to come close and implant my words in your Mind and you knowing it was me. I have always watched over you, my dear little one. It's been a long time since you came to the Earth and I had just left it when you were a baby. But we've covered a lot of ground since, haven't we? What can I say to help you?

We could talk of days gone by when I used not to know what was needed to be done here. When I came here I had not realised what it was like to be 'dead' and to me it was a revelation. I knew we had to be kind and helpful, but this business of being a Being of Mind was new to me.

We need to put things into perspective because seen from the Earth it must feel like a lot of hocus-pocus, of Beings of Light floating around with no shape or identity - but supposedly knowing what they are doing! The fact is we do know who we are and what we do. It is more a question of what or who we focus on, you see. It is just living for the moment. Living in the sense of sensing, being aware and wanting to do or know more. Just enjoying the moment, which automatically leads to or means we desire to achieve more or 'discuss' more. There will always be a never ending list of 'things' or activities or 'better states' to be in - even for just a short while of focusing on them.

'Better states' means states of Mind and emotion for most of the time. If one does not experience new states of thinking or feeling, it could soon become all very boring, because it is built in the nature of who we all are - we all are Beings of Creativity! By that we mean Beings who want to create, to achieve more, to uncover more ways of doing new things or experiencing new adventures - most of them within our Mind and our other aspects, our other facets of various personalities.

As the Mind develops new ways of inspecting itself by delving deeper into what there is or could be, it becomes a never ending (it seems!) game of multifaceted kaleidoscopes playing with each other and reflecting or digging into each other! We have so much scope within ourselves which we don't know about!

We can tell you that when your mum came over, though it will have been a sad day for you, we were and still are, delighted to have her over here with us - 'we' being your mum's mother and myself. We had waited so long for that time! It had been lengthy and arduous for her and very painful also, far too often! She would not let go of her body of flesh...because she thought she 'had to' stay near you all, to help you as much as she could! But it was very limited physically, wasn't it? She could not do much that way though she still loved you to the hilt! She is very cut up to be parted from you all. But now she has understood that she can do no better than protecting you and sending you strength and health from here, in a much better way than she would have done while still on Earth.

We have worked hard, she and I, to help her discover new aspects of herself and also to try linking up with you all on Earth. It has not always been easy for her but she is determined and worked very hard - always! So we've come a long way from the day she thought she had to hold a telephone in her new hands to talk to you! She's learnt a lot since!

412

But you can rest assured she'll have plenty more to do here, if she chooses to do so – and she will be kept happily occupied 'for aeons' if she wishes! This means she is certainly not likely to leave our world to choose to return to the Earth (if ever) until well after you have all come back here yourselves! There is too much for her to occupy herself. Do not fear she would not be there to welcome you and show you around!

It has already happened with your eldest brother. That was a shock for us all to see him suffer so much mentally and physically. We were so pleased to help him settle his Mind and his emotions when he arrived - as he had a bit of a turbulent Mind, wondering where he was in his 'dreams'. But all that got sorted out. He is fine now. We have great pleasure in seeing him adjusting nicely and happily!

Make the world understand we are all here in Peace and Love for each other. Those who are not are those who have not found it within themselves yet. That's because of what they have been doing on the Earth. There, they did not expand their Inner Knowledge, to the extent of letting their true Being come through to guide the Being of flesh which they used as a tool in their physical world.

You can only do your best at all times. It's not always easy but it is very satisfying, because it gives you inner balance and contentment. When the Soul and Spirit feel there is something lacking and not achieved, there is a longing or regret, then Peace eludes you. When you feel you can do no more for now, then you know you have tried hard. Subsequently, you may find more angles to deal with and then also do your best! This is all part of learning and learning is creative, because you improve your Self.

Your Self is a Being constantly creating! You are like that on Earth, or elsewhere too, whether in our world or in any other world you may choose to go to try and experience 'one day'. It is not just a question of 'popping over' somewhere to see what it is like, then pulling out at once. If you choose to go anywhere, you first learn what it may be like and what you may want to do there. Then you prepare yourself for the trip. That trip could have many possibilities or many ramifications and forks for you to choose from and to decide upon once there! It happens on Earth, it can happen elsewhere.

By elsewhere, I mean **other worlds which have a different texture to yours**. But that's not somewhere one would go unless it was already decided 'way back', as you'd say. That means one did not choose to come to Earth, one had chosen to go elsewhere instead. Because going to one place or the other - whichever it is - always implies becoming involved in **all** the new possibilities creating themselves as you go along in your new environment. So people who have chosen to come to Earth have many possibilities and choices to make and experience there. This is in order to complete as well as possible the development of their Higher Self, within the experience of this physical matter you know as the Earth World. But you would not just 'pop over' to another world simply 'to see what it's like'! That is the point I am trying to make.

May you understand, my dear little granddaughter of one life, that we are all behind you, trying to help and guide you, so that you feel you have achieved what you came for this time round. You will find us all again waiting for you when you decide to leave the Earth to have a well-earned rest - and hopefully with many experiences and achievements to be proud of!

We can only reiterate the motto of my life and your mum's: "Do your best". That's all you can aim for. Then you'll get constant peace of Mind and Soul. We love you all! Grandpa Léon.

****

FINAL THOUGHTS
by BRIGITTE RIX

This loving and heartwarming communication from my maternal grandpa - whom I have never met physically but who obviously watches over me and my family from the Spirit World - seems to be the best way to end this volume 2.

The first two volumes of 'I'm NOT DEAD: I'm ALIVE without a body' cover thirteen and a half years of wonderful, enlightening and at times mind-boggling conversations with my family and my Guide. This series all started when Mum astounded me in June 1999 by contacting me unexpectedly twenty-six hours after her passing, revealing how easy it had been for her to fly out of her body forever - which she left next to me on the hospital bed! She then continued to regularly and joyfully update me with her adventures in controlling and using her thoughts in that World of Mind and Light! Examining and 'peeling off' the layers of her recent physical life and delving more and more deeply into the mysterious and fascinating recesses of the Mind, helped her discover to her utter amazement that she had lived numerous past lives all over the globe - having been incarnated as numerous men and women over many centuries!

She has thus progressed a lot since her arrival, reaching a greater understanding of Reality! She has discovered she is not 'just my mum' - that was only one aspect of the multifaceted colourful kaleidoscope that her Real Higher Self is composed of! Like our own Higher Selves are too. Mum has grasped, at last, that she had actually chosen, as her 'life plan' and experience, to come to Earth this time round, just to be my brothers' and my mother. And the four of us had chosen indeed to be her children. Mum made an excellent job of it - lovingly and courageously throughout her Earthly life and beyond!

I am grateful and honoured to have her as my darling 'Maman' and proud of her great achievements. Her success is not visible in buildings or piles of money. Far better! The life she chiselled as my mum is one of the many faces of the multifaceted diamond of her Spirit. Whether in this recent life with me, or in 'past existences' as various other personalities, her fundamental Self has always tried to do her best whatever the difficult circumstances. Her guiding line was to act with Kindness and Compassion. Qualities of a true Spirit Being! Mum's achievements followed her, as she has now discovered, since they now radiate as the sparkling Light emanating from her Whole Self, the shining Eternal Spirit she is.

Looking back on those early days of her arrival in the 'Spirit World', I hope you realise, like I do, that death is not to be feared. The actual leaving the flesh is painless. As soon as we fly from what is only a flesh vehicle, we are at once free from any possible pain, we feel absolutely normal, in top health and looking younger if we wish to! No one is ever abandoned to cope on their own. Even if some people think they'll have nobody to welcome them on the Other Side of the 'veil', they will be pleasantly surprised when they are received warmly and lovingly by many caring persons there! The new arrivals can then enjoy freedom and peace and experience new exhilarating adventures in a World of Light, where their Mind is an exciting creative tool or toy! They will eventually analyse their recent Earth life and be helped to understand why they acted as they did - their Soul will be their own judge. Those who have caused wilful harm will eventually feel guilt, regrets and a desire to repair the damages somehow.

Since the parting can be a shock on both sides of the 'veil', the departed will be caringly helped to understand that grieving for those left on Earth is not helping them or their loved ones. So instead they will swiftly learn to send their love as a positive creative Energy, to improve the health and lives of those left behind. They will also grasp that the separation is only temporary. Not only will everyone be reunited one day, but meanwhile they always meet during the bodily sleep of those they love. And the rest of the time both parties are only a thought away from each other!

When we really love someone for who they are, then we want the best for them, even if it is hard for us! So let us be joyful that our liberated loved ones are free from any pain and illness, free from accidents and dangers, free from worries, free from man-made rules and regulations and duties and all the shackles life on Earth chains humans with!

Youngsters leaving the Earth at a young age are lucky to have escaped from heavy responsibilities and all those horrid balls and chains! Of course we'll miss them but let us be glad for them! They now have 'a whole new life ahead of them', guaranteed to be fun and exciting - and most of all they will always be FREE in a wonderful world full of wonders! Since we love them we must be happy for them and not grieve - otherwise they will feel our grief as heavy dark clouds spoiling their happiness and peace of Mind!

As my mum said: "You should be celebrating the day I arrived in this new world. I am so happy and free here! Be joyful for me, please! Meanwhile, whenever you think of me I receive your thoughts and your love, and be sure that I am always sending you all my love. Also, don't forget that we shall be together again, one day!"

****

Please visit my website for further knowledge:
www.italkwithspirits.com

417

Recommended Reading for further understanding:

• *I'm Not Dead: I'm Alive... Without a body -Volume 1* (*channelled by Brigitte Rix*)

• *Truths, Lies & Distortions:* Hidden Truths Revealed (*Spirit Teachers - channelled by Brigitte Rix*)

• *Dying To Be Me:* My journey from Cancer, to Near Death to True Healing (*by Anita Moorjani*)

• *Proof of Heaven:* A neurosurgeon's Journey into the Afterlife (*Dr Eben Alexander*)

• *Soul Survivor: The Reincarnation of a World War II Fighter Pilot* (*Bruce and Andrea Leininger*)

• *In Pursuit of Physical Mediumship* (*Robin P. Foy*)

• *Witnessing the Impossible* (*Diary of the Scole Experiment*) - (*Robin P. Foy*)

• *An Extraordinary Journey:* The Memoirs of a Physical Medium (*Stewart Alexander*)

• *Vibrational Medicine* (*Richard Gerber, M.D*)

• *Zerdin Phenomenal:* www.zerdinphenomenal.co.uk - Email: info@zerdin.co.uk - Telephone: +44 (0)1243 576063 - The Gatehouse, Priors Leaze Lane, Hambrook, West Sussex, PO18 8RQ. England

****

"When I am gone, release me, let me go,
I have so many things to see and do!
You must not tie yourself to me with **tears**!
Be happy that I have had so many years.

I gave you my love, you can only guess
How much you gave me in happiness.
I thank you for the love each has shown,
But now it is time I travelled on alone.

So grieve a while for me, if grieve you must,
Then let your grief be comforted by trust:
It is only for a while that we must part,
So bless the memories in your heart.

I will not be far away, for life goes on-
So if you need me, call and I will come:
Though you cannot see or touch me, I will be near.
And if you listen with your heart, you will hear
All of my love around you soft and clear.
Then, when you must come this way alone,
I will greet you with a smile and welcome you home!"

(Anonymous)

****

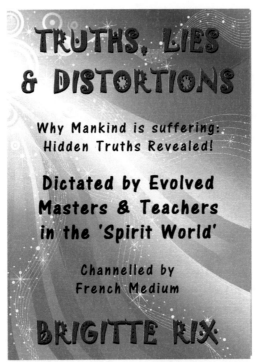

TRUTHS, LIES & DISTORTIONS

GROUND-BREAKING, AUTHENTIC KNOWLEDGE given by **Evolved Masters in the 'Spirit World'**, revealing **THE hidden Truths,** masked by centuries of man-made Lies and Distortions.

They have spoken to **encourage Mankind to open its Mind, to avoid being brainwashed by manipulative 'authorities', and to even challenge entrenched, unfounded or distorted man-made dogmas & theories.**

Those knowledgeable Teachers offer **answers to profound questions, and** many **mind-boggling revelations which MERGE THE BOUNDARIES OF SCIENCE & SPIRITUALITY,** including:

- *How & why we came to exist on Earth.*
- *There is no 'void'!*
- *What happens BEFORE we are born.*
- *Training course BEFORE BIRTH.*
- *Choosing a 'LIFE PLAN' to learn more.*
- *Spirit 'entering' the embryo.*
- *Reincarnation: Past lives make sense!*
- *Why our Mind can HEAL us.*
- *Why Mindsets affect events and our lives.*
- *Insight into: coma, suicide, euthanasia.*
- *Secret of viruses; organ transplants.*
- *LEY LINES, CROP CIRCLES, UFO'S!*
- *Other worlds and multi universes.*
- *CONSCIOUSNESS of Animals and Plants.*
- *Mind's Inner Levels and Dimensions.*
- *SELF-EMPOWERMENT: discover your inner spiritual wisdom.*

These Spiritual Masters dictated this entire book through the respected clairaudient medium, BRIGITTE RIX, who channelled their teachings by taking down at high speed the word for word dictation in 'automatic writing'. (350 pages) - **ISBN 978 1 898 680 604**

"This fascinating book gives a refreshing, alternative viewpoint from the common materialistic perspective. It is self-consistent, written with sincerity and offers eye-opening food for thought."
Gordon DALGARNO, BSc (Hons) Physics. *Senior Scientist Rowntree/Nestlé UK- Member/Institute of Acoustics - Adv.Cert. Kinesiology - Reiki Master.*

www.italkwithspirits.com

VOLUME 1
'I'm NOT DEAD: I'm ALIVE...without a body'

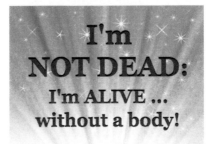

I'm NOT DEAD: I'm ALIVE ... without a body!

What's it like _after_ we die?

Find out from these
amazing & genuine
conversations with loved ones
alive in the Spirit World

Channelled by French medium

BRIGITTE RIX

BACK COVER of *'I'm NOT DEAD: I'm ALIVE...without a body'*

*"Console yourself, I have arrived safely.
Everything you told me is true..."*
These were the first words from my mother,
just 26 hours after her death.
This fascinating book is volume 1 of a lively diary,
charting the first 5 years of communications received
by the genuine medium Brigitte Rix from her mother,
father, husband and other people –
all in the Spirit World.

**This book is different from the rest.
It goes BEYOND proving that there is life after death.**

This 'travelogue', humorously narrated by Brigitte's mother, describes her step-by-step journey following her passing from Earth (with the words "I'm not dead – I'm alive without a body!") into a whole new world of mind-boggling discoveries of the Afterlife. The revelations from this 'author from beyond the grave' include her experiences of:

• Being reunited with family, friends and animals in the Spirit World.
• Discovering a 100-year-old family secret, that neither she nor Brigitte had ever known.
• Meeting other Spirit Beings who teach her how to adjust to this spiritual dimension.
• Learning how to manipulate the energy of her thoughts, to create her desired environment in the Spirit World – from changing the scenery of the decor of her ideal home to creating breathtaking natural landscapes!
• How colours can be experienced as sounds, while words transform into pictures.
• Reviewing her past lives and experiencing alternative versions of Earthly history.
• Learning how to fine-tune the frequency of her thoughts to be able to communicate with receptive people on the Earth plane.

Additional individual accounts by other loved ones and Spirit 'Guides' are included, providing further astounding insights into exactly what happens after we die – when we all finally get to 'go home'.

The book you are holding offers upliftment and reassurance that no parting is eternal – you will meet your loved ones again. People who 'pass over' into the Spirit World only lose their flesh body, but not their mind, personality and love for those still residing on Earth.

The Spiritual Energy – or 'Soul' – within each of us cannot be destroyed, it just passes into the next plane of existence.

This first volume sets the scene for the subsequent books, produced by Brigitte's gifted mediumship and her desire to spread the messages of love and knowledge from Spirit.

www.italkwithspirits.com   £10.99